KEY WEST

The Old and The New

KEY WEST

The Old and The New

By JEFFERSON B. BROWNE

A FACSIMILE REPRODUCTION
of the 1912 EDITION
with
INTRODUCTION and INDEX
by *E. ASHBY HAMMOND*

BICENTENNIAL FLORIDIANA FACSIMILE SERIES

UNIVERSITY OF FLORIDA PRESS
GAINESVILLE 1973

Library of Congress Cataloging in Publication Data

Browne, Jefferson Beale, 1857–1937.
    Key West, the old and the new.

    (Bicentennial Floridiana facsimile series)
    Includes bibliographical references.
    1. Key West—History. I. Title. II. Series.
F319.K4B8 1973   979.9′41   72-14327
ISBN 0-8130-0367-9

BICENTENNIAL FLORIDIANA
FACSIMILE SERIES
published under the sponsorship of the
BICENTENNIAL COMMISSION OF FLORIDA
SAMUEL PROCTOR, *General Editor*

FACSIMILE REPRODUCTION
of the 1912 EDITION
with PREFATORY MATERIAL, INTRODUCTION
and INDEX ADDED

BICENTENNIAL COMMISSION OF FLORIDA

GENERAL EDITOR'S PREFACE

THE citizens of Key West in 1912, the year that Jefferson Browne published his history, thought that they were on the threshold of a new era of growth and development. On January 22, 1912, at 10:43 A.M., the first official train of the Florida East Coast Railway arrived at Key West. Ten thousand people were present, yelling and cheering themselves hoarse. Many were seeing a passenger train for the first time in their lives. On the train was Henry M. Flagler who owned the Flagler System, and he was being hailed as a conquering hero. The *Miami Herald* enthusiastically called the extension of the railroad into Key West the "eighth wonder of the world," and spoke in glowing terms of what it would mean for Key West. The Jacksonville *Florida-Times Union* predicted: "Today marks the dawn of a new era. The Old Key West—one of the most unique of the world's historic little cities—is shaking off its lethargy and from today the spirit of progress and development will be greater than ever." It was in this spirit that Jefferson Browne, a member of one of Key West's most distinguished families, wrote his book.

Like the Bicentennial which the United States is preparing to commemorate in 1976, Mr. Browne in his history looked both to the past and to the future. Speaking for the nation, President Nixon sees the celebration of this nation's two-hundredth birthday as an opportunity for the people to look to our national heritage and accomplishments with pride, and to move toward the fulfillment of national goals yet to be attained. Mr. Browne was in no way writing in 1912 on such a grand scale, nor was his purpose so commanding, yet he did title his book *Key West, The Old and The New*.

Key West has a rich and colorful history. Settled in the 1820s, it soon became one of the most important cities in the state. Incorporated in 1828, it developed as a major shipping base. Schools were established in the 1830s, and in 1829 the *Key West Register* was founded, the first newspaper south of St. Augustine. In 1860 Key West was the second largest city in Florida, and there were more people living there than in Jacksonville or in Tallahassee. Several cigar factories and important military installations operated there. Mr. Browne notes much of this nineteenth-century growth and development in his book.

Jefferson Browne in 1912 was looking to a bright future for his community, but Key West failed to grow into a great metropolis; it did not become "America's Gibraltar" as had been predicted. The overseas extension of the railroad never enjoyed the volume of business that had been hoped for. Population remained small and relatively stable until after World War II. Although Jefferson Browne had hoped for a great prosperity for his community, he lamented the passing of "the old order, old ideas, old customs, old beliefs, old ideals—and the old people who cherished them." The physical features of Key West, at least in 1912, had not yet been marred. The crystal clear water, the blue skies, and the magnificent sunrises and sunsets were all there. These were the things in Key West which Mr. Browne felt would "not change with the onward progress of development," and would "attract newcomers as they fascinated the pioneers."

This blending of the old and the new is a basic theme of the Bicentennial. In establishing the American Revolution Bicentennial Commission, Congress specified that it should give special emphasis to the ideas associated with the Revolution—ideas that have vitally influenced the development of the United States, world affairs, and mankind's quest for freedom. To develop these concepts on the state level, the Florida Legislature established the Bicentennial Commission of Florida. A twenty-seven-member state commission was appointed, representing the Florida House and Senate and the important agencies of state government. The Lieutenant Governor, Secretary of Commerce, Secretary of State, Director of the Division of Archives, History and Records Management, Commissioner of Education, Director of the Division of Recreation and Parks, and a member of the State Board of Regents are on the Commission. In addition, ten persons, appointed by the Governor, also serve. Governor Reubin Askew is honorary chairman and Lieutenant Governor Tom Adams is chairman.

The Bicentennial Floridiana Facsimile Series, which is sponsored by the Bicentennial Commission of Florida, will publish twenty-five volumes of rare, out-of-print books and monographs. Representing the wide spectrum of this state's history from the First Spanish Period to the twentieth century, the series will make a major contribution to the knowledge of Florida history. Scholars with a special interest and knowledge of Florida history will edit each volume, write an introduction, and compile an index.

Professor E. A. Hammond, editor of this volume, is a member of the history and social science faculty of the University of Florida. A native of North Carolina, Professor Hammond is a graduate of the University of North Carolina at Chapel Hill. He is a distinguished scholar in medieval medical history. He has also written widely on a variety of Florida history subjects. A special interest is nineteenth-century Florida medical history. During the course of his research, Professor Hammond has delved into the history of Key West and South Florida. His work on Dr. Benjamin Strobel of Key West is definitive, and his articles on the early history of Sanibel and Captiva islands have appeared in scholarly journals. His interest in Jefferson Browne's book grew out of his varied research activities. Professor Hammond is presently gathering data for a medical history of Florida.

SAMUEL PROCTOR
General Editor of the
BICENTENNIAL FLORIDIANA
FACSIMILE SERIES

INTRODUCTION

THIRTY-FIVE years had elapsed after the publication of Walter C. Maloney's *A Sketch of the History of Key West, Florida,* when Jefferson Beale Browne, a native son of Key West, set about bringing the book up to date.[1] Having undertaken the revision, however, he decided to broaden its scope and rewrite the earlier work, extending the narrative to 1912. Maloney's *History* had been conceived as a brief account to be delivered as a public address in Key West as a part of the Independence Day celebration in 1876. It was Browne's intention to expand this work by including "all the available information on any subject connected with Key West, which is of interest to anyone," a pleasantly naïve proposal in the light of more recent historical scholarship. The ultimate result, *Key West, The Old and The New,* is nevertheless a significant history of one of America's most unusual cities.

At the beginning of the American occupation of the small island, which the Spanish had called Cayo Hueso, or Bone Key, its future appeared bleak. Archaeological evidence suggested an earlier habitation by aboriginal people, but there was little indication of extended occupation or stable culture. During the late eighteenth and early nineteenth centuries, Bahama-based wreckers had employed its excellent harbor as a lookout for unwary vessels making their way through the treacherous and unmarked Florida Straits from Cuba and the Gulf ports into the open Atlantic. To the first Americans in Key West, it became apparent that if United States occupation was to be economically feasible, this farthest major key must be protected by the military or police agencies of the federal government. And yet the Treasury Department whose responsibility it was to protect commerce in American coastal waters had given little official attention to the problem of patrolling Florida's more than 2,000 miles of shoreline. Key West and the other islands along the Straits seemed too remote to be of commercial importance.

Some seven years before the formal transfer of Florida to the United States, the island had come into the possession of Juan P. Salas by purchase from Don Juan de Estrada, Spanish governor of Florida. Salas had in turn sold his island to John W. Simonton, a merchant of Mobile. Litigation over ownership ensued in April 1822, when John Geddes, governor of South Carolina from 1818 to 1822, attempted to validate a claim to the property by sending an armed party to seize Key West and instituting a suit at law against Simonton and his associates. The Geddes claim was judged imperfect, however, and the court ruled in favor of Simonton.[2]

Shortly after he had purchased the island, Simonton disposed of three-fourths of it. One portion was sold to John W. C. Fleeming [Fleming], also a Mobile merchant; another was bought by John Whitehead, son of a banker of Newark, New Jersey; a third passed into the joint possession of John Mountain and John Warner, a commercial agent of the United States in Havana. The latter two sold their portion to Pardon C. Greene, a sailing master and native of Rhode Island. These four—Simonton, Whitehead, Fleeming, and Greene—were thus the original proprietors of Key West. Simonton, whose business interests were varied and prosperous, spent most of his time in Washington where his circle of friends and acquaintances included men of influence in government. He retained his portion of the island, however, and later bequeathed it to his wife, Ann. The other proprietors became prominent Key West merchants and citizens.[3]

These private proprietors readily understood that the success of their venture depended largely upon the protection which the American government could be induced to provide. Accordingly, Simonton, closest to the Washington scene, made certain that the Treasury Department understood both the military and commercial importance of Key West to the nation.[4] Consequent to this representation, Lieutenant Matthew C. Perry, commander of the U.S. Schooner *Shark,* received orders on February 7, 1822, from Smith Thompson, secretary of the navy, to sail from New York to Key West "for the purpose of making an examination of the Island, its harbors, its extent." Furthermore, he was authorized, if he thought it feasible, "to take possession of it in the name of the United States."[5] Some seven weeks later, Perry's mission had been accomplished. On March 28, he reported having taken formal possession of the island and renaming it "Thompson's Island" in honor of the chief naval officer, while assigning to its "capacious and sheltered" harbor the name "Port Rodgers," thus honoring Commodore John Rodgers, president of the Board of Navy Commissioners.[6] Both names soon fell into disuse. Perry concluded his report with a description of the island and an estimate of its importance as a commercial and military outpost.

In spite of such official encouragement, the prosperity of Key West was not assured. Its remoteness from the mainstream of American commercial activity discouraged investment, save in enterprises such as salvage and wrecking, in which, while risk was great, the promise of profit was also large. The agricultural potential of the island was negligible, and its water supply was inadequate, notwithstanding early claims that there were fresh water springs sufficient to the needs of settlers. When the frequent recurrence of fevers endemic to the area was added to these drawbacks, the prospects for successful settlement seemed dismal.

The first eight years of American occupation offered little encouragement. As the summers came, the fevers returned, and most settlers, and even the military detachments, deserted the area for the more healthful latitudes farther north. A notable example of such a removal was that of Commodore David Porter who, without authorization from Washington, sailed out of Key West with his ships and the majority of his naval personnel in October 1823. Only after he had arrived in the Chesapeake Bay did he notify Washington of his action.[7] Some left only for "the sickly season," others for good. Still, many courageous ones persevered, refusing to abandon their investments. Meanwhile, the outlook gradually brightened. By 1830, the census showed 517 persons in Monroe County, nearly all residing in Key West. Growth, while unspectacular, continued steadily. Along with a few outlaws, derelicts, and mere adventurers came thrifty and industrious men and women bent on making of Key West a prosperous business community and establishing a social structure not unlike that of other American towns.

One of the foremost of the latter group was William Adee Whitehead, the younger brother of John Whitehead; his arrival in Key West in October 1828 was an important occurrence. He immediately undertook to make an accurate survey of the island, setting forth in careful detail the plats and streets. His 1829 map includes the numbered plats with their dimensions and the designations of ownership.[8] This survey greatly facilitated the transfer of property. Secure, therefore, in the possession of the island property and enjoying the official protection of a naval unit—to be exchanged in 1831 for an army detachment—the proprietors were prepared to offer lots and business opportunity to persons willing to take their chances on this faraway subtropical isle.

People came to Key West, however, for many reasons. The wrecking business was in its heyday, and it lured many, notably sailing masters from New England and the Bahamas. Most were honest men; some were not. The establishment of Key West as a port of entry in 1822 and the appointment of a customs officer, in addition to the presence of a small military force, gave assurance to prospective investors that the American government stood ready to protect them in their ventures.[9] Within the next decade, merchant ships in increasing numbers were making Key West a regular port of call, and the federal government recognized in its location and harbor a strategic link in its defense operations. Imports valued at $140,585 were registered at its customhouse in 1829, and exports valued at $48,754 were shipped through its harbor the same year.[10]

Among the early settlers whose faith in Key West and whose business ability and civic interests contributed significantly to the success of the island was Fielding A. Browne, great-uncle of Jefferson Browne. Born in James City County, Virginia, about 1791, his introduction to Key West was entirely accidental.[11] On returning to Virginia from Mexico, where he had gone to settle the business affairs of his deceased brother, his ship ran aground on the Florida Reef. Brought ashore at Key West, he was compelled to tarry there until another vessel could take him home. He was favorably impressed with the possibilities of Key West as a business location, and he returned shortly thereafter to establish a salvage operation. The precise date of his arrival in Key

West has not been determined, but it may be assumed to have occurred before December 29, 1826; on that date Browne and several other citizens of the island petitioned Congress for the establishment of a federal district court in Key West.[12] By 1829, Browne's wharf and warehouse occupied a part of the waterfront between Duval and Simonton streets. In 1836, he was elected mayor. He was characterized by his grandnephew as "the typical Virginia gentleman, with the manners and pronunciation which distinguished them."[13]

On Christmas night 1830, Joseph Beverly Browne, nephew of Fielding A. Browne, arrived in Key West. Although only a lad of sixteen, he had graduated from the College of William and Mary, and had been invited by his uncle to join the Browne business firm. If it seems extraordinary that a boy so young had completed the college course, it should be recalled that academic standards and structures were not yet formalized. Young Browne's case was not exceptional for those times, although he was doubtless a gifted student.[14] He, too, had been born in James City County, Virginia. His father was John Eaton Browne, brother of Fielding. Under the auspices of his uncle, Joseph entered actively into the business and civic life of the town. In 1840, he was married to Mary Nieves Ximinez, a native of St. Augustine, who had come to Key West as a small child when her father, Joseph Ximinez, a shipowner, moved his business to Key West and set up regular shipping operations between Cuba and the settlements of southern Florida.[15]

Jefferson Browne referred to his parents with admiration and affection.[16] Since both enjoyed lengthy lives and their son was frequently in their company, his recollections were probably accurate. "Mrs. Browne," her son recalled, "was distinguished for her zeal in church, and all public enterprise in which the women of her day took part." His father had entered public life at an early age, having been a delegate to the St. Joseph Convention, called in 1838 to draft a constitution for Florida. Joseph was only twenty-four years old at the time. At twenty-six, he was appointed United States marshal, an office which he held for ten years and ultimately relinquished to become clerk of the United States District Court. He was a member of the Florida House of Representatives in the session of 1866, but with the formation of a "reconstruction" legislature he was not immediately returned to the House. In the fall of 1872, he was elected to the lower house, and he held his seat through the session of 1875.[17] He was remembered by his son as a "Jeffersonian Democrat and a Virginian . . . interested in public affairs," possessing tastes and a nature which "fitted him for public life and made him a marked man in the community as well as the state." Although he "belonged to the times of broad acres and wide hospitality like a souvenir from the past," he moved with dignity and ease in Key West, serving in public office with courage and honor.

Moderate success seems to have attended Joseph Browne's business endeavors. The United States Census of 1850 valued his real property at $12,000; the 1860 schedule added to that amount $8,000 in personal property. However these sums may be interpreted in terms of the inflated currency of more recent times, it is apparent that Jefferson was born into a middle-class family, enjoying from birth such social and educational advantages as well-to-do parents of that era could provide. The name Jefferson was not a random choice.

Born in Key West on June 4, 1857, he was the fourth child and only son.[18] His early education was in the private schools of Key West, but after the establishment of a public school he was enrolled there. He later attended Brookville Academy, Montgomery County, Maryland, and Kenmore University High School, Amherst, Virginia.[19] Soon after completing his course at the Kenmore School (probably about 1876), Browne returned to Key West to accept the first of his many public positions, when he became second assistant lighthouse keeper at the recently constructed Fowey Rocks lighthouse.[20] This important light warned of the reef along the entrance to the Florida Straits. Tending the light was not a demanding kind of duty, and young Browne filled his long and lonely hours with the reading of law books, becoming so absorbed in the subject that he remained at Fowey for fifteen months, it is said, without a single day's vacation. When, at the end of that period, he left to enroll in the law school of the University of Iowa, his preparation was so thorough that he was able to complete the course and obtain his law degree in less than two years.[21] He promptly gained admittance to the bars of Iowa and Florida.

Jefferson Browne's professional career was launched by his appointment as city attorney for Key West shortly after he returned in 1880. The following year, he undertook the dual role of attorney for both the city and Monroe County. He resigned these posts in 1886 to become postmaster of Key West, presumably his rewards from the Cleveland administration for loyal service in the Democratic Party. This position he relinquished in 1890 to run successfully for state senator. A measure of the trust he inspired among his associates may be found in the fact that he was elected president of the Senate at its first sitting on April 7, 1891.[22] He was again in the Senate for the session of 1893.

In the meantime, Browne's political horizon was extended by his election as a delegate to the Democratic National Convention, meeting in St. Louis in 1888. He was a delegate again in 1904 and 1908. In 1912, he served as Democratic elector for the election of Woodrow Wilson, in this instance as chairman of Florida's delegation. This impressive political success story was marred only by his failure to obtain the Democratic gubernatorial nomination in 1892 when the state convention selected Henry Laurens Mitchell.

Browne was appointed collector of customs in Key West in 1893, a post which he held four years. This was doubtless another reward for his service to his party. His next public post was that of chairman of the Florida Railroad Commission, to which he was elected in 1904. He worked in this capacity until 1907.

It cannot be denied that Jefferson Browne led a full and rewarding public life, nor can it be said that he ever came under censure for his public or private behavior. In addition to the offices and responsibilities mentioned, he was a practicing lawyer, qualified, as he stated on his professional card, "to practice in any court." His practice was carried on chiefly in Key West and Tallahassee. Beyond these activities, Browne also found time for participation in the social, fraternal, and religious life of his community. He was a member of the Benevolent and Protective Order of Elks, the first president of the Key West Rotary Club, and at one time a chancellor of the Knights of Pythias. For several years, he taught a Sunday school class in the Congregational Church of Key West. As he entered his successful campaign for a seat on the Florida State Supreme Court in 1916, the *Key West Morning Journal* stated, "Besides his legal attainments, Mr. Browne possesses to an eminent degree the judicial temperament, and in his practice has always been more interested in the proper determination of questions of Law and Justice than in mere victories at the bar."

Judge Browne's career in law had been one of distinction. His fundamental faith in American jurisprudence, his thorough training in the legal system, his sagacious approach to human problems, his gentleness of spirit, and perhaps also his reasoned political conservatism all had won for him a position of esteem among his fellow members of the Florida Bar Association. At its organizational meeting in Jacksonville on February 5, 1907, he was elected vice-president from the sixth judicial district, and reelected two years later. At the Tampa meeting of the association in 1910, he was elected president for the 1910–11 term. In whatever area of public service he undertook to labor, his qualities of leadership were recognized and utilized. It was not surprising that, upon his election to the Florida Supreme Court in November 1916, he was chosen chief justice.

Browne remained on the court until June 1, 1925, having sat as its presiding member until 1923. His reasons for resigning were simple and undisguised: he was sixty-eight years old and homesick for his native island. When the opportunity came to obtain the judgeship of the twentieth judicial circuit, permitting him to return to Key West and live among relatives and long-time friends, he seems not to have hesitated. Characteristically, this change was only the beginning of a demanding career as a circuit court judge. Even when the redistricting of the state's circuit court brought the Miami area into his province of responsibility and required that much of his time be spent in Miami, he accepted the additional burden and inconvenience without complaint. He was, in fact, presiding over a session of court in Miami on April 12, 1937, when he suffered the heart attack which was to prove fatal.

During the ensuing fortnight, as he lay in a hospital bed in the Miami Battle Creek Sanitorium in Miami Springs, Judge Browne apparently realized that the end was near. At his own request, he was carried home to Key West by ambulance on April 30. Death came at midmorning four days later as he dictated notes to his stenographer at his residence in the Air Station Apartments.

Notwithstanding the demands of his professional responsibilities, Judge Browne found time now and then to set forth in writing his basic legal and political philosophies. At least three of his papers have survived in the legal journals. They reveal not only the wide range of his interests and his learning but also the dominant attitudes which shaped his public life. None seems better to exemplify his fundamental thinking than his presidential address, "Our Progress Towards Absolutism," delivered before the Florida State Bar Association at its Pensacola meeting in 1911.[23] Herein is set forth the rational conservatism of his political orientation. From this we conclude that Thomas Jefferson was his political idol. The preservation of the integrity of the states as the main bulwark of people's rights against the absolutist encroachments of federal power was to Browne a major concern. No one spoke more eloquently on behalf of the states than Jefferson. Browne saw in Alexander Hamilton the arch-advocate of absolutism bent on destroying the governments of states, which he regarded as the instrumentalities for safeguarding the liberties of the people from the excesses of a radical democracy on one hand and the despotism of a highly centralized federal government on the other.

Even John Marshall, whom Browne later came to admire, was cited in this address as the perpetrator of dangerous precedents: "In 1801 . . . there occurred one of those circumstances . . . which gave our government its leaning toward absolutism, and since then we have continued in that direction with certain, although at times with halting, steps. This circumstance was the ascendancy of John Marshall to the Supreme Bench of the United States." Proceeding then to employ the supporting opinion of an unspecified historian, Browne added, "Jefferson had determined upon restricting the powers of the National Government in the interest of human liberty, and Marshall was bent upon enlarging the powers of government in the interest of nationality."

The judicial philosophy launched by Justice Marshall had by 1911, in Browne's opinion, borne its bitter fruit in the "New Nationalism" of Theodore Roosevelt and the rising clamor for extending the regulatory power of federal government. The liberal influence of Justice Holmes was already apparent—he had come to the Court in 1902—and, as Browne witnessed the trend in the Court away from the strict constructionism of the late nineteenth century, he found neither comfort nor hope in its behavior. In a succinct restatement of his thesis, he proclaimed, "There must be some power or some body of men occupying a middle ground between the people and the general government, capable of protecting the former from the aggressions of the latter." This, he thought, should be the role and duty of the states. Drawing upon his very considerable knowledge of the forces which had shaped the course of European history in the Middle Ages, he found an analogy (although an inept one) in the English experience of having the despotic threats of King John neutralized by baronial opposition. For America, the lesson was unmistakable. Fervently, he reiterated, "Our States are the ark of the covenant of people's liberties, as the barons in feudal days were the protectors of the rights of the English people from the aggressions of despotic rulers." In further support of his argument, Browne turned to the history of fifteenth-century France where he saw in the success of King Louis XI in undermining the power of the French nobility and usurping their appanages a fearful example of how despots are made. "The duchies were destroyed," he recalled, "but instead of greater liberty, the necks of the people were bent to the yoke of despotic rulers."

Browne had watched with alarm the steady encroachment of federal power upon what John Marshall had termed the "residuary sovereignty" of states. For this he blamed particularly what he called in his speech "the sapping and mining of the Constitution by judicial interpretation," to which intrusion Justice Marshall had opened the door. That the consolidation of federal power leading to the destruction of states' rights, and consequently of people's rights, should have been achieved through the agency of the highest court was to Browne the ultimate irony. To a historian who noted that Justice Marshall had a remarkable instinct of "what the law ought to be," he replied that this was a quality which befitted the legislator better than the judge. The latter should be concerned only with what the law is, not what it should be.

Still tracing "Our Progress Towards Absolutism," Browne found distressing trends in his native South. He looked with special disdain upon certain southerners who supported federal encroachment on states' rights by means of ever broadening interpretations of interstate commerce powers set forth in the Constitution. Although he does not identify them by name, they were in his judgment "hot-headed enthusiasts and demagogues . . . willing to exchange our birthright of State sovereignty for the mess of pottage of Federal control of railroads," thus opening the way for further erosion of the rights reserved to states and their people.[24]

To Judge Browne, the federal income tax and the direct election of senators, both soon to be incorporated into the Constitution as amendments sixteen and seventeen, were serious threats to the powers of states. The income tax, he said in his speech, was one of the fairest methods of raising revenue, but one which was "distinctively a State right and province." Furthermore, "the amendment we have to vote on contains a clause which is a most sweeping surrender of the rights and privileges of the States, giving as it does to Congress the power to tax incomes 'from whatever source derived' . . . and when we adopt the amendment we give to the Federal government one more agency to destroy the States." As for the direct election of senators, Browne felt, as had Jefferson, that some safeguard must be preserved against the occasional radicalism of the people on the one hand and the centralizing tendency of the general government on the other. How could the occasional whirlwinds of popular passion be contained other than by the disciplined control of a legislature-chosen Senate? He concluded with the warning, "With the election of Senators by direct vote, this fabric [safeguard] will be destroyed, and we will continue on the way of all the great republics of ancient times."

Only six years after these utterances, Jefferson Browne found himself in the highest judicial office of the State of Florida. Elected to the Supreme Court in November 1916, he was sworn in as chief justice in the early morning of January 2, 1917. Later that day, he performed his first official act when he administered the oath of office to the incoming governor, Sidney Johnston Catts. Browne was to become a distinguished jurist. One need only browse through the *Florida Reports (Cases Adjudicated in the Supreme Court of Florida)* for the years of his tenure to discern the rigorous reasoning, the wide legal knowledge, and the seasoned sense of justice which he brought to the deliberations of the court. On the occasion of his death, his long-time friend and law partner, William H. Malone of Key West, said of him, "Judge Browne's opinions while on the State Supreme Court bench have been referred to as legal classics. He had the distinction of having one of his dissenting opinions adopted as the decision of the Supreme Court of the United States."[25]

Although no hint of political predilection seems to have intruded upon his judicial opinions, Judge Browne continued to look with displeasure upon the political trends of his times. The progressivism of Woodrow Wilson's administration had run its course, but in his estimation the damage to states' rights was irreparable. Much of the disapproval which in 1911 he had directed at John Marshall was by 1920 reserved for Justice Oliver Wendell Holmes and the recently elevated Justice Louis Brandeis. In an article of that year, "The Super-Constitution," published in the *American Law Review*, Browne attacked with unconcealed bitterness the extension of "police power," the device by which he saw popular will undermining constitutional restraints. Declaring that "police power" was the power of absolutism and despotism, he proceeded to trace its development through the decisions of the Supreme Court from Marshall down to Holmes. It was in the decisions of state supreme courts, however, that he saw the greatest threat to liberty through the use of "police power." In the case of *Barbour* v. *State* (146 Georgia 667), he found an extreme and ominous expression of such a danger when the Supreme Court of Georgia reasoned, "But neither ownership, nor property rights, nor possession will be permitted to hinder the operation of laws enacted for the public welfare. Man possesses no right under the laws of constitution, State or Federal, which is not subservient to the public welfare."

Browne's attention was naturally drawn to the revolutionary events of contemporary Russia which had not at the time of his writing become stabilized. He was presumably acquainted with the theoretical extravagances of Marx, Lenin, and Trotsky, and had heard them echoed in the political harangues of the socialists of Western Europe, even in Britain, where Arthur Henderson professed to speak for British labor. But such exhortations to violence disturbed him not at all. He saw a greater threat in the silent revolution of court decision and legislative

xvii

enactment. In "The Super-Constitution," he wrote, "This country is no longer in danger from a revolution of force. . . . The voice of every Red within our gates raised in one loud acclaim against constitutional guarantees will be ineffectual to destroy them; while the doctrine of Mr. Justice Holmes in *Noble State Bank* v. *Haskell*, and the Georgia court in *Barbour* v. *State*, will blow away like wind all constitutional protection of life, liberty and property."

Browne feared that the time was near when radicals would no longer consider it necessary to nullify the Constitution. They would need only to control Congress and the legislatures, write such laws as served their purposes, and, when the Constitution should be invoked to restrain them, they would have as their champion "the apotheosized police power, at whose feet all constitutional guarantees must humbly kneel petitioning observance but impotent to demand it." These sentiments, thus expressed, were so representative of the conservative political thinking of the time that the prestigious *American Law Review* featured Browne's article in its issue of May–June 1920.

Though Judge Browne's literary talent is best represented in his professional writing and in the history reprinted in the present volume, he often wrote verse.[26] The following lines, apparently written following the death of his wife, Frances Atkinson Browne, or of his only daughter, Susan Nieves Browne Keating, are representative:[27]

On Parting from Her

Come grief, come woe, come sickness' threatening pall,
Naught more saddening than her absence can befall.
But like the rosy glow of breaking day
Her presence drives all carking cares away.
Her smile a sunbeam, her laugh an angel's song,
Her soul so pure, she never thought a wrong;
Too pure for mortal man, she scorns them all
Who at her feet in humble reverence fall.
God give her to me! God hear my earnest prayer!
Fill not my days with deep and bleak despair.
Not like a rainbow that for a moment cheers,
Then fades away and leaves the world in tears;
Nor like the evening clouds, with gorgeous rays alight,
Nor like the ships that hail, then pass into the night.
But let her presence be hope's beacon-light
That leads to love fulfilled, through darkest night.

One additional item from the pen of Judge Browne is worthy of mention, an article, "Across the Gulf by Rail," published by the *National Geographic Magazine* in 1896. It was patently written to publicize the expected advantages to Key West and the nation from the construction of an overseas railroad from the Florida mainland to the island city, a project in which Henry M. Flagler had already exhibited some interest and which would eventually materialize.[28]

Judge Browne's most significant literary undertaking, *Key West, The Old and The New,* was a labor of love. He knew Key West as few others have known it. His inquisitive and retentive mind had prompted him to collect every available scrap of information relating to the city's past. Connected by blood and marriage to two of the island's most prominent families, he had grown up with an awareness of who was who among its people. His many years of public life had exposed him to the economic and social developments not only of Key West but of the entire state. Though he may be considered a southern regionalist, he was by no means parochial in his vision. Through broad reading and travel, he was well informed on many matters of national and international interest. Still it was his love of Key West and the satisfaction he found in the friendly relationships he had established there that drew him ever back to the place of his birth and prompted him to rewrite the Maloney history.

Browne was obviously delighted with Maloney's *Sketch,* but as time passed he felt that a more complete history must be written. He did not reveal exactly when he made the decision to engage himself in the task, but it appears that for several years he collected the data which he would ultimately include. It cannot be claimed that Browne's history was superior to the Maloney work in literary quality. Browne himself would have made no such claim and, once he had acknowledged his indebtedness to Maloney, he proceeded to incorporate lengthy passages of the earlier book into his own text without further identification or even the guise of paraphrase. It must be stated, however, that neither work is of exceptional literary value. Both are, for the greater part, starkly factual. The chief historical merit of Browne's book is seen in the impressive body of data relating to every aspect of Key West's development from 1821 to 1912. His work is superior to Maloney's in that he was privileged to use as a point of departure the pioneer effort of his predecessor, that it was based on more extensive work in national, state, and local records, and that its *terminus ad quem* was 1912 instead of 1876.

Much of Judge Browne's history has been and will continue to be a source of satisfaction to genealogists whose searches lead them to Key West. His knowledge of family relationships was phenomenal, although much vital data such as dates of birth, marriage, and death have been omitted. Although the Key West elite, who were for much of the nineteenth century members of the Anglo-Saxon, Protestant community, are featured in his reminiscences, Browne has not neglected other social, religious, and ethnic segments. Included are treatments of the Cuban migrations and the Negro population. His public service had brought him into frequent contact with persons of all classes and ethnic origins, and he was mindful of their roles in the social structure. Browne, like so many Key Westers, was interested in people. The

xix

insularity of the town, which rendered it impossible for casual visitors to slip in and out unnoticed, seemed to intensify the interest, perhaps even the curiosity, of the inhabitants not only in mere sojourners but in each other. Besides, Key West was never populous; even by 1910 its residents did not number over 20,000.

Browne's table of contents, which he has designated "Index," lists thirty-four brief chapters and suggests the range of data included. The town's social and economic development claimed much of the author's attention. Politics is treated extensively and with scarcely any display of partisanship. Church history composes a comparatively large segment, as do military establishments. In every area, the approach has been personalized by the inclusion of names of individuals involved. Some readers may wish that Judge Browne had injected more critical opinion into his narrative, that he had been more analytical of the forces and motivations underlying historical change on the island. This was not his intent. He was writing a book about his acquaintances, friends, and relatives, and their forebears, inhabitants of the island city he had always loved. In such a work, there was no place for harsh judgments and scandal-mongering.

If Judge Browne loved Key West, the city reciprocated. Again and again, it demonstrated its confidence and affection by electing him to the public offices which he sought. It found him generous, compassionate, civic-minded, and (even though his last will and testament provides the only evidence in the matter) convivial. From this will, it seems proper at this point to quote the following provision: "My entire collection of wines, licquers [sic], cordials, etc., I desire distributed as nearly equal as possible [among the following friends]: In doing this I am not unmindful of the fact that the gift to each one will be small and that they are well able to buy all they want, but I would like for them sometime to pour out a draft and holding it up say: 'Here's to Jeff Browne.' "[29]

Jefferson Beale Browne died in Key West at midmorning on May 4, 1937, just one month short of his eightieth birthday. He belongs, along with Stephen R. Mallory and Dr. Joseph Y. Porter, among the most eminent sons of the island city.

E. ASHBY HAMMOND

University of Florida

NOTES

1. Walter C. Maloney, *A Sketch of the History of Key West, Florida* (Newark, N.J., 1876; facsimile edition, Gainesville, Florida, 1968).

2. Clarence Carter, ed., *Territorial Papers of the United States, Territory of Florida*, 26 vols. (Washington, 1956–62), 22: 382–83.

3. Jefferson B. Browne, *Key West, The Old and The New* (St. Augustine, Florida, 1912), p. 52.

4. Simonton's memorandum, December 7, 1821, to Treasury Department. In Carter, *Territorial Papers*, 22:411–12.

5. Ibid., 22:362–63.

6. Ibid., 22:385–86.

7. *American State Papers,* Class 6, Naval Affairs (Washington, 1832–61), 1:1118.

8. For each plat, Whitehead supplied a letter, F, G, S, or W, to indicate ownership by Fleeming, Greene, Simonton, or Whitehead (John). For some, names of recent purchasers were supplied. Earlier surveys had been made, but that of Whitehead was the most complete and reliable for the early part of the American occupation.

9. Senate Document, May 7, 1822, 21st Cong., 1st sess., no. 78, p. 1.

10. Ibid., p. 4. Although the town was yet to endure periodic epidemics and occasional destructive fires, its commercial success seemed assured.

11. The United States Census of 1850 lists him as a Key West householder, aged fifty-four. His death occurred on November 2, 1851.

12. Carter, *Territorial Papers*, 23:701.

13. Browne, *Key West,* pp. 52, 175.

14. According to the alumni records of the college, Browne's enrollment at William and Mary extended from 1826 to 1831. Letter to editor from Gordon C. Vliet, executive secretary of the Society of Alumni, William and Mary College, April 10, 1972.

15. Key West records of the 1830s reveal that Ximinez had business interests in the Charlotte Harbor area. Deed Record Book, A, Monroe County Clerk's Office, contains a record of the transfer of an island in Charlotte Harbor, Tio Sespas (the present-day Useppa), to Ximinez on January 23, 1833. United States Treasury Department records show him bringing cargoes from Cuba to Charlotte Harbor in 1835. See National Archives, Treasury Department, Letters Received from Collectors of Customs, 1835.

16. A biographical sketch of Joseph Beverly Browne appears in Browne, *Key West,* pp. 225–26.

17. Browne, *Key West,* p. 225. Browne was in error in recalling his father as a legislator from 1866 to 1870 and in failing to include him among the legislators of 1873 and 1874.

18. Biographical data principally from obituary notices in the *Key West Citizen,* May 4, 1937, and the *Miami Herald,* May 5, 1937.

19. Neither of these academies has survived and the dates of Browne's enrollments have not been determined.

20. Fowey Rocks, lying some six miles southeast of Cape Florida (Key Biscayne), got its lighthouse in 1878.

21. Records of the Alumni Association, University of Iowa, include the entry "Jefferson Beale Browne, LL.B., 1880." Letter to editor from Thomas L. Irwin, Jr., associate director, University of Iowa Alumni Association, April 26, 1972.

22. *Journal of the Proceedings of the Senate of the Regular Session of the Legislature of the State of Florida* (Tallahassee, 1891), p. 3.

23. This address was given on February 23, 1911. Since the proceedings of the bar association for the years 1910–19 were not published officially, it is assumed that this speech was privately printed in a limited edition. Two copies are known to exist: one in the Brooklyn Public Library, New York; the other in the Law Library of the University of Virginia, Charlottesville. Two other significant articles by Judge Browne are "The Super-Constitution," *The American Law*

Review 54 (May–June 1920):321–50; and "The American Law Institute, Its Organization and Purpose," *Proceedings of the Florida State Bar Association* (Miami, 1923), pp. 85–102.

24. It may be assumed that Browne had reference here to such southern political figures as Napoleon Bonaparte Broward of Florida, Hoke Smith of Georgia, and Braxton B. Comer of Alabama.

25. The editor has not identified this case. It was mentioned, along with other distinctions enjoyed by Judge Browne, by Malone at the time of the judge's death. See *Miami Herald,* May 5, 1937.

26. Only five of his poems have survived. They were printed in Vivian Yeiser Laramore, ed., *The Second Florida Poets: An Anthology of Forty-two Contemporaries* (New York, 1932), pp. 24–27.

27. Judge Browne was married June 18, 1889, to Frances Williams Atkinson of Kentucky. To that union was born Joseph Emmet Browne (b. April 30, 1890; d. May 7, 1940) and Susan Nieves Browne Keating (b. February 7, 1894; d. July 16, 1928). She was the wife of William B. Keating, a Key West physician. (The death certificate for Susan Keating, issued by the Florida Bureau of Vital Statistics, lists her birth date as February 8, 1894, and her death on July 15, 1928.)

28. *National Geographic Magazine* 7 (June 1896):203–7.

29. This will was transcribed and made available by Judge Helio Gomez and Mrs. T. O. Bruce of Key West.

Jeff. B. Browne

KEY WEST

The Old and The New

By JEFFERSON B. BROWNE

ST. AUGUSTINE:
The Record Company ◄═══► Printers and Publishers
1912

DEDICATION

IF THE memory of the name of Browne, transplanted from Virginia to Key West by my great-uncle, Fielding A. Browne, is kept alive by this work, I want the credit to be given to my Father and Mother, to whom in love and gratitude I dedicate this History.

Whatever of gentleness of character and intellectual culture I possess, I owe to my Father; to my Mother I owe the will to execute, and the desire to serve mankind.

They now rest side by side, after journeying together for near a half century, and I paraphrase, in humble reverence to them, the inscription which I placed on my Father's monument twenty-three years ago.

> "Those best of parents, how shall I repay
> The debt of love and gratitude I owe thee?"
> "By laying up our counsels in your heart."

As I lay down my pen, whatever pleasure the accomplishment of my task affords, it is saddened by the thought that their eyes will never behold the work which they inspired.

JEFFERSON BEALE BROWNE.

PREFACE

I HAVE written this history of Key West, believing that it would be interesting to the younger' generation, and to those who are to come after us, to know something of the people and events which filled the years that have gone.

My first intention was to copy Colonel Maloney's history, published in 1876, and bring it down to the present time.

In collecting the data, however, I found that there were a great many interesting events connected with the early history of Key West which Colonel Maloney had omitted, and concluded that if my work was to be as complete as was possible with available data, I would have to write it anew. This I have done, using, however, such data as his history contains, and at times preserving even his phraseology.

The brevity of Colonel Maloney's history is no reflection on his effort. He states that it was prepared on a few week's notice and was delivered as an address on the dedication of our city hall on July 4, 1876. It was impossible for him to have gotten together in that time the data which my work contains, in compiling which I have spent more than a year.

I have obtained information from the State, War, Navy and Judiciary Departments of the government at Washington, and from the Secretary of State's office at Tallahassee, Florida; from the New York, Boston and Congressional Libraries, and miscellaneous old publications. Information, embodied in a few lines may have been procured only by searching numerous records, and carrying on a voluminous correspondence. The historian who writes of Key West thirty or forty years from now, will have no occasion to cover the same ground.

I believe that this work contains all the available information on any subject connected with Key West, which is of interest to anyone. Where some trivial matters are mentioned, it is because they throw light on the habits and customs of the times, and may, perchance, brighten what may prove but a prosaic record of events.

With this explanation, I leave to posterity this compilation, as a tribute to the ancient order of things, and to the noble band of citizens who made this their home in the days of the Old Key West.

INDEX

THE BUSINESS PART OF KEY WEST

1. U. S. Military Cantonment. 2. Warehouses and Wharf of F. A. Browne. 3. Warehouses and Wharf of P. C. Greene. 4. Warehouses and Wharf of O. O'Hara. 5. Duval Street. 6. Front Street. 7. Fire Engine House. 8. Fleeming's Key and Naval Anchorage. 9. Turtle, Crab and Fish Market. 10. Blacksmith Shop. 11. Tops of Cocoanuts North of the Warehouse.

Looking North. Reduced from a pencil sketch by W. A. Whitehead, taken from the Cupola of the Warehouse of Messrs. A. C. Tift & Co., June, 1838.

KEY WEST

Looking South-East. Reduced from a pencil sketch by W. A. Whitehead, taken from the Cupola of the Warehouse of Messrs. A. C. Tift & Co., June, 1838.

1. Whiteheads Point. 2. Light-house. 3. Old Grave Yard. 4. Residence of F. A. Browne. 5. Custom House and Collector's Residence. 6. Jail. 7. Court House. 8. Whitehead Street. 9. Caroline Street. 10. Residence of A. Gordon. 11. Clinton Place. 12. Front Street. 13. Foot-bridge across Pond on the line of Duval Street. 14. House begun by Judge Webb, unfinished. 15. Residence of Judge Marvin. 16. Residences of P. J. Fontane and Patterson, one behind the other. 17. Residence of Mr. Weaver.

CHAPTER I

THE earliest recorded data about Key West is to be found in a grant of the island of Cayo Hueso on August 26, 1815, by Don Juan de Estrada, the then Spanish governor of Florida, to Juan Pablo Salas. The grant recited that it was "in consideration of the several services rendered by him at different times, much in the Royal Artillery Corps stationed at this fort, as well as the services rendered voluntarily and without pay at the office of the secretary under your administration."

Nothing was done by Salas in the way of settling or improvements and the island wore the same wild aspect that it had worn for ages, when on the twenty-first day of December, 1821, Salas offered to sell his right, title and interest to Mr, John W. Simonton,* of Mobile, who had met Salas in Havana. Having heard of the advantageous situation and capacity of the harbor, etc., Mr. Simonton was induced from the certain prospect of improvement throughout the country, by the cession of Florida to the United States, which his mercantile experience led him to foresee must advance the interests of a settlement at this point, to purchase the island for the sum of $2,000.00 on the nineteenth day of January, A. D. 1822.

Soon after making the purchase he sold one undivided quarter of his interest to Mr. John Warner, and Mr. John Mountain, respectively United States consul and commercial agent for the United States at Havana, and two other quarters to Mr. John Whitehead† and Mr. John W. C. Fleeming.‡ The interests of Messrs. Warner and Mountain were soon after transferred to Mr. Pardon C. Greene, who became a permanent resident of the island at that time.

Salas, however, had made a conditional sale to Mr. John B. Strong, who subsequently transferred his claim, such as it was, to Mr. John Geddes, who having the countenance of Captain Hammersley of the U. S. naval schooner, "Revenge," then in the harbor, effected a landing and took possession of the island in April, 1822.

A Dr. Montgomery and Mr. George M. Geddes were in charge of the party sent by Geddes to take possession in his name. It consisted of two white carpenters and three negroes, with provisions and lumber to build a shed. How long they remained on the island is not known, but as they were supported by Captain Hammersley of the United States Navy, the other claimants were helpless to do anything more than protest. A

---

* Appendix A.   † Appendix B.   ‡ Appendix C.

lawsuit resulted, which was finally terminated by a compromise. One of the legal documents connected with this claim states that the consideration given for the island, by Strong, was a small sloop of about thirty-one tons burden, called "The Leopard of Glastonbury," for which he had paid $575.00. Strong's title proved imperfect, and Salas, in order to obtain the restoration of the island to the Simonton claimants, conveyèd to him five hundred (500) acres of a tract at "Big Spring, East Florida."

There is no authentic record of the origin of the name Key West, of which two explanations are given. One, that it is the most westerly of the chain of islands or keys extending from the mainland—hence Key West; the other that it is a corruption of the Spanish words *Cayo Hueso* pronounced "Ki-yo Way-so," meaning bone island.

Mr. William A. Whitehead,* one of the earliest settlers of Key West, who surveyed and mapped the city in 1829, accepts the latter theory. He says:

"It is probable that, from the time of the first visit of Ponce de Leon until the cession of the Floridas to the United States, the islands or keys, as they are termed (a corruption of the Spanish word *Cayo*) which extended in a southwesterly direction from Cape Florida, were only resorted to by the aborigines of the country, the piratical crews with which the neighboring seas were infested, and the fishermen (many of them from St. Augustine) who were engaged in supplying the market of Havana from the 'finny tribes' that abound in this vicinity. Of the occasional presence of the first, we have evidence in the marks of ancient fortifications or mounds of stones, found in various localities (in one of which, opened some time since, human bones of a large size were discovered), and tradition has in addition brought down to us notices of them which deserve all the credit conferred upon the same authority, in other parts of the country. The oldest settler in this part of the country, one whose residence in the neighborhood of Charlotte Harbor dated back to about 1775, used to say, that in his early years he had heard it stated that some eighty or ninety years previous (probably about the commencement of the eighteenth century) the Indians inhabiting the islands along the coast and those on the mainland were of different tribes, and as the islanders frequently visited the main for the purpose of hunting, a feud arose between the two tribes, and those from the main having made an irruption into the islands, their inhabitants were driven from island to island, until they reached Key West. Here, as they could flee no farther, they were compelled to risk a final battle, which resulted in the almost entire extermination of the islanders. Only a few escaped (and that by a miracle, as they embarked in canoes upon the ocean) whose descendants, it is said, are known to have been met with in the island of Cuba.

Appendix D.

8

"This sanguinary battle strewed this island with bones, as it is probable the conquerors tarried not to commit the bodies of the dead to the ground, hence the name of the island, *Cayo Hueso*, which the English, with the same facility which enabled them to transform the name of the wine *Xeres Seco* into 'Sherry Sack,' corrupted into Key West. That the harbor of Key West was the occasional resort of pirates has been proven by the evidence of many who were connected with them in their lawless depredations, and by the discovery of hidden articles that could only have been secreted by them."

One of the matters intrusted to the commissioners appointed under the treaty of the cession with Spain, when the United States acquired Florida, was to pass upon the validity of the grant of the island to Salas, and they, having resolved it in his favor, and the same being confirmed by Congress, the title to all lands on the island of Key West, legally derived through Juan P. Salas and John W. Simonton, were perfected and forever settled. Owing to this, there is no confusion of ancient titles to Key West realty.

The establishment of a territorial government for Florida in March, 1819, was the beginning of the actual settlement and development of Key West. Several families from South Carolina and other States, and from St. Augustine who repaired here shortly after, were hospitably received by the proprietors, and building lots were given them within that part of the island intended to be laid out for the city.

On the seventh of February, 1822, Lieutenant M. C. Perry, commander of the United States schooner Shark, received orders to visit the island and take possession of it as part of the territory ceded by Spain, and on the twenty-fifth day of March following there was witnessed by the few residents then here the placing of a flag pole and the hoisting thereon of the flag of the United States, while at the same time its sovereignty over this and the neighboring islands was formally proclaimed. Lieutenant Perry named the island Thompson's Island, and the harbor Port Rodgers, the first in honor of the then secretary of the navy, Hon. Smith Thompson, and the other after Commodore Rodgers, the president of the naval board. From Lieutenant Perry's report to the navy department, it would seem that these names originated with him, and received the approval of at least three of the proprietors of the island, Messrs. Warner, Fleeming and Whitehead, who were present. These names, however, did not remain long in use; *Cayo Hueso* and its English substitute, "Key West," seemed to suit the fancy of the people more than the new names.

Commodore Porter of the navy, also took a hand in naming Key West and dated his letters from "Allenton," but this was even shorter lived than the others.

Key West lies in latitude 24°, 33', north, and longitude 81°, 48', west. Its topography, before its ponds and lagoons

9

were filled, was like that of other habitable keys near the Florida Reef, having a high ridge extending along its water front on the ocean or gulf side, where the deepest water lies, and sloping back to ponds and lagoons, beyond which lie high hammock lands. The early settlers naturally selected the high ridge on the deep-water side to build the city, and until the onward march of commercial progress and the development as a naval station drove them further back, the finest residences were built on and near the water front, from the present location of the United States Marine Hospital to the foot of Duval street. Back of the high ridge on the southwestern end of the island was a large lagoon which commenced in a swamp not very far from the southwestern end of the island and continuing along, nearly parallel with the beach, crossed Whitehead street near Caroline, and entered the water near the north end of Simonton street. Where it crossed White-head street it was so narrow that it was easily bridged for carts and carriages by a few planks. After crossing this street, it spread out into what was called a pond, which in 1836 covered about two acres of ground. Duval street then crossed this pond in about its center. The depth of water varied with the ebb and flow of the tide, but it was generally about twelve to eighteen inches deep. A foot bridge, made of piles and covered with planks, commenced within about 100 feet of the corner of Duval and Front streets, and extended to within about 75 feet of the corner of Duval and Caroline streets. A more substantial bridge about fifteen feet long afforded a passage across the entrance of the pond, about on a line with Simonton street, which was used by drays and other vehicles; it being the only way to get to and from the northwestern part of the island. There was also a small bridge across Whitehead street, which in 1850 was super-seded by a wagon road.

No attempt was made to get rid of the lagoon or pond because it was apprehended that if it should be closed to the flux and influx of the tides, other portions of the inhabited city would be subject to overflow, and to guard against this the charter of 1836 not only restricted the authorities of the city from filling up the streets, but the owners of lots covered by the pond were also restrained from filling them.

The hurricane of 1846 so altered the configuration of the island by washing up the sand, that the pond ceased to receive the tides, and the consequences apprehended not having occurred, the restriction against such filling was omitted from subsequent charters, and in November, 1853, an ordinance was passed requiring the respective owners of the submerged lots to fill them up.

These lots were in the hands of various owners, some of whom complied with the terms of the ordinance, others suffered the work to be done by the city, and paid the costs of the filling, whilst others refused to fill in or pay the expense incurred therefor.

10

The city was surveyed and mapped by Mr. William A. Whitehead in February, 1829, and like all new cities was more pretentious on the map than in reality. None of the streets extending southeasterly were cleared beyond Caroline street. On the 8th of October, 1831, the city council adopted a resolution giving free commission to the inhabitants of the town to cut and remove the woods standing on Eaton street, which caused it to be cleared of trees from Duval to Simonton streets. As late as 1837 Eaton street beyond Simonton was covered with its original small trees, heavy underbrush, vines, cacti, etc., but in that year the woods were cleared and the brush burned off on all that part of the island lying between Whitehead and Elizabeth streets, as far out as Fleming street.

The first street opened through to the South Beach was Whitehead street. Duval street was only cleared about half way between Eaton and Fleming street as late as 1836, and the only house on it at that time, after crossing Caroline street, was one belonging to Captain Francis B. Watlington. This house is still occupied by his immediate family, and though built in the early thirties, weathered the great hurricanes of 1835, 1846, 1909 and 1910, and sustained little damage.

A large part of this work was accomplished in one day by a party of fifty or more United States sailors sent on shore for this purpose by the commanding officers of the United States sloop Concord, and other vessels then lying in the harbor. Prof. Coffin, instructor in mathematics to the midshipmen, and leading townspeople, among whom were Judge Marvin, Mr. Jos. B. Browne, Mr. Stephen R. Mallory and Mr. Asa F. Tift, assisted in the work, which was done with a view to take away from the Seminole Indians, who were at war with the whites on the mainland, the means of concealing themselves, should they attempt an attack on the town.

The following from the pen of Judge William Marvin, for many years United States district judge at Key West, is interesting reading of the old days:

"About the persons I found living in Key West when I first landed there in October, 1836, from a little mail schooner, which sailed from Charleston (the whole population was then not very far from four hundred souls), James Webb, then about forty-five years old, was the judge of the Superior Court. He had been appointed by President Adams from Georgia. He was a good lawyer, an impartial judge and a genial gentleman. He resigned his office in 1839 and moved to Texas, where he was appointed by President Lamar, secretary of State. Texas had not then been admitted into the Union—it was the Lone Star. Mr. Alden A. M. Jackson was clerk of the court and Mr. Thomas Easton was marshal. They told in that day a good story of the marshal. He had been only recently appointed. He was calling in the court the names of the jurors. He did not know the sound of a single letter in Spanish. He had come from

Tennessee. He came to the name on the list—Joseph Ximinez. He called 'Joseph Eks-im-e-nez.' No person answered. Some one whispered to him to call 'Joseph He-ma-nes,' which he did. Whereupon Mr. Ximinez answered 'here' and walked up to the clerk's desk to be sworn in. 'Phoebus! What a name!' exclaimed the marshal.

"The only lawyers at that time at the bar were Mr. Adam Gordon and Mr. Wm. R. Hackley. Mr. Chandler had, a short time before, resigned the office of United States attorney and moved away. I had succeeded to his place. Mr. Wm. A. Whitehead was collector of the port, Mr. Adam Gordon deputy, and Mr. S. R. Mallory, inspector.

"The principal merchants were Mr. Fielding A. Browne, a Virginian; Mr. Pardon C. Greene,* from Rhode Island; Mr. Oliver O'Hara, from South Carolina, and his partner, Mr. Charles Wells, from New York. Mr. Wm. Shaw, Mr. Geo. E. Weaver and Mr. Philip J. Fontane were grocers and ship chandlers. Mr. Amos and Mr. Asa Tift kept a dry goods store. Mr. Alexander Patterson was an auctioneer, and kept a store located near a cocoanut tree at the foot of Whitehead street. Mr. William H. Wall kept a little store, had been married a a short time before to Miss Mabritty and lived in a small house on Whitehead street a little beyond Jackson Square, the farthest house out on that street. Mr. Lewis Breaker, the father of Mrs. James Filor, was a justice of the peace. Mr. John Geiger was pilot, captain of a wrecking vessel, a man of decided character and a sort of commodore among his compeers. Mr. Charles Johnson and Mr. Francis Watlington, both bright and intelligent men, were pilots and wreckers. I am not quite certain whether Mr. William Curry was living in Key West at the time I am writing of or not. I am inclined to think he came there at a somewhat later period. He was at one time clerk in Mr. Wall's store. At a still later period he formed a partnership with Mr. George Bowne in the business of buying and selling wrecked goods, and made money. But few people came from the Bahamas before 1836. Among the first to come were Mr. Wm. Curry's family, Mr. Samuel Kemp, Mr. John Braman, Mr. Benj. Albury, and Mr. John Lowe, Jr.'s family.

"Among the young men about town are to be named Amos and Asa Tift, Stephen R. Mallory, Joseph B. Browne, John P. Baldwin and Lieut. Benjamin Alvord, United States Army, afterwards paymaster general of the army. I do not know that these young fellows ever 'painted the town red,' for they were a well behaved and orderly set of young gentlemen; but they, or some of them, were known to be in the streets very often in the small hours of the morning, serenading some one or more of the young ladies of the town. Among these young ladies were Miss Mary Nieves Ximinez, who married Mr. Joseph Beverly Browne, Miss Whalton, Miss Breaker, and at a very

*Appendix E.

12

little later period, say in 1837-38, Miss Mary and her sister Miss Nona Martinelli. Nothing pleased Mallory better than to take his flute and get one or two friends, and Roberts, a colored man with his fiddle, to join him and go out into the beautiful moonlight nights and serenade some lady or ladies. Among the married ladies were Mrs. Wm. A. Whitehead, Mrs. Adam Gordon, Mrs. Wm. Randolph, sister of Mr. Fielding A. Browne, Mrs. George E. Weaver, Mrs. Joseph Ximenez, Mrs. Alexander Patterson, Mrs. Francis Watlington, Mrs. Johnson, Mrs. Whalton and Mrs. Ellen Mallory.

"Messrs. Charles Howe, Winer Bethel, Stephen J. Douglas, James Curtis, Thomas Ferguson, Walter C. Maloney, James Filor, Fernando J. Moreno, Senac, Charles and Asa Tift, James C. Clapp, Rev. Osgood E. Herrick and James Hicks all came to Key West after 1836. Mr. Howe was living at that time at Indian Key."

The first permanent settlers in Key West were Mr. Joseph C. Whalton and family, Mr. Michael Mabritty and family, Mr. Antonio Girardo and family from St. Augustine, Fla., and Mr. William W. Rigby and family and Mr. Richard Fitzpatrick.

A territorial government was established in Florida in 1819 and Key West then began to feel the benefit of an influx of population. Probably few new cities have ever started out with as high a class of population as Key West. Nearly all who came here had some means, and were people of culture and refinement. St. Augustine, Virginia, South Carolina, New York and Connecticut furnished their quota of the early population. Wrecking and fishing for the Havana market were the almost exclusive sources of revenue, and as they were both very lucrative occupations, many substantial fortunes were made.

The little colony at Key West was not without excitement at times. On December 7, 1831, the *Key West Gazette* said:

"Considerable excitement has existed here during this week occasioned by the riotous conduct of a number of the passengers from on board the wreck of the ship Maria. As soon as they arrived here, every accommodation which the place could afford was granted them; fifteen or twenty tents were pitched for their convenience, and a number of them were taken into different houses.

"On Thursday last, after a rather free indulgence to Bacchus, they, from some imaginary cause, became dissatisfied and threatened the lives of Captain McMullen and some of his crew. They evidenced their feelings that night, by the most boisterous behavior; in consequence of which the inhabitants at the lower end of the town were prevented from sleeping and were in momentary expectation of having their homes assaulted. On Friday afternoon they collected in such numbers on Browne's wharf that the proprietor was obliged to suspend business. Here a general battle ensued among them, in which it was difficult to tell who or how many were engaged, and a disfigura-

13

tion of eyes and noses followed, which by no means added to the engaging appearance of the party. The citizens generally became alarmed for the safety of their property. Under these circumstances letters were addressed by the proper authorities to Major Glasel, commandant of the post, and Captain Shubrick, of the United States sloop of war Vincennes, then in port, requesting them to co-operate in protecting the citizens of Key West from aggression. These calls were promptly answered; a detachment of marines under the command of Lieutenant Engle, from the Vincennes landed and remained during the night at the warehouse of Pardon C. Greene, whilst a detachment of United States troops under the command of Lieutenant Manning, patrolled the streets. As soon as it was known that steps were taken to prevent or suppress any riotous conduct, the mob dispersed and remained perfectly quiet, up to the time of their sailing on yesterday for New Orleans.

"Had not these steps been taken, it is more than probable that some serious mischief might have resulted, as the individuals composing the mob were generally under the excitement of liquor during their stay here.

"We understand that in consequence of this occurrence, and the prevalence of unfavorable winds, the Vincennes has been detained at this place longer than was contemplated on her first arrival.

"Since the above was in type, we have been informed that the disturbance originated with a Mr. Smith (one of the contractors), who had illegally exacted money from some of the unfortunate individuals. Upon the interference of some of our citizens he was compelled to disgorge."

A brief sketch of Key West, written in 1831, has this to say of the conditions prevalent here at that time: "The island was originally settled by persons from almost every country and speaking almost every variety of language they brought with them habits, manners, views and feelings, formed in different schools and in many instances totally dissimilar and contradictory. Some were attracted hither by considerations of interest alone, and for a long time, in consequence of their being no court or modes of legal restraint, they had no rules of conduct for their guide, except such as their own views of what would conduce to the attainment of their own wishes afforded. These conditions are now drawing to a close, and giving way to a different, and we are proud to say a happier state of things. The establishment of a superior court of the United States and the salutary lessons which are daily experienced from its judgment, have done much toward purging society of its impurities, and showing to the strangers that the mantle of the law is at all times ready to shield them and their property from imposition and fraud. Moral improvement is on the march; let but men of influence throw their weight upon its side and they will adopt the best method of promoting the prosperity and reputation of Key West."

On the fourth of May, 1832, Key West was honored by a visit from the great ornithologist, Mr. John James Audubon. It was the fifty-second anniversary of his birth. He had already published his chief work "*Birds of America*," which sold by subscription then for $1,000.00 per copy and is now worth over $5,000.00. It was while he was engaged in this work that he visited Key West and other points in Florida for data. He came here from Charleston on the revenue cutter Marion, the vessels of the United States having been placed at his disposal by the government.

The following sketch of him appeared in the paper published in Key West in 1832:

"Mr. Audubon—This gentleman left here in the revenue cutter Marion on Monday last for Charleston, calculating to touch on his way at the Florida Keys, and probably the mainland. It affords us great pleasure to state that this expedition has given him much satisfaction and added largely to his collection of specimens, etc. Mr. Audubon is a most extraordinary man, possessed of an ardent and enthusiastic mind and entirely devoted to his pursuits; danger cannot daunt, and difficulties vanish before him. During his stay here his hour of rising was three o'clock in the morning; from that time until noon and sometimes even until night, he was engaged in hunting among the mangrove keys, despite of heat, sand-flies and mosquitoes. On his return from these expeditions his time was principally employed in making sketches of such plants and birds as he may have procured. This was not an extraordinary effort for a day, it was continued for weeks, in short it appeared to constitute his chief aim, as it is his happiness. Mr. Audubon has adopted a most excellent plan of connecting with his drawings of birds such plants as may be found in the neighborhood where they are taken. We hesitate not in giving it as our opinion that his work on ornithology, when completed, will be the most splendid production of its kind ever published, and we trust that it will be duly estimated and patronized. The private character of Mr. Audubon corresponds with the nature of his mind and pursuits—he is frank, free and generous, always willing to impart information, and to render himself agreeable. The favorable impression which he has produced upon our minds will not soon be effaced."

Mr. Audubon was the first ornithologist to find the white-headed pigeon in the United States, although it was well known in Cuba.

This bird is still found in Key West and is plentiful on the keys in this vicinity, a circumstance worthy of note, as the wild pigeon is almost extinct in other parts of the United States.

It resembles the domestic pigeon, in habits and flight, rather than the passenger pigeon, that almost extinct species.

15

They do not go in flocks, but separately and in twos and threes. They are a dark rich blue-black "having the upper part of the head pure white, with a deep rich brown edging at the lateral parts of the crown." The young have no white on their heads, that distinguishing feature not appearing until the birds are four months old. This bird comes from Cuba in the latter part of April and remains on the keys where it breeds, until about the first of October. It is not found elsewhere in the United States.

Mr. Audubon painted the whiteheaded pigeon on a bough of what is called in Key West the "Geiger Flower," botanically known as the "Rough-Leaved Cordia." Of this plant, which is now abundant in Key West, there were only two specimens in 1832, and they were in the yard of Dr. Benjamin B. Strobel.

During this visit Mr. Audubon discovered a new variety of pigeon hitherto unknown to ornithologists, of which he says: "I have taken upon myself to name this species the 'Key West Pigeon,' and offer it as a tribute to the generous inhabitants of that island, who honored me with their friendship." It is sometimes called the "partridge pigeon," from its resemblance to the partridge or quail in its habits and coloring. Like the whiteheaded pigeon, its natural habitat is Cuba, whence it once came in quantities to Key West and the adjacent keys, but is rarely found here now. Only a half a dozen specimens have been procured in the last thirty years, one of which was shot by Mr. J. W. Atkins, manager of the Telegraph and Cable Company, an amateur ornithologist of some repute. Mr. Audubon calls it the "most beautiful of woodland cooers," and on observing for the first time "the brilliant changing metallic hues of its plumage" was so inspired with the difficulty of copying nature in this instance that he exclaimed "But who will draw it?" His painting, in the "Birds of America," shows it to be a most beautiful bird, but it is obvious that Nature laughed at man's effort to put on canvas what God had limned.

On February 22, 1832, the one hundredth anniversary of the birth of Washington, a banquet was given by the patriotic citizens of Key West, in honor of that occasion. The program and toasts were of high order and deserve to be perpetuated in history; not only as a lesson in patriotism but as an illustration of the thoroughness of the journalism of that day.*

AFRICAN SLAVES

In May, 1860, the United States gunboats Mohawk and Wyandotte captured two slavers, the Wildfire and Williams, and brought them into this port with their cargoes of three hundred Africans.

A barracoon was constructed at Whitehead's point, about where the principal sand battery now stands, and several large barracks built for them. These fronted the shore

*Appendix F.

16

a distance of about 140 yards from high water mark, and every day the Africans would go in a mass and bathe. As their clothing was scant, consisting of merely a clout, they had none of the inconveniences of modern surf bathers. The dormitory for their accommodation was two hundred and twenty-five feet by twenty-five feet, and this was divided into nine large rooms, so that the sexes and children of different ages could be separated. They were fed in squads of ten, seated around a large bucket filled with rice and meat, each armed with a spoon to feed with. Thirty gallon tubs well supplied with cool fresh water stood in each room. The percentage of sick among them was enormous. Nearly all were suffering with ophthalmia, while many were totally blind. A hospital one hundred and fourteen by twenty-one feet was erected, which at one time had as many as one hundred and eighty patients. The hospital was in charge of Doctors Whitehurst, Skrine and Weedon, under whose care most of the sick were restored to health.

The Africans were cared for by the Federal authorities but were the recipients of many acts of kindness from our citizens. Hundreds visited them daily, carrying clothing, food and other things for their comfort and pleasure. The first burial was of a child six weeks old, whose young mother was barely in her teens. Her devotion to her offspring made her an object of much sympathy to the visitors to the camp, and upon the death of the child, our people provided a handsome coffin to bury it in. The interment took place some distance from the barracoon, and the Africans were allowed to be present at the services, where they performed their native ceremony. Weird chants were sung, mingled with loud wails of grief and mournful moanings from a hundred throats, until the coffin was lowered into the grave, when at once the chanting stopped and perfect silence reigned, and the Africans marched back to the barracoon without a sound.

In December, 1867, Key West was honored by a visit from Mr. Jefferson Davis, late president of the Southern Confederacy, and his wife, Varina Howell Davis. Mr. Davis' long confinement in Fortress Monroe had broken his health, and he was advised to go to Cuba for the winter. He embarked from Baltimore for Havana via Key West, and spent the day here. He and Mrs. Davis were the guests of Hon. Joseph B. Browne. A delicate and thoughtful attention was shown them by Colonel W. C. Maloney, Sr. He sent a basket of fruit from his garden to ornament the dinner table, and requested that it be presented with his compliments to Mr. Davis, after the dinner. In the center was a fruit of the cocoanut tree, surrounded with its spiral stemmed blossoms. The delicate green of the anone, contrasted with the brown of the sapodillo, and the yellow and red of the mango gave the needed dash of color; the whole effect was enlivened by a generous sprinkling of the bright pink of the West India cherry—the favorite fruit of the donor's

17

2

Beauvoir Miss.

14th May 1881

My dear friend,

Your kind letter was by some accident mislaid and has been but quite lately recovered, it has been read with much gratification. My Wife and I have often recurred to our hospitable reception at your Father's house, and though we well remember you, it would not have been surprising because of your tender age if you had forgotten us.

Please accept my most cordial wishes for your welfare and happiness and believe me ever truly and respectfully yours

Jefferson Davis

garden. Colonel Maloney had been an uncompromising Union man during the war, and his intense nature made him a bitter partisan. But the war was over, Mr. Davis was a private citizen, his health was broken, and he had suffered the hardships of a long prison life, and, what was a still more weighty consideration with Colonel Maloney, he was a guest of the city and entitled to all consideration.

An incident of this visit, trifling in itself, is indicative of Mr. Davis' gentleness of character and disinclination to wound. While out driving with his host, they stopped at a friend's home to get a ripe sapodillo for Mr. Davis to taste. He broke it in halves, and on taking a bite, quietly and without any expression of distaste, put the two parts together, and continued his conversation. On being asked if he did not like the fruit, said: "I cannot say that I care for it particularly, but I fancy some people are very fond of it."

Illustrative of his extreme punctiliousness, this incident is given:

In 1880 a group of students in the State University of Iowa were boasting of the distinguished people of their acquaintance. One of them spoke of knowing Mr. Jefferson Davis who had been a guest at his father's home in Key West. The claim was good naturedly challenged, and a wager laid, to be determined upon the young man receiving a letter from Mr. Davis which would verify his statement. The student wrote to Mr. Davis in April, 1880, and after waiting two months, received no reply, and paid the bet. More than a year afterward a letter came from Mr. Davis stating that through some accident the letter had been mislaid, but upon it being lately recovered was promptly answered. At this time Mr. Davis was engaged in writing his great work, "The Rise and Fall of the Confederacy," and notwithstanding the fact that his mind was engrossed with his great subject, he was concerned lest he might have been guilty of an act of discourtesy, and hastened to make reparation, although a year had elapsed since he received the letter.

In 1880 General U. S. Grant, accompanied by General Phil H. Sheridan, paid Key West a visit, on his return from his tour around the world. He came on the steamship Admiral from New Orleans bound for Havana. It was a day memorable in the history of the island—all stores were closed, and it was made a general holiday.

He was met by a committee consisting of Mr. John Jay Philbrick, Hons. Frank N. Wicker, George W. Allen, Eldridge L. Ware, Joseph B. Browne, G. Bowne Patterson, Judge James W. Locke and many others. A drive over the island, a public reception, and a banquet were part of the functions provided for his entertainment. The banquet was served in the St. James hotel, as it was then called, prepared by Mr. L. Y. Jenness. The menu was printed on silk American flags; the red, white and blue color scheme being carried out in the badges and decorations.

President Cleveland also paid Key West a visit at the expiration of his first term, 1889. He was accompanied by Ex-Secretary of State Bayard, Postmaster General Vilas and General Fitzhugh Lee, then governor of Virginia. They spent only a few hours in the city, but during that time they were shown around the island in carriages, and held a public reception in the Russell House.

In 1902 Hon. William Jennings Bryan was a visitor in Key West, and delivered an address. As there was no hall large enough to hold all who wanted to hear him, he spoke in the open air at the corner of Elizabeth and Fleming streets.

CHAPTER II

KEY WEST was peculiarly fortunate in its early settlers. Unlike the usual pioneers, they were not mere hewers of wood and drawers of water, but were people of culture, education and refinement, and, as was natural for such a community, they early directed their endeavors towards moral and intellectual development.

In March, 1831, just two years after the city had been laid out, a resolution of the town council, proposed by Mr. William A. Whitehead, called for a public meeting of the citizens to adopt measures for obtaining the services of a clergyman, and among the duties required of him was the opening of a school, and the earliest school established in Key West was by the Rev. Alva Bennett in 1834-5, he being the first clergyman to have a charge on the island. It was kept open a little less than a year, as Mr. Bennett returned north in April, 1835, and died soon afterwards. It was evidently well patronized, for Colonel Maloney in his history states that "Mr. Bennett realized from it about $30.00 per week."

The next school, as appears from an advertisement in the Key West *Enquirer* in April, 1835, was kept by Mr. Alden A. M. Jackson, the son-in-law of Judge Webb, in the county court house. The terms were from $2.00 to $4.00 per month according to the branches studied.

During the pastorate of the Rev. Mr. Dyce of St. Paul's church he conducted a school at the same place.

In 1842 Mrs. Passlague, a relative of Mrs. William Pinckney, opened a school, which she conducted for a year or two only. She was a French lady of rare intellectual attainments.

In 1843 a provision was made for paying from the county taxes for the education of children whose parents were unable to pay. About thirty pupils were at that time taught at the public expense. The amount allowed was $1.00 per month for each pupil, the teacher providing his own school room.

A school was taught by Colonel W. C. Maloney, Sr., on a lot situated on the western corner of Front and Fitzpatrick streets. The building was a two-story house, built in the style then quite common in Key West, and frequently seen in the West Indies, with *jalousies* on both floors.

In 1845 Mr. and Mrs. Turner came to Key West from the north, and opened a school in the court house, which they conducted for several years.

In 1852 Lieutenant Daniel Beltzhoover, a United States army officer, stationed at this post, taught a class at the barracks. Shortly after this Mr. John M. Bethel opened a school on Eaton street, in a building near the corner of Eaton and Simonton streets, adjoining the First Methodist church. Most of the present generation of older men went to school to him. After the Civil War he returned to Nassau, where he held for thirty years the position of secretary of the Colonial Parliament, and on his retirement, he came again to Key West and opened a night school. Two of his pupils are among the prominent men of Key West, Hon. William H. Malone, Jr., and Hon. Charles L. Knowles. He was educated in England, was a teacher of the old school, believed in thoroughly grounding his pupils in the fundamentals, and considered the strap a necessary adjunct to getting knowledge into a boy's brain.

In 1852 Miss Euphemia Lightbourne, the sister-in-law of Judge Winer Bethel, opened a school that became one of the leading institutions of Key West. In 1865 her niece, Miss Mellie Bethel, became her assistant, and on the death of Miss Lightbourne in 1887, Miss Bethel conducted the school alone. It closed its doors permanently in 1911, after sixty years operation, during which time it never missed a term. Its influence will continue during the lives of the present generation.

Other excellent private schools were kept by Miss Ann Elizabeth Browne, and Miss Josephine Ximinez, and many of our most cultured women studied under them.

PUBLIC SCHOOLS

1870 marks the beginning of the public or free school system in Key West. A school was opened on the first floor of the Masonic Temple on Simonton street. Mr. Eugene O. Locke, now clerk of the United States district court for the southern district of Florida, a brother of Judge James W. Locke of that court, was the first principal. He was succeeded by Mr. Thomas Savage of Boston, who afterwards became a member of the law firm of Allen, Long and Savage, of which Governor Long of Massachusetts was a member. In 1874 a large three-story building was erected on a lot in the rear of Simonton street, between Fleming and Southard streets, called Sears school. It accommodated about five hundred pupils. Mr. Justin Copeland was principal, with a corps of eight teachers. In 1909 it was abandoned and torn down.

Succeeding principals of Sears school, in the order of service, were Mr. Barnes of Baltimore, Mr. Wyman, Mr. F. J. Cunningham, Mr. Taylor Lee, Mr. W. J. Cappick, Mr. Adolph Van Delden, Mr. John A. Graham, Mr. Byrne, Mr. Yancy, Mr. B. C. Nichols, Mr. Bonnington and Mr. M. P. Geiger.

A public school for the education of the negro children was opened in 1870, called Douglas school. William M. Artrell, a negro from the Bahamas, was the first principal.

In 1887, under the administration of Dr. R. J. Perry, county superintendent of public instruction, a public school was opened on a lot on Grinnell street, between Division and Virginia streets. It was called "Russell Hall" in honor of Hon. Albert J. Russell, then State superintendent of public instruction, a prominent Mason, a distinguished Confederate officer and a fine orator, who devoted his life to the cause of education.

The first principal of Russell Hall was Mr. Taylor Lee. He served one full term, was reappointed, and in his second year was principal of both Sears school and Russell hall. He died on December 22, 1888.

He was succeeded as principal by Miss Lovie Turner, who held that position continuously until the close of the term, of 1911, when she resigned. She made a fine record and was loved and respected by the pupils and patrons of the school.

In 1900 Russell Hall was moved from Grinnell street to a lot on the corner of White and Division streets, and remodelled into a commodious colonial structure.

In 1909 a handsome concrete building was erected on the corner of Southard and Margaret streets called Harris high school. It took the place of Sears school in Monroe county educational work. The site cost sixteen thousand dollars and the building forty-two thousand dollars. On the completion, Sears school house was torn down, and its name abandoned.

Harris high school was dedicated on July 4th, 1909, and addresses were delivered by Mr. Jefferson B. Browne, Mr. W. Hunt Harris, Mr. William H. Malone, Mr. Charles L. Knowles, Mr. Virgil S. Lowe, Mr. J. Vining Harris, Dr. J. N. Fogarty, Major Hunter, United States army, and Commodore W. H. Beehler, United States navy.

CATHOLIC SCHOOLS—CONVENT OF MARY IMMACULATE

In 1868 the Sisters of the Holy Names of Jesus and Mary, a Canadian organization, came to Key West and opened a school for white girls in a large frame building on the corner of Whitehead and Division streets, which had been occupied as a barracks during the Civil War, where they taught for over ten years.

In 1878 they laid the foundation for a new convent to be erected on a part of tract twelve of the original survey of Key West, extending about six hundred feet along Division street, contai 1ing about eight and a half acres. The building is of native coral rock quarried on the island, the main part of which cost thirty-five thousand dollars. In 1904 it was enlarged to nearly twice its original size by the addition on the northeast end, at a cost of twenty-two thousand dollars. It is the handsomest educational building in the State of Florida, and a monument to the devotion and heroism of the good women who founded and maintained it.

Many of the sist rs died at their post of duty of yellow fever, and only once has it closed its doors—in 1898 when the holy sisters placed the convent, two school buildings and their personal services as nurses at the disposition of the naval authorities for hospital purposes.

Among the first to receive the loving care of the nuns was Father Chadwick, chaplain of the Maine. On his recovery he celebrated mass in the convent chapel, using the chalice given him by the crew of the Maine, and which had then just been recovered.

Of all the good women who gave their services for the success of this institution, one sister, by reason of her great ability and long service, deserves special mention—Sister Mary Theophile, who spent forty years in the educational field of Key West.

The convent conducted by sisters of the Catholic church is a religious institution, but non-sectarian in its teachings, and is liberally patronized by families of Protestants, and the great majority of our highly educated and accomplished women received their education at the convent of Mary Immaculate. Its influence on the morals and character of the women of Key West is infinite.

The same community of sisters in 1881 established St. Joseph's College for white boys. The college building, on the corner of Simonton and Catherine streets, stands on a lot which extends along Catherine to Duval street, owned by the Catholic church.

In 1869 a parochial school for white boys was established, conducted by a lay teacher, Mr. W. J. Cappick, under the supervision of the resident priest.

In 1870 St. Francis Xavier's School for the education of negro children was opened.

A Jesuit college for the higher education of boys was established in 1904, and is conducted by the Jesuit priests.

HARGROVE INSTITUTE

In 1898 Bishop Warren E. Candler of Atlanta, Ga., of the Methodist Episcopal Church South, representing the Woman's Board of Home Missions, came to Key West, and interested a number of gentlemen in a proposition to establish a seminary of learning here.

He appointed a committee on ways and means, consisting of Dr. Cornelius F. Kemp, Messrs. George L. Bartlum, Charles R. Pierce, Alfred Bates Curry and Jefferson B. Browne. Several meetings were held by them at the residence of Rev. J. P. DePass, where plans for raising money, securing a lot and founding the institution were worked out.

The seminary began in a modest way in 1899 in a rented building formerly the residence of Mr. Martin L. Hellings, near the light-house. The next year it was moved to the Gato residence on Division street, near the North Beach.

The first building erected on the property purchased for

24

the seminary on United street, was completed in 1901. It was a large colonial frame building, with recitation rooms, dormitories and living quarters for the faculty.

Its first principal was Miss Mary Bruce, to whose indomitable will and energy the success in launching this institution is mainly due. She was succeeded in 1905 by Miss Emily J. Reid who resigned in 1908, since which time the institution has been under the management of Professor Arthur W. Mohn. Under him the institution has thrived, and ranks as one of the first in the State.

In 1910 a principal's residence was erected, and in 1911 an administration building called Bruce Hall was completed. It is built of artificial stone, and contains twelve recitation rooms, two music rooms, a chemical and physical laboratory, a library room, the principal's office and a chapel or auditorium with a seating capacity of over six hundred, the largest in the city. Its large roof garden, where open air entertainments can be held, is one of the most attractive features, and in this climate one of the most useful.

The colonial building has been recently remodelled, and named Ruth Hargrove Hall. It is now used mainly as a dormitory and has accommodations for fifty teachers and students. An attractive kindergarten cottage stands at the rear of the lot.

Additional land was purchased in 1910 and in 1911, and the school tract now contains three acres.

The institution was first called Ruth Hargrove Seminary, but in 1910 the name was changed to Hargrove Institute.

CHAPTER III

THE DESIRE for religious worship, which is a dominant trait of the English speaking people, manifested itself in the earliest days of the settlement of Key West, and the people gathered together in the old court house in Jackson Square and held non-denominational services. Occasionally, when some clergyman would be transiently on the island, his services would be engaged and the islanders worshipped God with no thought of the denomination of the pastor.

On the 7th of March, 1831, the first movement was made to have a clergyman regularly domiciled at Key West. A meeting of the town council was held on that day and a motion made by Mr. William A. Whitehead, requesting the council to call a meeting of the citizens of Key West for this purpose. In pursuance thereof a meeting was held on the 9th day of March, and Judge James Webb of the United States court presided. A committee of six was appointed, consisting of Hons. James Webb, David Coffin Pinkham, judge of the county court of Monroe county, William A. Whitehead, collector of customs of the port of Key West, Col. Lachland M. Stone, United States marshal for the Southern District of Florida, Dr. Benjamin B. Strobel, surgeon of the army post, Dr. Henry S. Waterhouse, postmaster of Key West, to ascertain as far as practicable how much could be raised by subscription for the support of a minister, and the number of children who would attend the school to be established by him, and to communicate with the bishop of the Episcopal church of New York, requesting him to procure and send a clergyman here. In their letter they express proper consideration for the comfort of the clergyman, and say: "The minister would not be required in any year, that he should stay a greater portion of the months of August and September than would be entirely agreeable to himself."*

On October 13, 1831, another public meeting was held and the committee reported that they had communicated with the Rt. Rev. Benjamin T. Onderdonk, Protestant Episcopal Bishop of New York, and although the letter appeared in a religious magazine published by the Episcopal church in New York, no person had been appointed, nor had they received any reply from the bishop. The committee recommended that their efforts having failed of response from the Episcopal bishop, that they invite a clergyman of some other denomination.

*Appendix G.

Key West was unfortunate in its selection of a bishop to whom to apply for a pastor, as Bishop Onderdonk on the 3rd of January, 1845, after a sensational trial, was "suspended from all exercise of his episcopal and ministerial functions."

ST. PAUL'S EPISCOPAL CHURCH

The Episcopal church was the pioneer religious organization in Key West, and the entire population who desired a church to be established here, united for the purpose of public devotion under the name of the Protestant Episcopal Church, and many united with it who had not previously been of that faith.

Rev. Sanson K. Brunot, of Pittsburgh, Pa., the first clergyman to hold services in Key West, arrived here December 23, 1832. He came with letters of introduction from the Rt. Rev. Benjamin T. Onderdonk, bishop of New York, and Mr. S. J. Whitehead of New Jersey. He was only 24 years old and had not been long in the ministry. He accepted the call largely on account of his ill health, many of his family having died of consumption, and he thought thus to avoid becoming a victim to that disease. He was warmly welcomed on the island and became the guest of Mr. William A. Whitehead. During his stay the parish was organized, and an act of association was drawn up and a charter obtained from the territorial council on February 4, 1833. The official title of the organization was "The Rector, Wardens and Vestrymen of St. Paul's Church, Key West."

On Christmas day, 1832, was heard for the first time on the island, the beautiful service of the Episcopal church, by a regularly ordained priest.

After the morning service the following named persons were enrolled in the first Episcopal congregation: Mr. James Webb, Mr. William A. Whitehead, Mr. David C. Pinkham, Mr. Fielding A. Browne, Mr. Thomas Eastin, Mr. Alexander Patterson, Mr. A. H. Day, Mr. John W. Simonton, Mr. Adam Gordon, Mr. William H. Shaw, Mr. J. R. Western, Mr. William H. Wall, Mr. Theodore Owens, Mr. Eugene Trenor, Mr. L. A. Edmonston, Mr. Henry K. Newcomb, Mr. Francis D. Newcomb, Mr. Henry S. Waterhouse, Mr. Amos C. Tift, Mr. E. Van Evour, Mr. John Whitehead, Mr. Pardon C. Greene, Mr. Oliver O'Hara, Mr. George E. Weaver, Mr. Philip J. Fontane, Mr. John J. Sands, Mr. Stephen R. Mallory, Mr. Francis B. Watlington, Mr. Charles M. Wells and Mr. John P. Baldwin.

At the first election of wardens and vestrymen held April 5, 1833, Mr. James Webb and Colonel Oliver O'Hara were elected wardens, and Messrs. Fielding A. Browne, Pardon C. Greene, Alexander Patterson, David Coffin Pinkham and William A. Whitehead were elected vestrymen.

Mr. Brunot's health soon began to fail and after officiating only a few times, frequent hemorrhages put a stop to further public services. Feeling that his end was approaching and desiring to pass his last days in his old home, he left Key West in May, 1833, and died soon after his arrival in Pittsburgh.

Before leaving he advised the vestrymen to apply to the Missionary Society of New York for aid. In July, 1833, the vestrymen adopted Mr. Brunot's suggestion, and the Missionary Society appointed Rev. Alva Bennett of Troy, N. Y., and contributed $200.00 a year towards his salary, to which the parish added $500.00 a year. Mr. Bennett arrived in Key West in October, 1834, and remained until April, 1835.

On November 16, 1834, during Mr. Bennett's pastorate, the holy communion was first celebrated in Key West, in the court house, in Jackson Square, where services were held.

Mr. Bennett was succeeded by Rev. Robert Dyce who was also appointed by the Board of Missions and arrived in Key West in September, 1836. In 1837 Mr. Dyce made a tour of the country to solicit funds for the church and succeeded in raising $3,000.00.

On the 5th of May, 1838, Mrs. John William Charles Fleeming, wife of one of the original proprietors, gave to the vestry of St. Paul's church a tract of land having a frontage of two hundred feet on the southeast side of Eaton street, from Duval to Bahama street, and extending on Duval and Bahama streets two hundred feet; "the lot to be used for church purposes and the pews in the church to be free."

On the 10th of July, 1838, the vestry voted to erect a church building to be constructed of the native coral rock. It was to be forty-six feet long, thirty-six feet wide and twenty-two feet high on the inside, and to contain thirty-six pews and a gallery at one end.

The vestry went to work with a will, and by December 23d of the same year four hundred and fifty pieces of the native coral rock had been quarried and placed on the grounds. On the 3d of March the church was so far completed that the pews were sold at auction. The church cost $6,500.00.

On February 14, 1839, Mr. Dyce resigned charge of the parish and was succeeded by Rev. A. E. Ford. Mr. Ford left in 1842 and was succeeded by Rev. J. H. Hanson, who remained in charge until May, 1845, when he resigned. During this time the work on the church was nearly completed.

In October, 1846, the Rev. C. C. Adams was called and appointed missionary by the Domestic Board of Missions. Mr. Adams started for Key West via Savannah and St. Augustine. Before leaving St. Augustine he learned that the church had been blown down by the hurricane of October, 1846, and at the suggestion of the provincial bishop of Georgia he came to Key West "to ascertain the character of the parish and if he found it as being unworthy an effort to rebuild, to so report to him, and abandon it, otherwise, to go abroad and beg for funds to rebuild." After arriving at Key West Mr. Adams decided on the latter course, but first received assurances from the vestry that the new church should be forever free. He left Key West January 11, 1847, having assumed charge on that date.

He returned the following December with about $3,300.00. A frame church was then erected and the first service was held in it on July 30, 1848. The church was consecrated January 4, 1851, by the Rt. Rev. C. E. Gadsden, Bishop of South Carolina.

Four pews at the back of the church were set apart for the use of negroes, both free and slave, who were members of the Episcopal church. The practice prevailed until in 1888, when a negro Episcopal church, St. Peters', was erected, since which time they have attended that church, except a few of the old negroes who would not sever their relations with the church of their youth. At the celebration of holy communion they wait with old time respect for the white people to commune, and then go reverently to partake of the sacrament.

On January 5, 1854, the parish declared itself self-supporting and severed its connection with the Missionary Society. On April 1, 1855, the Rev. Mr. Adams resigned.

In December, 1856, E. O. Herrick was made rector, which position he occupied until he resigned in January, 1870, to accept an appointment as chaplain in the United States army. He was, for many years stationed at Fortress Monroe, where he was rector of the Church of the Centurian on the military post at that station. He died at Watertown, N. Y., October 1, 1907.

In December, 1857, during Mr. Herrick's pastorate the present rectory was built at a cost of $4,500.00. In 1860 the church was enlarged at a cost of about $4,000.00.

The following are the names of the succeeding rectors and dates of services:

Rev. Wm. T. Saunders, from July, 1870, to June, 1872.

Rev. J. S. J. Higgs, incumbent of the parish of San Salvador, from December, 1872, to the latter part of January, 1873.

During the winter of 1873 the Rev. Charles A. Gilbert visited Key West and held services.

Rev. John Reuther, from March, 1873 to 1874.

Rev. J. L. Steele, from 1874 to October 13, 1878, when he fell a victim to yellow fever.

Rev. J. B. Baez, a Cuban resident of Key West, who had been ordained a minister, held services until the appointment of a new rector.

Rev. Charles A. Gilbert, who had visited Key West in 1873, was called, and was in charge of the parish until November 8, 1880, when he, too, fell a victim to yellow fever.

Rev. Charles Stewart, from November, 1880, to May, 1881, when he resigned.

Rev. Chas. F. D. Lyne, from December 4, 1881, to February 13, 1886, when he died after a life of long and useful service.

29

Rev. J. D. Baez again filled the pulpit from February to June, 1886.

Rev. John B. Linn, from July, 1886, to 1890.

Rev. Gilbert Higgs, from 1890 to June, 1903. Mr. Higgs shares with Mr. Herrick the distinction of the greatest length of service of the pastors of St. Paul's Church; each having served faithfully for thirteen years. Mr. Higgs married Miss Clara Herttell, of Key West, and died in Atlanta, Ga., the 7th of September, 1911, and his remains were brought to Key West for burial. Funeral services were held in the parish school house on the church lot September 11, 1911, the burial service being conducted by Rev. Charles T. Stout and Rev. A. R. E. Roe.

Mr. Higgs was born in St. George, Bermuda. He was a man of great energy and fine artistic taste, and found time from his clerical duties to lay off the church grounds in an ornamental garden, which during his pastorate was one of the show places of the city.

After Mr. Higgs' resignation the parish was without a priest until June, 1904, when the Rev. James J. Cameron came to Key West and remained until June, 1905.

Rev. Samuel Duncan Day was here from June to August, 1905.

Rev. B. F. Brown, from June, 1906, to August, 1906.

Rev. John F. Porter, during September and October, 1906.

On the first Sunday in December, 1906, the Rev. Charles T. Stout took charge of the parish and is the present pastor.

The first Sunday school was organized November, 1832, and in January, 1833, there were between fifty and sixty children in attendance.

In 1851 a Ladies' Missionary Society was formed in the parish. Its officers were: Mrs. J. Y. Porter, president; Mrs. S. J. Douglass, secretary; Mrs. Joseph B. Browne, treasurer; Mrs. Kells and Miss Lightbourne, directresses.

In 1847 a frame church was erected about midway of the block fronting on Eaton street, which was destroyed in the great fire of 1886. In the same year another frame building of like dimensions was erected and furnished with a set of chimes, which would have done credit to a much wealthier congregation. At that time they were the only chimes in the State. They were paid for by private subscriptions—several of the large bells being presented by individual members. Among those who presented bells were Mr. Wm. Curry and Mr. Horatio Crain. The church was liberally supplied with handsome memorial windows and tablets.

On October 11, 1909, the sixty-third anniversary of the hurricane of 1846 (which destroyed the stone church), this church was destroyed by a hurricane. All the bells of the chimes except the smallest were saved, together with several of the handsome memorial tablets, which will be restored when the new church is erected.

A parish meeting was held on March 6, 1911, to devise ways and means for rebuilding St. Paul's church and a committee appointed, consisting of Hon. Geo. W. Allen, Hon. W. Hunt Harris, Hon. Joseph N. Fogarty and Mr. Frank H. Ladd, Mrs. Joseph Y. Porter, Mrs. J. W. Allen, Mrs. George L. Lowe and Miss Etta Patterson. Funds have been raised, plans accepted and work on the new church will begin in 1912.

St. Paul's church has seven hundred baptised persons on its rolls and three hundred communicants. Its Sunday school has two hundred scholars.

ST. JOHN'S CHURCH

On the 20th of December, 1875, a number of distinguished Cubans, among whom were Hon. Carlos M. de Cespedes, Alejandro Rodriguez, afterwards mayor of Havana, and General of the Rural Guards in Cuba, Messrs. Teodoro Perez, Joaquin Leon, Juan B. Baez and others, met in St. Paul's church for the purpose of organizing an Episcopal church in which the services would be held in Spanish, and a petition to that effect was submitted to Rt. Rev. John F. Young, Bishop of Florida, and on the first of January, 1876, Mr. Juan B. Baez was authorized by the bishop to act as lay reader for the new congregation.

On March 20, 1877, he was ordained deacon by Bishop Young, and on March 9, 1879, was regularly ordained priest by Rt. Rev. Benjamin Whipple, Bishop of Minnesota.

The new church, called St. John's Episcopal Church, began with about two hundred members and continued its work under Rev. Baez's pastorate until a short time before his death. Owing to his previous ill health, the congregation gradually fell off, and with his death no further services were held, and the church, as an organization came to an end.

HOLY INNOCENTS CHURCH

As early as 1892 the apparent need of an Episcopal church, more accessible to the members of that denomination residing in the vicinity of Division street, impressed the Rev. Gilbert Higgs, and he tried to meet the necessity by holding services at the residence of Mr. Clement Knowles, Sr., as often as was compatible with his duties as rector of St. Paul's. This he continued for a year and a half, assisted by Mr. James M. Jones as lay reader, and by other members of the Brotherhood of St. Andrew.

The first Sunday school was opened in Russell Hall school house on June 23, 1895, with twelve scholars. Dr. Higgs was superintendent; Mr. James M. Jones, assistant superintendent; Dr. William J. Bartlum, secretary, and Mr. St. Clair Crain, treasurer; Mrs. Edward B. Rawson, librarian, and Mrs. Benjamin Tynes, organist. Mrs. Rawson and Mrs. Susan Folker were the first teachers of the new Sunday school. The organ used was loaned by Mrs. G. Bowne Patterson.

31

On August 13, 1895, the Missionary District of Southern Florida purchased from Mr. Benjamin Tynes a lot on the corner of Virginia and Grinnell streets, fifty by one hundred feet, the contract price of which was fifteen hundred dollars. The term of payment were twenty-five dollars cash and five dollars a month, without interest. By special effort the entire indebtedness was paid by Easter, 1903, Mr. Tynes generously deducting one hundred dollars from the original purchase price. There was a small building on the lot, which was fitted up and used for Sunday school and church services. Bishop Gray made his first visit to the new church February 2, 1896. The sacrament of confirmation was first administered on April 28, 1897, to a class of eight.

On March 19, 1900, the cornerstone was laid for a church, donated by Mrs. Joseph Y. Porter, as a memorial to her father, Mr. William Curry. It was completed in October, 1900, and the first services held by the Rev. Walter C. Cavell, November 4th of that year. As there was an indebtedness on the property for part of the purchase price of the land, the church was not consecrated until February 2, 1904, but services were regularly conducted in the interval.

The name "Holy Innocents" was adopted because of the preponderance of little children in the congregation.

For a time the minister lived in a rented house, but in February, 1904, a lot on Grinnel street was purchased from the Monroe county school board, for eight hundred dollars, and a vicarage erected which was completed July 15th of that year, when the pastor and his wife moved into their new home.

The succeeding ministers of Holy Innocents were Rev. William Curtis White, who served for nearly five years; Rev. Arthur Browne Livermore, Rev. Charles F. Sontag, Rev. Arthur T. Cornwall and Rev. A. R. E. Roe, the present priest. The Right Rev. Anson R. Graves held services during the winter and spring of 1910, and the Rev. George Ward officiated for a few months in 1911.

To Judge Livingston W. Bethel belongs great honor and credit for his untiring work for the success of Holy Innocents. Never a service has been held when he was in the city that he was not present, and when pastorless, he officiated as lay reader and kept the congregation together. He has been senior warden ever since the church was first established.

ST. PETER'S EPISCOPAL CHURCH (COLORED)

The history of this parish begins about forty years ago Numbers of colored church people had emigrated from the Bahamas, and finding no place of worship of their own, decided to hold services amongst themselves, going from house to house as opportunity offered. On December 14, 1875, a meeting was called and presided over by Bishop John Freeman Young of Florida, and the title of "St. Peter's" adopted as the name of the new parish. A vestry was elected which appointed Dr

J. L. Steele the first rector. From this time on the work grew rapidly, and services were held in various rooms and halls, with sacraments at St. Paul's.

After Dr. Steele's death in 1878, matters stood still for a time, but revived with much energy in April, 1887, when Bishop Weed sent as rector Rev. C. D. Mack.

Plans were laid for purchasing land for a church lot, and in December of the next year Father McGill, who had then taken charge, began the erection of a church hall, which building eventually became St. Peter's Church. The entire cost of building, furnishing, and memorials was borne by the members of the church. J. L. Kerr, a colored priest, did faithful work for over fifteen years.

In October, 1909, the church was badly damaged by a hurricane, the restoration costing over five hundred dollars. The next year a second storm entirely destroyed the church, and from the ruins has been erected a fair sized hall, which is used for devotional purposes.

Funds are being raised to replace the church by a substantial concrete building. The membership is one of the largest in the city, the communicants numbering over five hundred, with three hundred Sunday school children, besides various guilds, etc.

In 1908 Rev. A. R. E. Roe became rector of St. Peter's, but resigned in the fall of 1911 to accept a call as priest of Holy Innocents.

CHAPTER IV

CATHOLIC CHURCH

EARLY items about the Catholic church are very scarce, as no history of it has been left at Key West. The earliest data is obtained from the baptismal, marriage and funeral registers, which date back something over half a century.

In the early forties Key West was in the diocese of Savannah, Ga., and priests sent by the bishop of that place, came once or twice a year to administer the sacraments. On October 10th, 1846, a priest from Havana celebrated high mass in the city hall, a two-story building erected over the water at the foot of Duval street, the first floor of which was used as a meat and fish market.

Among the earliest priests who officiated at Key West were Rev. Fr. Corcoran about 1847, and Rev. Fr. J. F. Kirby in 1851.

The first Catholic church in Key West was on the southwest side of Duval street, about one hundred feet from the corner of Eaton street. It was dedicated by the Rt. Rev. Bishop Francis Xavier Gartland on the 26th of February, 1852, and the sermon was preached by the Rev. Fr. Hunincq, a Belgian priest. It was called the "Church of St. Mary, Star of the Sea." Since it first shed its light in Key West it has, like a star of the sea to the wandering mariner, been a star of hope and comfort in times of despair and sorrow, and a star of joy to those who have lived in its teachings. The church was repaired and enlarged in 1870, and a large pipe organ installed.

This church had among its early congregation many negroes, some free and some slaves, belonging to Catholic families from St. Augustine. For them was assigned a part of the church separated from the whites. This custom still prevails in this church, which numbers among its members many of the best negro families.

The first to be appointed resident priest was Father J. N. Brozard on November 8, 1852. With him during 1852 was Father Ed. Quigley, and in 1853 Father J. T. O'Neil. In 1854 Father Quigley was pastor, and in 1855 Father Ed. Murphy and Father J. Barry officiated. In 1856 Father Kirby and Father Clemens Prendergast were here administering the sacraments. In 1857 Bishop J. Barry, then bishop of Savannah, accompanied by Father Prendergast and Father Ed. Aubrie (of the society of Priests of Mercy, a Catholic religious order), visited Key West and administered the sacrament of confirma-

34

tion.   In 1858-9 Fathers J. J. Cabanilla, Marius Cavalieri,
Felix Ciampi, who belonged to the society of Jesus (Jesuits),
officiated at Key West. They were probably only visiting priests
or here on a special mission, as Father Ciampi was a renowned
preacher in Philadelphia at that time.

Bishop Augustine Verot was consecrated Vicar Apostolic
of St. Augustine, Fla., April 25, 1858; transferred to Savannah
in 1861, and appointed First Bishop of St. Augustine, when
Key West became part of St. Augustine diocese.

In February, 1860, Father Sylvanus Hunincq came as
pastor to Key West. He died that summer of yellow fever,
having ministered to many during the epidemic of that year.
A marble slab was inserted in the wall of the church to commemorate his life and services to humanity. He was much loved
by people of all denominations for the great catholicity of his
charity. In the same year Father James Hassan was appointed
rector. He was succeeded in 1864 by Father Jos. O'Hara, who
was succeeded by Father O'Mailley. From 1867-9 Father J. B.
Allard was pastor and Father P. La Rocque was his assistant.
Father La Rocque is now bishop of Sherbrook, Canada. Father
Allard died in 1874, and in the absence of Father La Rocque,
who went to finish his studies, Father A. F. Bernier was in charge.
Father Hugon was in charge from 1875 to 1877.   From here
Father Hugon went to Tallahassee where he has ministered
for the last thirty-eight years to a small but devoted, devout
and cultured congregation. In that year Father La Rocque
returned and had as his assistant Father Fourcard, who died
of yellow fever in 1878. In 1879 two Jesuits, Father Avenione
and Father Encinosa came from Havana to assist the priest,
and they also died of yellow fever. At this time Father
Spandenari became assistant to Father La Rocque. From 1880
to 1890 Father Ghione had charge of the church without any
assistant, but in the latter year Father Bottolaccio came as
his assistant.   In 1897 Father Ghione went to Italy and left
Father Bottolaccio in charge. Shortly afterwards he advised
Bishop Moore that he would not return to Key West, and the
bishop made arrangements with the Jesuit Fathers of New Orleans
Province, to take charge of the Key West church.   Father
A. B. Friend, S. J., arrived in Key West February 15, 1898,
where he has since officiated with the exception of a short interval
when he was stationed at Miami, during which time, the church
was in charge of Rev. Father Schuler.

On the 20th of September, 1901, the church that was erected
in 1852 on the lot on the southwest side of Duval street, between
Eaton and Fleming streets, was destroyed by fire. From that
time until August 20, 1905, the Catholics worshipped in one of
the buildings put up on the convent ground by the government,
for a hospital during the Spanish-American War.

The new Catholic church is a handsome concrete structure
which was begun February 2, 1904, and dedicated August 20,

1905, by the Rt. Rev. W. J. Kenny, D. D., Bishop of St. Augustine. The design and character of construction are the work of Father Friend, to whose energies and ability is the church also indebted for financing its construction. It is situated on the corner of Division street and Windsor Lane, and built of concrete made from the coral rock dug from the lot on which the church is built.

CHAPTER V.

THE METHODIST church was introduced into Key West by the Wesleyans from the Bahama Islands, and as late as 1845 the congregation was composed almost entirely of people from the British West Indies, there being but one American among them.

In 1837 among the very many worthy persons who came to Key West from the Bahamas, was Mr. Samuel Kemp, who though long dead, still lives in the sacred regard of our people. He was a Wesleyan Methodist and worshipped with those who resorted to the court house for that purpose for some time, but later erected at his own expense (assisted in the labor by some of his neighbors who were mechanics) a small building for public worship on land owned by himself on Eaton street near William. This was the first place of public worship in which the denomination known as the Wesleyan Methodists congregated in this city, and was the foundation of the Methodist church here.

"Father Kemp," as he was usually called by reason of his advanced age and somewhat clerical demeanor, officiated as pastor of this small congregation, and was often assisted in the devotional exercises of his church or chapel, by Captain Ogden of the United States army stationed here at the time.

The congregation becoming too numerous to be accommodated in this small building, a larger one was erected on a lot on the southeast side of Caroline street, between Simonton and Elizabeth streets.

In 1844 a break in the Methodist Episcopal Church of the United States occurred, which resulted in the formation of the Methodist Episcopal Church South. It grew out of the contention of the abolitionists that the general conference had the power to depose from the Episcopacy one who had previously been elevated to that rank. The Rt. Rev. James Osgood Andrew had married a lady who inherited some slaves from her first husband, and it was demanded of him that he get rid of them or desist from the exercise of his office. In Georgia, where Bishop Andrew resided, the law prohibited the manumission of slaves. Notwithstanding this a resolution was introduced in the conference that "The Rev. James Osgood Andrew be and he is hereby affectionately requested to resign his office as one of the Bishops of the Methodist Episcopal Church." After several days discussion a substitute for this motion was offered by two members of the Ohio conference, to the effect "That it is the sense of this general conference that he desist from the exercise of his office so long as the impediment exists."

On May 31st a motion was made to postpone any further action in the matter until the next general conference, and the southern members to a man supported it, as did a few of the conservative members for the Middle and Northern conferences, hoping thus to avoid the schism which the abolitionists were bent on effecting. It was defeated by a vote of ninety-five to eighty-four.

Finley's substitute, deposing Bishop Andrew from the Episcopacy, was then adopted by a vote of one hundred and eleven to sixty-nine. This action accomplished what the abolitionisst had been working for—a separation of the Northern Church from that of the South—and a plan of separation was adopted June 8, 1844. By this plan all the property within the limits of the Southern organization when formed was to be free from any claim by the general conference. The Southern church was also to receive an equitable share of the common church property, etc.

A Southern conference was called to meet in Louisville, Ky., on May 1, 1845, and on May 15th the Methodist Episcopal Church South was duly organized. It may not be out of place here to show the bad faith of the Northern abolitionists. In 1848 the general conference of the Northern section of the Methodist church repudiated the plan of separation, and the Church South was forced to go into the courts to maintain its rights under the plan. Suits were brought in the United States circuit courts in New York and Cincinnati. In the New York suit a decision was rendered in favor of the Church South, but in Cincinnati the case went adversely to them. It was carried to the Supreme Court of the United States, where on April 24, 1854, by a full bench—Mr. Justice McLean, a Methodist declining to sit in the case—the judgment of the circuit court in Ohio was reversed, and the plan of separation sustained in all its provisions.

The Methodist Episcopal Church South having begun its existence in 1845, it thus appears that Rev. Simon Peter Richardson, who was sent to Key West by the Florida conference in 1845, was the first minister of the Methodist Episcopal Church South to officiate in Key West, although Rev. Andrew Graham was stationed here the year before.

Mr. Richardson thus describes the condition of the Methodist Church and its congregation at Key West in 1845:

"By the conference of 1845 I was appointed to Key West station. Brother Graham of California memory, was stationed there the year before, and gave me a very unfavorable account of his ministry on the island. He told me there were thirty-two grog-shops there, and that he had encountered many difficulties. The whiskey men had threatened to wash him, which meant to tie a rope around his waist and shoulders and from the wharf to cast him into the water and then haul him in, and then cast him out again. It is a terrible ordeal to put a man through. He eluded their grasp by taking refuge on the boat that brought him over. He suffered many other indignities that were heaped upon him during the year. His church building was a small unceiled structure twenty by thirty feet. His flock was composed of Wesleyan Methodists from the West India Islands. There was but one American among them, and the more I thought over the treatment he had received, the more indignant I became. The devil made a flank movement on my piety and consecrated life, until I felt that if I ever heard of any attempt to 'wash' me they would smell fire and brimstone. I resolved that I would wipe up the earth with the first man that insulted me. The devil had got complete control of me.

"I was the only regular preacher on the island. Other preachers were occasionally there, but the Catholics came regularly to my church. When I reached the island I was met by several of the brethren, who kindly conducted me to my boarding place, with one of the best families I ever knew. They held family prayers three times a day. I looked around for trouble but found none. Everybody was polite and kind to me. I soon began to cool down and feel repentance for my sins.

"In a few days the judge, lawyers, doctors and prominent citizens called to see me, a reception I never had before nor have had since. I was invited to the Masonic lodge and chapter, and made chaplain of both. My little chapel was soon filled with the women, the men standing around outside. This brought prominently before the public mind that I must have a larger church. I collected about four thousand dollars, and from the rock of the island put up and paid for a large stone building; but it was not covered in when that ever-to-be-remembered storm came and prostrated all to the ground, a mass of ruins, and carried my little chapel entirely away, out to sea, and we never saw nor heard of it any more.

"This was the condition of affairs in October. I took the lumber and what I could bring from the wreck of the stone church and put up a small building to preach in, and large enough for my Sunday school.

"I was married in 1847. I had been married only a few weeks when the Catholic priest and the Episcopal and Baptist preachers came to the island, and all determined to go to the mainland and collect money to build churches, because of the storm. This was one of the trials of my life. I had the island largely under my control. Many of the best families had joined the church but had nothing left after the storm. They were utterly helpless to build, and if those preachers succeeded in building the people would have to go to their churches, having nowhere else to go. I had spent one of the hardest year's work of my life to make it a Methodist town, and had succeeded far beyond my expectations; but I saw that all was lost, in that still formative state, unless I had a church large enough to hold my congregation together. I had had a hard experience in getting money abroad to build my St. Augustine church. I could not see how I could well leave my young wife, for I knew I should be kept months away. But go I must, I did not consult feeling nor the relations of my young wife. I simply informed her that I would have to leave her with her good mother for a time until I could get money to build a new church. I left on the first vessel for New Orleans."

Mr. Richardson canvassed all the principal cities of the South and succeeded in raising over three thousand dollars. He thus describes his return to Key West.

"I had the lumber sawed at the mills in the upper part of the city, and engaged a sloop to take it to Key West. I never believed in spirit-rappings or any other superstitions, but I had a distinct presentiment that that vessel was going to be wrecked. So strong was my impression that I left a duplicate of the bill at the mill. I went to the insurance office and proposed to insure. The agent dissuaded me, declaring there was no danger on the coast at that season of the year. The captain said he would be glad if he could get wind enough to carry his vessel to Key West. But with all this, I insured. I still felt a presentiment that the vessel would be wrecked. On July fifth I left Charleston, with thirty-two hundred dollars in gold, on a United States propeller for Key West. The thermometer stood at one hundred and five in Charleston. The brethren declared I would burn up at Key West, but when I reached the island the thermometer stood at eighty-seven. I immediately employed workmen to commence the building, but my vessel failed to put in her appearance. Finally I saw a large yawl coming into port with flag up. It was the captain of the sloop on which I had shipped the lumber, or a part of it, for the church. His vessel was wrecked on the Florida reef, and was a total loss. I soon had the bill duplicated and sent forward and collected my insurance. I had the church built storm-proof, and by October it was finished, paid for, and I was in it and preaching. The church I built remained for fifty years, and was removed only a few years ago and another erected. We now have four churches on the island. Mine was the third church we had built during the two years I was there."

The church built by Mr. Richardson in 1847 was afterwards lengthened to sixty feet and could accommodate eight hundred persons.

In 1877 plans were adopted for a church to be built of native coral rock, and the corner stone laid in the latter part of the year. Work was to progress only as funds were in hand. At the end of three years the walls were up about twenty feet, a temporary covering put on, and the congregation began worshipping in it. This was during the pastorate of Rev. John C. Ley. In his work, "Fifty-two Years in Florida," he says: "The plan after

I left was finally changed, the congregation becoming discouraged in regard to carrying out the original design, and finished it up as a one-story building."

Rev. C. A. Fulwood has to his credit the longest term of service as pastor of this church. He served from 1872 to 1876, both inclusive, and again in 1888. Rev. E. A. Harrison comes next with four years; Rev. J. C. Ley also served four years, from 1877 to 1880, and Brother Henry Hice three years, 1895 to 1897. Brother R. Martin with three years, from 1883 to 1885; Brother Barnett, 1886 to 1887; Brother J. P. DePass in 1898 and 1899, were distinguished ministers who left their impress on the comunity as well as their congregations. Rev. J. D. Sibert is the pastor in 1911.

SPARKS CHAPEL

In 1868 the Methodists having decided to introduce instrumental music in their church, about thirty members severed themselves from the congregation and formed a new organization. Those enrolled for the new church were: Mr. Joseph P. Roberts and Mrs. Emma Roberts, Mr. T. B. Russell and Mrs. Sarah Russell, Mr. Benjamin Russell and Mrs. Sarah Russell, Mr. Philip Albury and Mrs. Mary N. Albury, Mr. Randall Adams and Mrs. Catherine Adams, Mr. George Curry and Mrs. Mary Curry, Mr. Joseph Ingraham and Mrs. Elizabeth Ingraham, Mr. Samuel Kemp, Mr. John Demeritt, Mr. Jabez Pinder an Mrs. Druscilla Pinder, Mr. Joshua Pinder, Mr. William Saunders and Mrs. Elizabeth Saunders, Mr. Benjamin Roberts, Sarah Thompson, Sarah Curry, Mr. Thomas Adams, Mr. John Roberts and Mrs. Margaret Roberts.

It was called Sparks Chapel after Rev. J. O. A. Sparks, its first pastor.

A lot on the corner of Fleming and William streets was procured and a frame building erected, which was used as a place of worship until 1887, when the new church was built, under the pastorate of Rev. W. H. F. Roberts. The deed of gift to the land contained a clause intended to prohibit the use of instrumental music in any church erected thereon. Rev. Mr. Sparks drew the deed, but it was not properly worded and failed of its purpose, and in 1892 instrumental music was introduced in the chapel, over the objection of some of the older members. The first service in the new church was held September 5,1887, During Rev. S. Scott's pastorate the church was remodeled and made very attractive both inside and out.

On October 11, 1909, it was totally destroyed by a hurricane, and for over two years the congregation worshipped in Harris high school auditorium. On the second anniversary of its destruction, work was begun on the foundation for a new church which will be completed in 1912.

Beginning in such a modest way, Sparks Chapel has main-

tained a healthy and normal growth, and been in the forefront
of the most aggressive evangelical work in Key West.

MEMORIAL CHURCH

In 1886 a small band of earnest Christians, members of the
First Methodist church and Sparks Chapel, who lived too far
to attend services with much regularity, organized a congregation, and met for the worship of God in Russell Hall school.
Their first pastor was Rev. John A. Giddens, who was then living
in Key West on account of ill health.

In 1887 they bought a lot on the corner of Watson and
Virginia streets, and the old Sparks Chapel building moved thereon, and Memorial Church, M. E. South, began its mission for
good. In 1903 they bought an adjoining lot, and erected a
pastor's home.

Among the members of this church were Mr. T. J. Pinder and
family, Mr. Blake Sawyer and family, Mr. William McClintock,
Mr. Hubert Roberts and family, Mr. E. E. Archer and Mr.
Benjamin Carey.

The membership is now one hundred and ninety-two,
and two hundred and fifty scholars are enrolled in the Sunday
school.

The Rev. T. H. Sistrunk, the pastor in charge, is a gifted
orator, with the courage of his convictions, and aggressive in
all movements toward civic uplift.

CUBAN METHODIST MISSION

The Methodists were among the first of the Protestant
churches to make converts among the Cuban refugees, and the
Rev. H. B. Someillan was ordained minister and placed in
charge of the Cuban Mission. It was not until 1877 that they
had a church of their own. In that year Rev. J. C. Ley, pastor
in charge of the First Methodist Church, interested Bishop
Pierce in the importance of providing a place of worship for this
congregation, and through him a thousand dollars was furnished
by the Missionary Society, and a lot purchased on the corner
of Duval and Angela streets. The small house situated on the
lot was remodeled and furnished, and has since been the place
of worship of the Cuban Methodist congregation. Rev. H. B.
Someillan was the pastor for many years. He was succeeded by
Rev. A. Silviera. Miss Annis Pyfrom, a highly cultured, talented,
Christian woman, devoted some of the best years of her life in
work connected with this mission. She conducted a parish school
which wielded a great influence on the Cuban population.

One of the first preachers to the Cuban Mission was the
Rev. Van Duzer, who died of yellow fever in the epidemic of 1875.

CHAPTER VI

THE earliest recorded data of any Baptists meeting for worship in Key West, was on December 20, 1842, when "agreeably to appointment, after prayer and deliberation, the brethren met at the residence of J. H. Breaker for the purpose of ordaining Brother Charles C. Lewis to the gospel ministry. Prayer was offered by Brother Breaker on behalf of the candidate, during which the laying on of hands was performed by Brothers Elim Eldridge, J. A. Wolfe and O. T. Braman. Charge was then given by Brothers Breaker and Asa Sawyer, and the right hand of fellowship by all the brethren present."

This method of ordination was not strictly in accord with Baptist usage. After leaving Key West, Rev. Mr. Lewis was pastor of the Asia Minor Church, as it was locally designated, but properly, the Second Baptist Church of North Stonington, Conn. At the first meeting, this church acquainted the North Stonington Baptist Association with the manner of Mr. Lewis' ordination, and inquired if a reordination would be necessary. The old fathers after mature consideration, decided that Mr. Lewis was scripturally and regularly ordained, and thus placed the stamp of regularity on the acts of the little band of Baptists on the island, and established Mr. Lewis' title to being the first pastor of the Baptist church in Key West.

As there were no Baptist churches in Florida with which the Key West church could be associated, they applied for membership in the North Stonington, Conn., Association, and were willingly received. For many years they annually corresponded with this association, until it was ascertained that the church in Key West had a member who owned slaves, and they were notified that if they permitted slave owners to be members of their church, they could not continue their membership in the association. The Baptists here saw no reason to exclude from membership a person who was holding property sanctioned by the constitution and laws of the United States and the State of Florida, and upon their refusing to comply with this demand, were dropped from the North Stonington Union Association.

Subsequently the church sent Pastor-elect J. H. Breaker to Mobile for regular ordination. On December 23d of the same year they met for covenant meeting at the residence of Mr. J. H. Breaker, who was chosen clerk. Articles of faith and covenant were read, and ten persons examined and received for baptism, Catherine and Lavinia Johnson, John Pent, William Richardson, John Park, Reason Duke, Druscilla Duke, Mary Arlege, Martha B. Arlege and Susan Sands, who were baptized on Sunday, Christmas day, 1842. This was the first baptism by immersion performed on the island.

The formal constitution of the church took place March 11, 1843. Six persons, members of churches in Connecticut, Mr. J. H. Breaker, Mr. Ben Sawyer, Mr. O. T. Braman, Mr. J. A. Wolfe, Mr. Asa Sawyer and Mr. Elim Eldridge, with several others, solemnly entered into a covenant as the "Key West Baptist Church."

The first celebration of the Lord's Supper by the Baptists occurred March 26, 1843. There is no record of the election of any pastor at this time, but the records state that "in April, 1843, Elder Lewis left the church to go north on account of the ill health of his wife, and the church was left without a pastor."

In November, 1843, Elder Tripp assumed the pastoral care of the church. He preached twice on Sundays at the court house.

The first movement towards building a house of worship was made April, 1844, and the pastor was sent north to solicit funds for that purpose. He met with little success, abandoned the work, and never returned to Key West. The church, though pastorless, maintained regular prayer services. In 1845 Rev. Mr. Doolittle took charge, and it is recorded that "He preached twice on the Sabbath in the Episcopal church." This did not seem strange to the Christians who were in Key West at that time, although it may appear so to denominational people of today. In April, 1847, Mr. Doolittle returned to his northern home, when Mr. J. H. Breaker became pastor, and preached at the court house, and in the Methodist chapel.

During Mr. Breaker's pastorate the first meeting house was contracted for; the price being six hundred dollars. This house was opened for worship January 2, 1849.

From 1852 to 1890 the records of the church are lost. The church however, was not prosperous, the constant change of pastors preventing any progress.

During the Civil War the white Baptists drifted into other churches, and the church building was taken possession of by the negro Baptists, who held services there until the fall of 1879, when Rev. William F. Wood, who had been a chaplain in the Union Army, came to Key West and revived interest in the Baptist church. He continued as pastor until early in 1900, when he went to Fernandina, where he died. During his pastorate in Key West he served as a missionary in Cienfuegos, Cuba, for about two years. He was the first evangelical missionary to that island.

In 1866 the church building was destroyed by fire, and the present Baptist church was shortly afterwards erected, largely through the generosity of Mr. John White, who was for more than forty years a member of the congregation. A handsome memorial window to him now adorns the front of the edifice.

The names of the succeeding pastors are Reverends H. M. King, W. W. Bostwick, J. L. D. Hillyer, R. F. Hart, W. H. House, T. J. Porter, James L. Rogers, H. H. Sturgis, J. W. Tucker, M. A. Clonts, who served twice as pastor, W. A. Norwood who served a few months in the interim, and Earl D. Sims. Rev. C. E. W. Dobbs, the present pastor came here in September, 1910.

During Mr. White's life, and the pastorate of Mr. Wood the church thrived to a remarkable degree, and became one of the foremost evangelical influences in the city. After Mr. White's death the congregation not being wealthy, funds for the support of the church were hard to raise, and it was difficult to secure and keep the services of a pastor, so the congregation gradually dwindled away.

During the pastorate of Rev. M. A. Clonts it regained its old time membership. Mr. Clonts first came to Key West in August, 1901, and stayed until October, 1902. Mr. Norwood succeeded him and served nearly a year. The church was again left pastorless from August, 1903, until Mr. Clonts returned in April, 1904. It was then that the church started on its present era of prosperity. During his pastorate the old First Baptist Church was formally dissolved, and the Eaton Street Baptist Church organized on March 23, 1905. On March 3, 1901, the old church unanimously voted to transfer the property to the Home Mission Board of the Southern Baptist Convention, but nothing was done towards the transfer until Mr. Clonts' second pastorate, when it was finally consummated. The church was then repaired and improved by the addition of the new front, with its attractive columns, and a pastorium was erected. Mr. Clonts ended his pastorate here September 30, 1908, and had a church for a short time in Jacksonville. He has since been engaged in life insurance, and has prospered.

Rev. Earl D. Sims was pastor from June, 1909, until July 31, 1910.

The church under the pastorate of Rev. C. E. W. Dobbs, has grown in membership and grace, and is now one of the strong religious influences on the island.

The Baptist pastors of Key West have had the hardest tasks of any of our ministers, as each one has found the small congregation badly scattered, and have had to

> "Watch the things they gave their lives to, broken,
> And stoop and build them up with worn-out tools."

FIRST CONGREGATIONAL CHURCH

The First Congregational Church is one of the later institutions of worship in Key West. Like some of the others it had its origin in a disagreement among the members of an older church. Sparks Chapel, one of the Methodist churches, had a subsidiary organization among its members, known as "The Band of Prayer," one of the leaders of which was suspended from the church on a matter of discipline. Thirty-one other members of the band voluntarily withdrew, and without immediately perfecting any other church organization, met for worship at the homes of the different members. Finally in July, 1892, the leaders of this churchless band of Christians determined to organize an independent church. The Rev. Charles W. Fraizer was called to advise the brethren, and on July 20, 1892, the church was organized, with Rev. Mr. Fraizer as its first pastor, at the home of Mr. Samuel Roberts. The meetings were thereafter held in an "upper room" used as a sail loft. Mr. John A. Harris was the first convert of the church, his regeneration having taken place at the initial meeting of the Band of Prayer. It was through him that the church obtained its present site on William street, upon which the commodious brick church was erected.

The corner stone was laid by Rev. S. F. Gale, home missionary superintendent of the denomination for Florida, on the twenty-seventh of June, 1903. From the small beginning of thirty-two members this church has become one of the foremost places of worship of the city. The present membership is two hundred and fifty-six. Mr. Fraizer served as pastor from July, 1892, to September, 1901; Rev. Charles Campbell from September, 1901, to September, 1902; Rev. William E. Todd from October, 1902, to September, 1903; Rev. H. R. Vau Anken from November, 1903, to May, 1905; Rev. Neil McQuarrie from May, 1905, to October, 1908. Rev. H. B. Gibbons from October, 1908, to October, 1911.

One of the peculiarities of this church is that its membership has always had a preponderance of male members.

CHRISTIAN SCIENTISTS

In 1897 some of the devout disciples of Mrs. Eddy met at the residence of Mrs. Elenor Hellings, on Duval street, to hold services in accordance with the custom of that sect.

Under the influence of this little band of Christians several converts were made, and it became necessary to secure larger quarters for their services, and in 1899 they moved to the Masonic Hall on Simonton street, where they worshipped until 1911.

In 1904 a church was organized with fifteen charter members: Mrs. Elenor Hellings, Mr. and Mrs. F. A. Beckman, Mrs. Rosalie Maloney, Mrs. Ida Atkins, Mr. H. T. Mathews, Mrs. E. May Mathews, Mrs. Mary E. Maloney, Mrs. Annie L. Delaney, Messrs. Theodore L. Kinsey, H. J. Kinsey, O. C. G. Urban, Alfred A. Berghell, Ira M. Richardson and Mrs. Elizabeth Knowles.

In 1911 they bought a lot on the corner of Division and

Georgia streets, and erected thereon a concrete church, where services are now conducted. Their membership is nearly forty.

SALVATION ARMY

About fifteen years ago the Salvation Army sent a captain to Key West to begin their customary warfare against vice. In season and out of season, through good report and evil, too, they have worked hard and diligently. They work in the Master's vineyard apart from the others, and reach a class that would never hear religious admonition but for them.

In 1907 Hon. W. Hunt Harris permitted them to use, free of rent, a lot on Margaret street, where they erected a tabernacle for indoor worship.

CHAPTER VII

THE first graves were made on the western beach between the town and Whitehead's point; most of them in the space between Emma street and the Marine Hospital building. A visitor to the island in 1830 described them as being marked by "a few plain stones to tell that the possessors of the little tenements below once lived and died," but the majority have merely the stones marking the length of each, but

> "Who sleeps below? Who sleeps below?
> Is an idle question now."

Prior to 1835 there was no clergyman regularly stationed on the island, and burial services, in common with other rites of the church, were conducted by laymen.

That anyone should have been an "old citizen" as early as 1831 seems strange, but the local paper of that day published a notice of the death on "Friday, the 13th of May, of Robert B. Stanard, Esq., formerly of Virginia, and one of the *oldest inhabitants of our town*." The funeral services were conducted by Mr. Wm. A. Whitehead. His remains were placed in the cemetery near the Marine Hospital.

In 1831 a committee was appointed by the town council to select a proper site for the permanent location of a general burial place. Part of tract fifteen, lying between the termination of Whitehead street on the South Beach and Lighthouse Point was selected and used until 1847. The destructive hurricane of 1846 not only added to the number of the dead, but disinterred many who had been buried in the old tract. This circumstance gave rise to the necessity of seeking another place for sepulture.

As late as 1855 interments were occasionally made in St. Paul's Episcopal churchyard.

In 1847 the city purchased the greater part of what is now the City Cemetery, which lies to the northeast of Passover and Windsor Lane. The cemetery has been enlarged from time to time by the purchase of adjacent tracts. It lies now in a thickly settled part of the city, surrounded by residences and tenement houses.

In 1868 the Rt. Rev. Father Verot, the Bishop of St. Augustine, secured from the city council, the grant of a tract of three hundred feet square in an unoccupied portion of these grounds, for the consideration of "one dollar," and as the conveyance reads, "to be devoted to the exclusive use of a Catholic

48

burying ground, by and under the control of the said Bishop and his successors in office."

The disinterment of human bones on the southeast side of the island, where excavations were being made for public improvements a few years ago, gave rise to the impression that a public burying ground had once been located in that vicinity. These remains, however, were those of the Africans who were brought to Key West in two captured slavers in 1860; a number of these died here, and were buried some distance from the barracoon, at the place where the bones were found.

A custom prevails in Key West not practiced elsewhere in the United States, of closing the doors of stores while a funeral procession is passing. All business along the line of march is suspended, and the last tribute of respect thus paid to the dead.

4

CHAPTER VIII

THE MUNICIPALITY

THE first act incorporating the City of Key West was passed January 8, 1828.

On November 8, 1828, this act was repealed and a new one incorporating the Town of Key West was passed. It incorporated all the free white inhabitants of that part of the island of Key West comprehended within the limits prescribed by the plan of the town then on file in the clerk's office in the county; being all that portion of the island beginning at the junction of White street with the waters of the harbor, and extending along White street to Angela, thence southwesterly along Angela to Fort Taylor reservation, thence northwesterly to the waters of the harbor, and thence along the shore line back to White street.

The government was vested in a board of seven town councilmen, to be elected by the free white male persons over the age of twenty-one years, who had resided three whole months within the proposed limits. The president of the body, in addition to his duties as such, acted as mayor and exercised the powers, and received the fees and emoluments of a justice of the peace for the territory. The council had usual municipal powers, and the unusual ones of "appointing pilots, regulating pilotage and enforcing all laws of the territory as well as those of their own enactment."

The first charter authorized levying license taxes, but gave no authority for a tax upon realty. This was a source of much controversy, the large landed proprietors being opposed to taxing their realty, as the major part of it was unproductive, and they were freely donating lots to induce settlers to come to Key West.

The incorporated town gave place in 1832 to the incorporated city by virtue of a charter granted by the territorial council in that year. It provided for the selection of a mayor and six councilmen. Twelve months residence was required for voters. The first mayor elected under this charter was Colonel Oliver O'Hara.

It provided for a tax on real estate of not more than one half of one per cent on its value. It also authorized a per capita tax on "free negroes, mulattoes and slaves."

Under it members of the council were fined for being absent from meetings, and on April 4, 1835, at the suggestion of Mr. Adam Gordon, mayor, the amount assessed and paid for fines

50

was donated to the Sunday school library at Key West and its receipt duly acknowledged by Mr. William A. Whitehead, superintendent. Note the difference in the public spirit of the old and the new Key West! Our forefathers considered that those who offered their services as members of the city council should attend to those duties or be fined for non-attendance. Under the present charter councilmen are paid four dollars a meeting for working for the city, for whose development and welfare, should be given voluntarily the best services of every citizen.

The members of the town council elected under this act were Mr. David Coffin Pinkham, president; Mr. Pardon C. Greene, Mr. Benjamin B. Strobel, Mr. William A. Whitehead, Mr. Joseph Cottrell, Mr. Fielding A. Browne and Mr. George E. Weaver. The town council being empowered to elect the other city officials, elected Mr. William H. Wall, clerk; Mr. P. B. Prior, marshal, and Dr. Henry S. Waterhouse, treasurer. Dr. Waterhouse afterwards moved to Indian Key, and on January 17, 1834, he and his young son were drowned by the upsetting of a small boat in which they had embarked for Matecumbie.

Mr. Prior did not qualify as marshal and Mr. Stephen R. Mallory, who afterwards became United States senator, and secretary of the navy of the Southern Confederacy, was elected and served in his place.

Under this charter an ordinance was passed by which negroes were not permitted to be on the streets after half past nine o'clock at night, without written permission (if free) from the mayor or an alderman, and if a slave from his master or mistress, under penalty of being whipped or put to labor on the public streets for three days.

Negroes, whether free or not, were not permitted to play the fiddle, beat a drum, or make any other kind of noise after bell-ring without written permission from the mayor or an alderman.

Every citizen was empowered to apprehend any negro violating this ordinance, and take him before the mayor or an alderman and obtain an order committing him to jail.

No stores were permitted to be open after bell-ring. The city bell was rung for five minutes before half-past nine every night. It was amusing to see a belated negro sprinting for home on hearing the bell ring, in order to get there before it stopped, and hear some bystander cry out,

> "Run nigger, run,
> The patrol catch you."

This charter was the first that authorized the assessment of real estate for purposes of taxation, and the assessment roll showed the value of realty to be $65,923.75. The improved portion was assessed at $61,005.00, and the unimproved which included all the rest of the island, was assessed at the rate of twenty-five dollars an acre, a total of $3,918.75. The taxes

51

collected on this assessment amounted to $329.61; the expense of the government being borne largely by the revenue raised from license taxes. The charter gave no authority to levy taxes on personal property.

The number of buildings within the city limits in 1832 was eighty-one, including sheds for the storage of wrecked cotton and other articles, blacksmith shops, etc. The two principal buildings were the warehouses of Pardon C. Greene and Fielding A. Browne; the assessed value of each was $6,000.00, including the land and wharfs.

In 1835 the city charter was abolished by the territorial council through the influence of certain parties whose intended action was unknown to the citizens generally. The repealing act provided that all ordinances should remain in force.

As soon as this action became known a petition was sent to congress protesting against it. The congressional Committee on Territories to whom the matter was referred, having reported against the action of the territorial council, that body in 1836 reenacted the charter.

Prior to 1828 a survey of the island was made, but when the proprietors sought to appropriate their several portions in accordance with the division previously agreed upon between Messrs. Simonton, Greene, Fleeming and Whitehead, it was found that the surveyor had left the island without furnishing them with any courses, distances or other data, whereby their prospective properties could be defined.

Mr. William Adee Whitehead, a young civil engineer, who had come to Key West to go into business with his brother, was engaged to survey the island and lay out the town, which he completed in February, 1829.

The streets, other than those bearing the surnames of the original proprietors, were named by them to perpetuate the memories of their relatives, friends and distinguished citizens. "Eaton" was named after Hon. John A. Eaton, secretary of war in President Jackson's cabinet; "White" after Hon. Jos. M. White, territorial delegate in Congress for Florida; "Duval" after the governor of Florida; "Grinnell" after the merchants of that name in New York; "Southard" for a senator and secretary of the navy; "Caroline," "Margaret," "William," "Thomas" and "Emma" after brothers and sisters of Mr. John Whitehead. "Frances" after a daughter of Mr. Fleeming; "Ann" after Mr. Simonton's wife; "Elizabeth" after a relative of Mr. Greene; "Fitzpatrick" after Mr. Richard Fitzpatrick, a then resident and for several years a delegate from Monroe county to the territorial council. "Clinton Place" after De-Witt Clinton of New York, and "Jackson Square" after Andrew Jackson. The little mangrove island just across the harbor was named Fleeming's Key after one of the original proprietors.

In April, 1836, the first election under the new charter was held, and Mr. Fielding A. Browne was elected mayor and Mr.

William R. Hackley, Mr. Alden A. M. Jackson, Mr. Pierce P. Fellows and Dr. D. Platts elected councilmen. The total vote cast at this election was thirty-nine, the population being something less than three hundred. The total vote cast in the city election of November 14, 1911, was two thousand, four hundred and forty-seven.

In 1838 a novel question of taxation arose. The charter of 1836 authorized the levying of occupational taxes which were promptly paid by the leading business men of the city without protest. In the early part of 1838 an ordinance was passed levying an occupational tax to raise revenue for the year 1838 and Mr. John P. Baldwin, Mr. George E. Weaver, Mr. John H. Sawyer and Mr. P. J. Fontaine addressed a communication to the mayor, Mr. W. A. Whitehead, protesting against the enforcement of the ordinance, contending that occupational licenses once granted were for an indefinite time, and that the city had no right to require those who had been granted licenses in 1837 to take them out again. That if they could be required to do so annually, the city could also "compel them to take out licenses daily or hourly, at the pleasure of the council."

Mayor Whitehead replied to this protest in a document* remarkable for close analysis and cogent reasoning and completely and thoroughly disposed of their contention.

Judge Marvin, who was at first inclined to agree with the contention of the merchants, upon reading Mr. Whitehead's reply, said to him: "You may be perfectly right, for I am not at all tenacious of my opinion."

Mr. George E. Weaver said, "I am perfectly satisfied as to the power of the corporation since reading your communication."

A number of the merchants, however, persisted in their refusal to pay licenses, and Mr. Whitehead requested that a meeting of citizens be called by the city council "to determine whether the laws should be enforced or the charter dissolved." The council not complying with his request, he called an election for mayor, and announced his intention to resign his office in favor of whoever was elected.

Feeling ran high, and those who were opposed to Mr. Whitehead's construction of the charter, picked up a low, illiterate character, the keeper of a sailor grog shop, named Tomaso Sachetti, who could hardly make himself understood in English, and ran him for mayor, for the double purpose of placing an indignity on Mr. Whitehead, and nullifying the objectionable ordinance. The low element, elated at the prospect of one of their ilk being mayor of the city, rallied to Sachetti's standard, and as he also had the moral support of a few of the prominent citizens, no self-respecting man could be induced to run against him. He was chosen without opposition, and on the fourteenth of March was notified of his election by Mayor Whitehead,

*Appendix H.

53

who at once resigned as mayor, and turned the office over to Sachetti. Sachetti's reply on the same date was written by Mr. Charles Walker of whom Mr. Whitehead says: "He was a lawyer from New York, a loco-foco, an agrarian, a disorganizer, etc."

Mayor Whitehead left Key West shortly after this and never returned; and although he retained his interest in the place until his death in the early eighties, he never got over his treatment by the people of the city he had helped to found, and to which he had given his best abilities to develop and improve. Key West thus lost one of its foremost citizens, a victim to a spirit—still too prevalent—which seeks to belittle and injure the man who dares oppose public opinion, or who bravely maintains his position against popular clamor.

In 1846 after the admission of Florida into the Union, another charter was adopted, which regulated the affairs of the city until 1869, when it was superseded by the General Act of Incorporation for Cities.

About this time Key West started on its career of industrial development, coincident with the Cuban migration. The population rapidly increased from three thousand in 1860, to upwards of twelve thousand in 1870; hundreds of buildings were erected far beyond the old city limits. Under the general laws of the State, the city limits could not be extended without the concurrent vote of a majority of those living within the city, and those living within the territory to be annexed. Several attempts were made to extend the city limits, but the population outside were unable to see what benefits were to be derived which would compensate them for the increase in taxation, and voted against the extension.

Those outside the city limits were as orderly and law-abiding as those within, and were happy and prosperous without the so-called privileges of a city, and in addition were free from molestation by city policemen. There were no greater number of offences committed outside than within the limits.

In 1876 a commodious city hall was built, and its dedication on July 4th was attended with much pomp. Colonel W. C. Maloney, Sr., delivered an address which was published as an historical sketch of Key West. It was the first attempt at compiling for the use of posterity the events that had shaped the destinies of this island. The hall was destroyed by fire in 1886, and a larger one of brick built on the site of the old. The ground floor was designed for a market, and for several years was so used, but at this time there is only one stall in use. Since the fire engine house was destroyed by the hurricane of 1909, the ground floor of the hall is set apart for an engine room, and for other uses of the fire department.

When the pond, which covered most of that part of the city bounded by Simonton, Caroline, Whitehead and Greene streets, was ordered filled, several of the owners failed to comply with the ordinance, and the work was done by the city, and the lots sold to pay the expense. The lot on which the city hall stands was acquired in this way, and such was the city's precarious title, until Colonel Maloney, acting for the city, and Mr. Moreno, the agent of, and Mr. Mallory, the attorney for the heirs of Mr. John W. Simonton, to whom the lots belonged, affected a settlement; or rather Miss Florida Simonton, the sole surviving heir of Mr. Simonton, through her trustee, Miss Mary B. Jones, gave the property to the city on June 21, 1871.

In 1889 the legislature granted a special charter to the city of Key West, and included the entire island within the corporate limits. The government was to be by nine commissioners appointed by the governor, and they were to appoint all the other officials. The president of the commissioners performed the functions of mayor in addition to his duties as commissioner. The first mayor under this system was Hon. Walter C. Maloney, Jr.

This charter authorized a bond issue for paving and street improvement, and a contract for grading, paving and curbing certain streets was let to Mr. G. J. Baer. The work was progressing smoothly when a policy of obstruction was adopted by the engineer. The legal representatives of the contractors appeared before the commissioners on several occasions, protesting against this policy, and made every effort to have the work proceed according to contract. Failing to obtain relief from the commissioners, he gave up all effort to proceed with the work, and brought suit in the United States court, where he obtained a judgment for one hundred and seventeen thousand dollars. In 1899 a bond issue of one hundred and forty-eight thousand dollars was floated to pay this judgment with accrued interest and costs.

In 1891 the charter was amended, and provided for the appointment by the commissioners of a mayor who should not be one of their body, and for the election by the people of a clerk, marshal, tax collector, assessor, treasurer, etc.

In 1907 a new charter was granted to which amendments have been made from time to time, according to the fancies of the members of the legislature, the caprice of ward politicians, or the demand of agitators. It has been demonstrated, however, that change is not necessarily progress, and those who are least qualified by ability and experience to suggest amendments to the organic law are the most eager to propose them.

In 1910 the city voted a bond issue of one hundred and ninety-two thousand dollars for paving or sewerage purposes, and a contract was awarded to the Southern Asphalt and Construction Company to pave all that portion of the city lying southwest of Caroline street; Division street from Duval to White street, thence along White street northwest to the water; Fleming from Whitehead to White street, and Simonton as far as Fleming street, with brick; and Duval street from Caroline to Division street, with asphalt block. The first brick in the new pavement was laid by Mr. Charles R. Pierce of the board of public works on December 11, 1911.

The total bonded indebtedness of the city is something over six hundred thousand dollars; the assessed value of all property in 1900 was two million six hundred and seventy thousand nine hundred dollars, and in 1910 was four million two hundred and thirty thousand nine hundred dollars. During that decade over two hundred thousand dollars' worth of real estate was condemned and taken over by the United States government.

From 1832, the date of the first charter of the city, the following citizens have successively been elected to the office of mayor: Mr. Oliver O'Hara, Mr. Fielding A. Browne, Mr. William A. Whitehead, Tomaso Sachetti, Mr. Pardon C. Greene, Mr. Philip J. Fontaine, Mr. Alexander Patterson, Mr. Benjamin Sawyer, Mr. Walter C. Maloney, Mr. Fernando J. Moreno, Mr. John P. Baldwin, Mr. John W. Porter, Mr. William Curry, Mr. Philip J. Fontaine, Mr. Alexander Patterson, Mr. Benjamin Sawyer, Mr. John P. Baldwin, Mr. William Marvin, Mr. Alexander Patterson, Mr. E. O. Gwynn, Mr. William S. Allen, Dr. D. W. Whitehurst, Mr. Henry Mulrennan, Mr. Joseph B. Browne, Mr. William D. Cash, Mr. Winer Bethel, Mr. E. O. Gwynn, Mr. Carlos M. de Cespedes, Mr. Livingston W. Bethel, Mr. Robert Jasper Perry, Mr. E. O. Gwynn, Mr. William McClintock, Mr. R. Alfred Monsalvatge, Mr. James G. Jones, Mr. J. W. V. R. Plummer, Mr. James A. Waddell, Mr. Walter C. Maloney, Jr., Mr. Robert J. Perry, Mr. James A. Waddell, Mr. John B. Maloney, Mr. George L. Bartlum, Mr. Benjamin D. Trevor, Mr. George L. Babcock and Mr. Joseph N. Fogarty.

The surviving mayors are Mr. William D. Cash, Mr. Livingston W. Bethel, Mr. John B. Maloney, Mr. George L. Bartlum, Mr. George L. Babcock, Mr. Benjamin D. Trevor and Dr. Joseph N. Fogarty, the present incumbent.

When Dr. Fogarty finishes the term for which he was elected November 14, 1911, he will have the honor of having held the office of mayor for a longer period—six years—than any of his predecessors.

Mr. Cornelius J. Kemp, Mr. William B. Curry, Mr. Frank H. Ladd, Mr. Edward E. Ingraham, Mr. William M. Pinder, Mr. Charles W. Lowe and Mr. J. R. Valdez compose the present city council.

On the board of public works are Messrs. William R. Porter, Jefferson B. Browne, Joshua Curry, Charles R. Pierce and Shirley C. Bott.

ARTESIAN WELL

In 1895 the city undertook to secure a supply of fresh water, and an artesian well was sunk in Jackson Square to a depth of two thousand feet. Samples of the borings were taken every twenty-five feet from the surface to the bottom. A set of these samples was furnished by Mr. Alexander Agassiz to Mr. Edmond

Otis Hovey, who prepared a very full and exhaustive report for the zoological society of Harvard College. Mr. Hovey says that the samples indicate a shallow water origin for much of the material. The most solid rock passed through came from a depth of from one hundred and fifty, to one hundred and seventy-five feet from the surface inclusive. No traces of fresh water were found.

CHAPTER IX

MONROE COUNTY

IN 1821 when Andrew Jackson was governor of Florida, he, with the approval of the authorities in Washington, divided the State into two counties, Escambia and St. Johns. The former comprised all that part of the State lying west of the Suwanee river, and the latter all lying east and south.

Monroe county, named after President Monroe, the sixth county to be established, comprised no insignificant portion of the territory. It embraced all that part lying south of a line commencing at Boca Gasparilla river on the Gulf of Mexico, and extending up the northern margin of Charlotte Harbor to the north of Charlotte river; thence up the northern margin of that river to Lake Macaco; thence along the northern margin of that lake to its most eastern limits; thence in a direct line to the headwaters of the Potomas river; thence down that river to its entrance into the ocean, together with all the keys and islands of the Cape of Florida.

In 1828 the first division of the Territory of Florida into counties was made for representative and other purposes (the territory before that time having been governed by the organic laws of congress, and a council authorized by that act). In February, 1836, out of these magnificent boundaries Dade county was established and so named to perpetuate the memory of Major Dade who with his command was massacred on December 28, 1835.

Its southern line commenced at the western end of Bahia Honda, and ran in a direct line to Cape Sable; thence in a direct line to Lake Macaco, thus cutting off from Monroe county all of the keys north of Bahia Honda, and all of the eastern portion of the southern peninsula north of Cape Sable. This caused much dissatisfaction, as a very appreciable part of the population of Monroe county resided at Indian Key, and their business, domestic and social relations were entirely with Key West.

In 1859 the boundaries of Monroe county were again changed, and a portion of the county on the mainland was cut off to form a part of the new county of Manatee.

By the act of 1866 the northern boundary of the county commenced at the mouth of Broad Creek, a stream separating Cayo Largo (as it was then called) from Old Roads Key, and extending thence in a direct line to Mud Point. This change gave back to Monroe county all the islands from Old Roads

Key to Bahia Honda which had been taken by the act of 1836. On the thirteenth of May, 1887, the county of Lee was created out of that part of Monroe county north of the line, which separates townships 53 and 54 south.

Prior to the organization of Dade county, Monroe was bounded on the north by Mosquito county, which was created December 29, 1824. The name Mosquito was not distinctive enough, however, for a county which shared with all the other counties in the State the privilege of being inhabited by these diminutive citizens, and in January, 1845, the name of Mosquito county was changed to Orange county.

Before there was any survey made of Key West or the town chartered, there was erected on Jackson Square a building known as the county court house which was altered and improved at the expense of the United States in 1830 and occupied by the United States court until it moved into a building on Wall street. In 1831 the territorial council appointed Col. Lackland M. Stone and Mr. Wm. A. Whitehead commissioners to erect a stone jail and brick cistern, and a lot was purchased by them, which was part of lot two in square sixty-four, on which to erect the jail.

In 1832 Col. Stone removed from Key West, and Mr. Fielding A. Browne was appointed commissioner in his place. Bids were called for to erect a jail twenty-six by sixteen feet with two rooms and cistern adjoining. Bids were received from Mr. Richard Fitzpatrick for $3,200.00 and from Mr. John W. Simonton to erect the jail without the cistern for $1,699.00. A lot for the erection of the jail had previously been purchased, but as the amount appropriated by the legislative council for the jail and cistern was but $2,000.00, it was decided to build the jail near the court house on Jackson square where a cistern had already been built. The jail, which was on the Thomas street side of the square, was built of native coral rock, the walls being three feet thick. In 1845 this jail was abandoned, and one of similar construction erected on Jackson Square near the corner of Fleming and Whitehead streets. The old jail on Thomas street was standing as late as 1871, but in its dilapidated condition was of no use except to afford a shelter to wandering herds of goats.

The second stone jail in turn gave way in the march of progress (or crime?) to a larger and more modern structure in 1880. In 1907 a concrete wall ten feet high was built around the rear wing of the jail. In 1910 its capacity was again increased.

In 1875 a small one-story brick building was erected for an office for the clerk of the circuit court. In it was a fire-proof vault for keeping county records and court documents. It was so used until the new court house was completed in 1890.

In 1889 the wooden court house that linked the old Key West with the new—where Christians of all denominations had worshipped God, and sung praises unto His Holy Name;

where young children had been carried to have their lives dedicated to the service of Christ, with the sign of the Cross; where the sacred marriage ceremony had been performed; and the requiem for the dead mingled with the sobs of the afflicted; where secular and Sunday schools had been taught, and the territorial and State courts performed their functions—was torn down to make way for the commodious brick court house which now stands on the square.

The day before the demolition of the old court house a number of citizens gathered there, on invitation of the county commissioners, and participated in what might be regarded as the funeral services of the old structure. Short speeches were made by Mr. Eugene O. Locke, Mr. Jefferson B. Browne, Mr. Walter C. Maloney, Jr., and Mr. W. R. Carter, member of the Hillsboro county bar.

The erection of a court house and jail on Jackson Square has fostered the erroneous impression that it is the property of the county. Jackson Square is the property of the city as much as the streets, and is held by the same title and from the same source. No deed or grant in writing to this square was ever made by the original proprietors, but in the division of the island the block bounded by Whitehead, Southard, Thomas and Fleming streets was treated as common or public property, and shown on the map delineated by Mr. Wm. A. Whitehead in 1829, as Jackson Square, named in honor of Andrew Jackson. The delineation and its recordation was a dedication to the use of the public, and the city holds it in trust, as it holds the streets, for public purposes only.

Col. W. C. Maloney, one of the great lawyers of his time says: "In this connection, a matter of moment to all of you, seems to demand a passing notice, inasmuch as it is believed to be but little known, and less understood by the community generally, and some of the officers of government especially, than it should be, and which affects the interests of the people inhabiting that portion of the island particularly subject to the jurisdiction of the 'City of Key West,' under and by reason of its corporate powers. I allude to the proprietary and possessory title in and to 'Jackson Square.' There are those of you who are under the impression that, because of the fact that there is no instrument of writing, in the shape of a conveyance from the original proprietors of the island to the city authorities granting the 'fee,' as the lawyers term it, coupled with the fact that the county court house and jail have been erected upon it, that the title to the square is not wholly in the 'city.' Let me assure you that your condition as owners of this square is much better than it would have been if the original proprietors had given an absolute deed of it in 'fee' to the city, for in that case it might have been sold from under your feet, and the money expended for a banquet to entertain the king of the cannibal islands, or some other illustrious dignitary from abroad.

"The proprietors of the island, foreseeing that Key West must become the county seat of Monroe county, and the most fitting place for the exercise of the judicial powers of the United States in admiralty and maritime affairs, wisely made room in your city for the accommodation necessary to these purposes, and in the plan of the city 'Jackson Square' is delineated, and in the division of the island between the original agrarian proprietors, it was treated as 'common' or 'public' and the plan of the city with this delineation, being made the incorporated area of your city by charter, gave to you in your corporate capacity all the proprietary rights vested in the original proprietors, save that of alienation, and vested in you, and you only, the right of possession.

"You hold this square and also 'Clinton Place' by the same terms by which you hold the streets running through your city, not by express grant, but by an 'implied use,' or 'usufruct.' You can only lose your right when you suffer them to be used for other than public purposes, consistent with the nature of the usufruct."

In 1876 Mr. Wm. A. Whitehead made this contribution to the literature of the proprietorship of Jackson Square:

"On laying out the town it was first thought desirable that the public square should be located nearer the water, and the block between Fitzpatrick street and Clinton Place was thought of. Another project was to locate it at the 'Middle Spring,' as it was then called in Square 61, but the fact that there was already a building on what is now Jackson Square, erected, if I mistake not, for the use of the county authorities before the survey was made or the town chartered, led to the selection of that square for the purpose. As you say in your address, there is no document emanating from the proprietors conveying the fee of the streets and squares, nor do I recollect that anything was said or thought of, at the time, relating to the control of Jackson Square. That, as well as the streets, was informally dedicated to public uses, and that there should ever arise any difference of opinion, in regard to its control, between the authorities of the county and the authorities of the town was never thought of. The former were virtually in possession, and I do not believe that any application was made to the town authorities for permission to erect the jail. I am not qualified to discuss the legal points that may be involved, but knowing as I do the views and wishes of all the original proprietors, I do not hesitate to affirm that it was their intention that the square should be used for any legitimate purpose, either of town or county; and representing as I do, one fourth of the proprietary interest, I would be pleased to join those representing the other interests, in signing any document that might legally and effectually determine the rightful control. As such a course is probably impracticable, I would take the liberty to suggest the appointment of a commission, composed of an equal number of representatives of the city and county authorities (with the judge of the United States district court as umpire, in case of any disagreement), charged with all needful control of the premises. I think the circumstances fully warrant some such concession on both sides."

Mr. Whitehead's wise recommendation was never adopted and the control of, or jurisdiction over Jackson Square, still remains in this uncertain condition.

Clinton Place, the small triangular plot at the intersection of Front, Whitehead, and Greene streets, was dedicated by the original proprietors to the use of the public in like manner as Jackson Square. In 1886 the Army and Navy Club of Key West erected a granite monument to the officers and men of the Union army, navy and marine corps, who died at Key West from 1861 to 1865. A concrete coping has since been constructed around it by the Federal government, which is permitted by the city authorities to have the care and maintenance of the plot.

Although the construction of a jail was one of the first public acts of the county authorities, an incident occurred in 1828, a narrative of which was published in a Northern paper, indicating how little use there was for it at that time, which sheds light on the easy going ways of the people, and their respect for the supremacy of the law:

Samuel Otis was the keeper of the jail, which was a small frame building quite distant from the settled part of the town. A man by the name of Ayres, who was in the habit of getting drunk, had come to Key West. He was taken in custody by Captain Otis and carried to the residence of Col. Greene, who was one of the magistrates, who upon being told that Ayres was drunk again ordered him put in the lockup, after the following conversation had taken place:

"Well, Squire, Ayres has been drinking again! Shall I take him to jail?"

"You may do with him what you please, Capt. Otis," replied the justice, not well pleased at the moment with the interruption.

"Just as you say, Squire," was the answer of the obsequious officer, and he forthwith announced to the gentleman in attendance that he must proceed to jail.

"Rot me if I do, Capt. Otis. Ain't I a free citizen of this here republic? I tell you I won't go unless I please, and I don't please unless I get my clothes."

"Well Ayres, where are your clothes?"

"Why they are down in the old shed by the water, and there they may stay for all me, for I won't go to get 'em; that's flat, Capt. Otis."

"Will you stay here, then, Ayres, while I go."

"No, I won't; how can you 'spect a man to stay here in this hot sun?"

"Well, Ayres, I don't want you to stay here, then; but while

I go after your clothes, do you go to the jail, knock at the door, and Peter will let you in."

Peter, the jailer, was no less a person than one of three mutineers who had been sentenced by the Admiralty court to six months imprisonment, and had stayed there because the judge had commanded him to do so. He was the factotum of Capt. Otis, kept the keys and locked himself in after every necessary opening of the prison doors.

Ayres proceeded to the jail and knocked and when Peter asked who was there he replied "It's me—open the door! Otis says you must let me in, and though I don't like altogether to be shut up with such fellows as you be, I 'spose I must, for they say it's law."

Upon that, the doors opened "grating harsh thunder," and the prisoner within admitted the prisoner from without.

In 1900 the county bought a plot of land opposite the United States army post, and erected an armory for the use of the local military company. Shortly afterwards the Supreme Court of the State decided that it was the duty of the State to provide armories, and that the county had no authority to expend money for that purpose. In 1903 the legislature refunded to the county the sum of $10,000.00 which had been expended for the armory. With this money the county road, which traverses the entire length of the island, was built.

The finances of the county are in excellent condition.* The present county officers are: James R. Curry, chairman; W. R. Porter, E. Monroe Roberts, Braxton B. Warren and Domingo Milord, members of the board of county commissioners. Eugene W. Russell, clerk circuit court; Hugh Gunn, county judge; Clement Jaycocks, sheriff; Thomas O. Otto, tax assessor; Theodore A. Sweeting, tax collector.

*Appendix I.

CHAPTER X

COURTS

THE early settlers of Key West were not people to sit down and wait for things to come to them. In 1827 the Senate of the United States passed a bill for the establishment of a territorial court at Key West with admiralty jurisdiction. The passage of the bill was opposed by the people in the northern part of the State, and they had reasonable prospects of defeating it, when Mr. John W. Simonton went to Washington and presented a memorial to Congress urging its passage.*

In 1828 congress passed the bill establishing a territorial or federal court at Key West under the title of the "Superior Court of the Southern Judicial District of the Territory of Florida." Its jurisdiction extended over that part of "the territory which lies south of a line from Indian river on the east and Charlotte Harbor on the west, including the latter harbor."

It had civil and criminal jurisdiction, as well for offences against the laws of the Territory of Florida, as of the United States, and embraced admiralty and maritime jurisdiction, thus superseding the jurisdiction of local and inferior magistrates, as well as the special commissioners for the adjudication of questions of salvage, arising out of the frequent wrecks occurring in this vicinity. The establishment of this court, the first term of which commenced November 3, 1828, led to the migration hither of a number of lawyers, but the business of the court not proving very extensive, the stay of most of them was of limited duration. Considerable amusement was excited at the time by an announcement in the newly established newspaper called the "*Register*," of the arrival of a vessel from Middle Florida with "an assorted cargo, *and seven lawyers*." Just how many of these lawyers remained is lost to history, but that they were men of ability the records of our courts abundantly show. Few cities of a population of twenty-five thousand can boast of a bar superior to that of Key West in the days when the population was less than a thousand.

Mr. William Allison McRea, Mr. James Webb, Mr. William Marvin, Mr. L. Windsor Smith, Mr. Adam Gordon, Mr. Samuel J. Douglas, Mr, Edward Chandler, Mr. Stephen R. Mallory, Mr. William R. Hackley, Mr. Walter Cathcart Maloney, and others, were men of the highest character, distinguished alike for their ability as lawyers, and general intellectual attainments.

---

*Appendix J.

Dignified and courtly, scrupulous and conscientious, they placed the profession of law on the high plane tradition tells us it once occupied.

Judge James Webb of Georgia had the honor of being commissioned first judge of the superior court in 1828. He retired from office in April, 1838, and went to Texas, and became secretary of state of that republic prior to its admission into the Union. He was succeeded by William Marvin, Esq., in 1839, who occupied the bench of this court until Florida was admitted into the Union in 1845, when Isaac H. Bronson, Esq., was commissioned judge for the whole State. In 1847, when the district court of the United States for the Southern District of Florida was created, Judge Marvin was appointed judge of this court and presided over it until 1863, when he resigned.

Judge Marvin was a man of towering intellectuality and grandeur of character. While on the bench he published a book entitled "A Treatise Upon the Law of Wreck and Salvage," which became a standard authority in the admiralty courts of England and the United States, and it occupies today a unique position among the treatises on the law of salvage. After his retirement from the bench he wrote a work on "General Average" which is an authority on this subject. Later he wrote "The Internal Evidences of the Authenticity of the Four Gospels." In this work he brought to bear his great judicial mind in the analysis of his subject.

At the close of the war he was appointed provisional governor of Florida by Andrew Johnson. In 1865 he was elected United States senator from Florida, for the term which would expire March 3, 1867. Thad Stephens and his crowd, however, had no use for men of Judge Marvin's calibre and character, and his election was nullified by reconstruction, and he never took his seat.

On the resignation of Judge Marvin in 1863 he was succeeded by Thomas J. Boynton, one of the youngest men ever appointed to the bench of the United States. He was a man of rare ability, culture and refinement. He came to Key West for his health, which had been greatly impaired by intense application to other sciences in addition to that of the law, but his health not improving, he resigned his position and returned north, where he soon died.

Judge John McKinney was appointed in 1871. To him Col. Maloney, in his history, pays this tribute:

"With melancholy feelings is the name of this gentleman introduced; modest, dignified, urbane, diligent and learned, he gave promise of much usefulness: alas! how short his judicial career. Leaving the island with the expressed intention of removing his family hither for permanent settlement, he failed to reach the city of New York alive; his death is reported to have occurred just previous to the arrival of the steamer in which he was a passenger."

The present incumbent of the United States district court for the Southern District of Florida, Judge James W. Locke, was appointed by President Grant February 1, 1872, and is the oldest Federal judge, in point of service, on the bench.*

From the date of establishment of a Federal court at Key West until in the seventies, the amount of business on the admiralty side of the court was very large, but as steamships gradually took the place of sailing vessels, and light-houses were built on the most dangerous points of the Florida Reefs, the number of wrecks gradually diminished. The amount of salvage business before the court is still quite large as compared with that of other districts, but is light compared with early days.

The act of congress creating the court for the Southern District of Florida in 1847, prescribed that the judge of this court should reside at Key West, but in 1896, congress repealed that part of the act of 1847, and the judge has since lived in Jacksonville.

In 1894 the territorial limits of the Southern District of Florida were enlarged, and they now include all of the State that lies east of the Suwanee river, and the counties of Madison and Hamilton west of the Suwanee.

During the Civil War and again during the Spanish-American War, there was considerable business on the prize side of the court, and many important and novel questions were therein adjudicated.

The national bankruptcy act has also increased the work of this court, but the general civil and criminal business is inconsiderable. Only three persons have been convicted of capital felony during its existence, one of which occurred in this city, and two on the high seas. Two were capitally punished and the other was sentenced to imprisonment for life.

Norman Sherwood, the first man hanged in Key West, had a *recontre* with a man named Jones on the fifth of July, 1830. After they were separated he went away, but returned in an hour with a pistol, avowing his intention of killing Jones. Bystanders again interfered and induced him to leave, but he returned shortly still determined to kill Jones. Mr. John Wilson, who was Sherwood's friend and partner, then stepped up and asked him to give up his pistol; he refused and said he would shoot any man who attempted to take it. Wilson then laid his hand on Sherwood's shoulder and again asked him to give it up, when Sherwood shot him, and he died a few minutes later. Sherwood remarked that "he regretted Wilson's death, but it was his own fault as he had told him that he would shoot anyone who attempted to take the pistol from him; for he firmly intended to shoot Jones and would permit no man to prevent him; that Wilson had attempted to do this and he shot him, believing he had a perfect right to do so."

The prisoner was defended by Messrs. Thurston and Braden.

*Appendix K

66

He was found guilty of murder in the first degree, and hanged on the tenth of December, 1830.

The place where Sherwood was confined was insecure, and he had several opportunities to escape, and on being asked why he had not done so, replied: "They want to hang someone for a pattern, and I guess I'll gratify them."

How thoroughly the grand jurors of those days did their work of "inquiring into the body of the county" is shown by their presentment, December 5, 1834, in what they designated "A List of Grievances." Some of these grievances still exist, but others sound strange to modern ears.

They complained that "the jail was in bad condition; the mortar used for the wall being mostly sand and good for nothing, the walls filled with loose stones and no mortar mixed with them, and entirely unfit for the purpose for which it was designed."

"That the officials whose duty it was to keep persons charged with offences, suffered them to go at large when they ought to have been confined."

"That the territorial limits of this county were not properly defined and fixed."

"That foreigners and persons from beyond the boundaries of this territory were permitted to take fish in this district and county, and did not pay any tax or revenue to the territorial county."

"That wrecking vessels were not allowed salvage upon the duties on the goods saved from wrecks."

"The want of a marine hospital where sick and disabled seamen could be comfortably situated and properly cared for."

"That grog shops, coffee houses, billiard rooms and other places were kept open on the Sabbath. These places encourage the idle and profligate, and the same are highly destructive to the morals and good order of society."

"The introduction of free negroes and mulattoes in this county, which is contrary to the policy of protection which had long been established and adopted in the southern section of the United States."

"We also believe and feel confident that this particular district and county is more exposed to the detestable views of fanatics and abolitionists attempting to tamper with and corrupt our slave population than most places."

"The want of a road to some point on the mainland in this county whereby the citizens may be able to communicate with the seat of government in the territory."

"Against a law passed in 1833 whereby the guns and boats of persons who live and may be found on the keys are exempt from execution. The grand jurors believe that no distinction should be made between those living on the keys or the mainland."

"We present as a grievance that boats not engaged in trading or commerce, but which are farm or plantation boats, if over a

67

certain size, should be required to get papers from the custom house and have a captain appointed under the restrictions which trade and commerce are subjected to."

"Against requiring persons who live on the mainland to attend court in Key West as jurors."

This statement of grievances was sent to our representative in Congress, with a request to lay it before the president of the United States, and use his exertions to having the grievances herein complained of redressed.

Shortly after the admission of Florida to the Union, the United States court was moved from the county court house to a stone building belonging to Wall & Pinckney, fronting on Wall street, back of the building now occupied by Monsalvatge & Reed on Front street. This building was destroyed by fire in 1859, and the court moved to the "Stone building" situated on the corner of Caroline and Whitehead streets, now used as a United States marine guardhouse. In 1885 it was moved to a building then belonging to Mr. John W. Sawyer, on the corner of Front and Fitzpatrick streets, which was destroyed in the fire of 1886. This was most unfortunate, as all the original papers and many records of important cases were lost. Court was next held in a building on the corner of Duval and Charles streets owned by Williams and Warren, where it remained until the Government building on Front street, at the foot of Greene, was completed in 1891.

STATE COURTS

Prior to 1845 when Florida was admitted into the Union, all law business was transacted in the territorial court, and it was not for some time thereafter that there was any business of importance in the State courts.

After Statehood, justice was administered by a Circuit and a Probate Court. Monroe county was in the Southern Circuit, and the first judge was William Marvin, who was appointed in December, 1845. He held the office only three months, and was succeeded by Judge George W. Macrae. In January, 1848, Judge Joseph B. Lancaster assumed the judicial toga. He was succeeded in 1853 by Judge Thomas F. King, who was followed in 1865 by Judge James Gettis.

In 1865 James Magbee became judge. During his incumbency there occurred one of the most remarkable proceedings ever witnessed in a court of justice. He was incarcerated in the city prison in Tampa for being drunk, and while there issued a writ of habeas corpus, commanding the mayor, J. E. Lipscomb, to bring the body of James Magbee before His Honor, James Magbee, to show by what authority he was depriving him of his liberty, and caused it to be served on the mayor, who treated it with merited contempt. When the judge was released, he issued a rule for the mayor to show cause why he should not be punished for contempt of court in refusing to obey the writ, and made public his intention to send the mayor to jail. People from all parts of the county came to town to protect the mayor from the threatened outrage, and the court house was filled with armed and determined men.

At the hearing the judge overruled the defendant's plea and sentenced him to jail. In an instant Mr. Lipscomb snatched a double barrelled shotgun from one of the bystanders and leveled it at the judge, but before he could shoot, he was surrounded by his friends and escorted out of court in defiance of the judge, and the mob of negroes assembled for his support. No attempt was afterwards made to enforce the order. Judge Magbee was a reconstruction judge, and this incident one of the minor outrages of that era.

Judge Winer Bethel, of Key West, succeeded Judge Magbee on April 6, 1875, and served until his death, March 30, 1877. Next came Henry L. Mitchel, who presided over the court until he went on the Supreme bench in 1889. Succeeding judges and their terms of service were G. A. Hanson, 1889 to 1891; Henry L. Mitchell, 1891 to 1892; G. B. Sparkman, 1892 to 1893; Barron Philips, 1893 to 1899; Joseph B. Wall, 1899 to 1911.

In 1911 the Eleventh circuit was created, consisting of Monroe, Dade and Palm Beach counties, and Livingston W. Bethel, the present incumbent, was appointed judge. He is a son of Judge Winer Bethel, who presided over the Circuit Court for Monroe county thirty-five years ago.

Judge Wall's death on December 19, 1911, removes the last survivor of those who have presided over the court in Monroe county, as judge of this circuit.

The first clerk of the Circuit Court was Colonel Walter Cathcart Maloney, and the first sheriff was Mr. John Costin.*

PROBATE COURT

The first judge of the Probate Court was Mr. Adam Gordon, who served from August 15, 1845, to December of the same year, and was succeeded by Mr. Benjamin Sawyer, who held office until Judge Winer Bethel was appointed in January, 1858.

COUNTY COURT

In 1868 the County Court took the place of the Probate Court and Judge James W. Locke was appointed judge, who served until February, 1871, when Mr. Charles S. Baron was appointed, and was followed by Judge Angel De Lono in 1870. In 1888 James Dean, a negro lawyer from the mainland, was elected but was removed from office in 1889 by Governor Fleming for malfeasance in office. Judge De Lono was appointed to the vacancy, and was succeeded by Judge Andrew J. Kemp in 1893. In 1900 Beverly B. Whalton was elected judge and held the office until his death in January, 1910, and was succeeded by Mr. Hugh Gunn, the present incumbent.

*Appendix L.

CHAPTER XI

KEY WEST AS A NAVAL BASE

IN FEBRUARY, 1822, Capt. L. T. Patterson and Lieut. Tuttle of the United States navy arrived with orders from the government to survey the coast and harbor, and they were soon followed by various government vessels that brought stores and materials, and by the end of the year the island was a regularly constituted naval depot and station, under the command of Commodore Porter. A resolution was adopted in the house of representatives in Washington requesting the President of the United States to inform the house:

"What appropriation will be required to enable him to fortify Thompson's Island, usually called Key West, and whether a naval depot, established at that island, protected by fortifications, will not afford facilities in defending the commerce of the United States, and in clearing the Gulf of Mexico and the adjacent seas from pirates."

To this Hon. Smith Thompson, secretary of the navy, for whom Captain Perry had named Key West, replied:

"That the geographical situation of the island referred to in the resolution has for some time past attracted attention, and been considered peculiarly important both as a military position and in reference to the commerce of the United States.

"The commander of one of our vessels, cruising in that quarter was accordingly directed last winter to touch at this island and take possession of it as a part of the territory ceded by Spain to the United States, and to make such general examination as might be useful in forming an opinion of the advantages of the place, and the propriety of a further and more particular survey. From the report of Lieutenant Commander Perry, who was charged with this duty, it has been satisfactorily ascertained that this position affords a safe, convenient and extensive harbor for vessels of war and merchant vessels. His instructions, however, did not require him to make so minute a survey as was necessary, in order to judge of the extent to which this place might be safely and advantageously occupied and improved as a naval depot.

"These are some of the obvious benefits in time of peace; but its advantages in time of war with any European power having West Indian possessions, are still more important, both as it respects the protection of our own commerce and the annoyance of our enemy. An enemy with a superior naval force *occupying this position, could completely intercept the whole trade between those parts of our country lying north and east of it, and*

those to the west, and seal up all our ports within the Gulf of Mexico.
It may, therefore, be safely answered, to one branch of the inquiry
made by the resolution, that if this island is susceptible of defence,
a naval depot established there would afford a great facility in
protecting our commerce. It is believed, however, that it is
susceptible of defense, at an expense that would be justified by
the importance of the place; but to form any tolerably satisfactory
estimate of the amount, an accurate survey and calculation, by
competent engineers, is indispensably necessary.

"This island is considered so advantageous and convenient
a place of rendezvous for our public vessels on the West Indian
station, that it is intended to make it a depot for provisions
and supplies for the expedition against the pirates, lately authorized by congress, to be secured in temporary buildings, under
the protection of a guard of marines."

Commodore Porter's communications to the department
abound in expressions, which show his high appreciation of the
advantages likely to result from the occupation of the island
by the United States as a naval station. Under date of May 11,
1823, when asking for an increased number of vessels and men,
he said:*

"From the importance of the trade of Cuba and the Gulf of
Mexico, the whole of which is protected from this place, with a
force not equal to one frigate, I presume my requests will not
be considered extravagant. The arrivals and departures of the
American vessels from the port of Havana alone average about
thirty a week, and those from Matanzas about twenty. Not
a day elapses but that great numbers of American vessels are
to be met passing through the gulf, and since our establishment
here, they daily in numbers pass in sight of us. I mention these
facts to give you an idea of the importance of this station, and to
show the propriety of augmenting the force by the additions
which I have asked."

Under date of November 19, 1823, he said: "The fixing an
establishment at Thompson's Island for rendezvous and supplies
has had a most happy effect in attaining the object had in view.
Its vicinity to Havana, placed as it were, in the thoroughfare
of vessels sailing through the gulf, making it, in many points
of view, an object of great importance to the United States."

Commodore Rodgers thus mentions the island under date
of November 24, 1823: "Nature had made it the advance post
from which to watch and guard our commerce passing to and
from the Mississippi, while at the same time, its peculiar
situation, and the excellence of its harbor, point it out as the most
certain key to the commerce of Havana, to that of the whole
Gulf of Mexico, and to the returning trade of Jamaica; *and I
venture to predict, that the first important naval contest in which
this country shall be engaged will be in the neighborhood of this
very island.*"

*Appendix M.

71

Seventy-five years afterwards this prophecy was fulfilled, and with Key West as a base, our fleet engaged in the most important naval contest ever fought in the gulf, destroyed the Spanish fleet, and drove Spain from the Western Hemisphere.

Sickness prevailed during the summer of 1823 to a great extent, and the reports of naval officers to the department, and from the department to the president, are replete with explanations as to the cause, and apprehensions as to the effects upon the permanency of the establishment. "Had the necessary number of medical men been furnished this year", wrote Commodore Porter, "the squadron would have been no doubt in a great measure saved from the deplorable consequences which have resulted, as the disease, in its commencement, was completely under the control of medicine; but I regret to say that several perished without receiving any medical aid whatever, and without even seeing a physician."

He further reports that "with the exception of one case of yellow fever, only bilious fever prevailed until June 20th, and the cases yielded readily to the agency of medicine, at which time it assumed a highly malignant form.

"This disease now commenced on board the store ship Decoy, which was rendered unhealthful by the impurity of her hold. A quantity of ballast was put on board from this island, containing shell-fish and sea-weed, which by the heat of the tropical climate, was thrown into a state of putrefactive fermentation. Two of the cases, however, which occurred on board this vessel were contracted by imprudent exposure to a noonday heat in the streets of Havana."

The secretary of the navy, under date of September 21st, drew the attention of the president to the impropriety of abandoning the island. "It ought not," said he, "readily be deserted. It is very desirable to save it." And Commodore Rodgers wrote a letter to the Secretary on the sixteenth of November, containing these sensible passages:

"United States Schooner Shark, Hampton Roads, Nov. 16, 1823.—From the little experience I have had, my opinion is that the climate of Thompson's Island is similar to that of the West India islands generally; that its air is perhaps less salubrious than some, but more so than others; and notwithstanding the objections which may be urged against it, on account of particular defects arising from its surface, and the many salt and fresh water ponds which it is said to contain, still, that it is, from the excellence of its harbor and *its peculiar station on the map of the Western Hemisphere*, too important an object, in a political and commercial point of view, to be suffered to remain unoccupied and unregarded, for, admitting its climate, in its present unimproved state, to be as unfriendly to health as even that of the colony of Surinam, it is, notwithstanding, susceptible of being so improved, or at least, the dangers attending it so much diminished by artificial means (such as I will hereafter describe), as to render the objections to it, if not harmless, at least comparatively small."

These remonstrances had the desired effect and prevented the abandonment of the island as a naval base.

The first use of Key West as an active base of naval operations was in 1822, when Commodore David Porter commanded the squadron organized to suppress the pirates of the West Indies, known as "Brethren of the Coast." Prior to his assuming command, no satisfactory progress had been made—the draught of the war vessels being too great to follow the buccaneers into the shallow bays, coves and rivers in which they sought refuge when pursued. Operations were conducted in this unsatisfactory manner for two years when Commodore Porter in command of the West Indian Squadron, inaugurated a new plan of campaign. First, he selected the island of Key West as a base of operations, and erected a storehouse, workshop, hospital and quarters for the men. He then detached and sent north the big, useless frigates and supplied their places with eight small light draught schooners and five twenty-oared barges. These last were appropriately named Mosquito, Midge, Gallinipper, Gnat, and Sandfly. Of the old squadron he retained the Peacock, John Adams, Hornet, Spark, Grampus and Shark. Thus was gathered at Key West a fleet of twenty-one craft, eminently suited for the work of driving from the sea forever the dreaded "Brethren of the Coast."

In order to make his barges available, it was necessary to tow them until he fell in with the buccaneers, and when they attempted to escape in shallow water, man the barges and go in pursuit. For this purpose he procured an old New York steam ferryboat, the Sea Gull, and her use for naval purposes is the first instance of a steam propelled vessel being used in the United States navy. In this way, Captain Porter captured and destroyed a number of the buccaneers' vessels, who made their final rendezvous at the Isle of Pines. Here he attacked, captured or destroyed most all of them. Some that escaped put into the Port of Fajardo, Porto Rico.

The buccaneers paid tribute to the Spanish government, and left the commerce of that nation unmolested, for which they received its moral support. Commodore Porter followed the buccaneers into Fajardo, and upon the military authorities refusing to give them up, sent a punitive expedition ashore, and taught the Spanish authorities a needed lesson. Thus was ended piracy in the Caribbean Sea.

Spain complained of his action at Fajardo, and he was court-martialed and sentenced to six months suspension, whereupon he resigned and entered the service of the Mexican navy, and later was connected with the Turkish navy, and while holding this position, the United States in atonement for the injustice which had been done this gallant and efficient officer, appointed him consular agent of the United States in Turkey, where he died in 1843.

While engaged in the suppression of piracy in the Caribbean Sea he became impressed with the importance of Key West as a naval base and so reported to the secretary of the navy in 1829.*

In 1856 a United States naval depot and storehouse was commenced at the corner of Whitehead and Front streets. In 1857 when the walls were ready to receive the roof, work on the building was suspended, and it remained so for several years for want of an appropriation by congress. At the outbreak of the Civil War it was in this unfinished condition.

In 1861 the U.S.S. Atlantic, having conveyed Federal troops for the relief of Fort Pickens, touched at this port for a supply of coal but finding none, was compelled to sail to Havana.

On three occasions has the importance of Key West as a naval base been demonstrated. During the Civil War more ships were stationed at Key West than at any other port in the United States, and but for its occupancy by the Northern forces as a naval base, the result of the war might have been different. In 1873 when the capture of the Virginius threatened war with Spain, nearly every available ship in the navy was hurried to Key West, which was made the base of all operations. In 1897, on the breaking out of the war with Spain, every available naval vessel was again sent to Key West, and the Oregon and Marietta made their record run from California to the all important Key West.

Its position on the Straights of Florida—through which four thousand vessels pass annually, and the commerce of all the gulf ports—commands the protection of American commerce in any war. In all past history this position has been of the greatest importance, and no matter where on the Western Hemisphere the war may be, the American commerce in the Straits of Florida will have to be protected from Key West as a naval base.

Whether the inexplicable zeal of certain naval authorities to develop Guantanamo (a port in a foreign country), at the expense of one of our own ports, will be sanctioned by congress, or continue after the personnel of the naval board is changed, is problematical.

Vague theories, personal preferences, individual hostilities, and opportunities for speculation, may give Guantanamo a temporary advantage over Key West, but actual war will again demonstrate that this place commands the route on the Key West-Porto Rican strategic line of force, and that it commands all approaches to the Gulf of Mexico, the Caribbean Sea and Panama Canal, and as a distinguished naval historian says, the government will recognize "the capacity of the Florida Reef as an advantageous naval station—a sort of Downs or St. Helen's Roads, in the West Indian seas."

---

*Appendix N.

74

In 1881 the naval wharf was rebuilt; iron piles being substituted for the wooden ones and a steel pier constructed. This work was done by Lieut. Robert E. Peary, the discoverer of the North Pole, who spent a year in Key West. The pier was demolished in the hurricane of 1910, and a more substantial concrete one was completed in 1911.

In 1895 the Navy Department bought the property that was the home of the two Stephen R. Mallorys, father and son, both of whom represented Florida in the senate of the United States. The old house, which was a center of social and intellectual life, was torn down to give place to coal bins.

In 1890 a double house was built by the Navy Department for the use of the commandant and paymaster of the station. It proved too small for two families and is now used exclusively for the commandant, at the present time Admiral Lucian Young.

In 1902 the United States government condemned for naval purposes all that part of the island lying southwest of Whitehead street between Fleming and Fitzpatrick streets, except the Mallory property, and the old home place of Mr. Joseph Beverly Browne, on the corner of Caroline and Whitehead streets, which the government bought in 1858, and the strip of water front acquired in 1854, on which the machine shop, commandant's quarters and coal bins had previously been erected. On the property condemned, the Navy Department now has buildings for the various departments of the service, and residences on Whitehead street for the paymaster and civil engineer. A distilling plant with a capacity of fifteen thousand gallons per day was constructed in 1898, and in 1910 a concrete reservoir of one million, five hundred thousand gallons capacity was erected on the Whitehead street side of the navy yard. In 1906 a wireless telegraph station was constructed, which is one of the most powerful in the world, and messages sent from here have been caught by the Mare Island station, a distance of twenty-six hundred miles.

Standing on the naval reservation at the corner of Whitehead and Caroline streets, is one of the oldest buildings in Key West, and for many years had the unique distinction of being the only one not built entirely of wood. It was known as "The Stone Building," being built of cement from a cargo of that material wrecked at Key West. It is a quaint three-story structure with a high pitched roof, having a narrow balcony supported by consoles of solid cement, extending the entire side on Whitehead street. On the gable end was once a similar balcony, but it has been taken down, and only the consoles remain. Above the side balcony is a large plaster mask of the builder, Mr. John G. Ziriax, who kept the foremost bakery of his day. Before it acquired the cognomen of the "Stone Building" it was known as the "Ziriax Building". It is now used as a marine guard-house.

Another building on the Naval Reservation which connects the old and the new Key West, stands about two hundred feet southwest of the Marine Guard-house. It is a type of the old style Key West architecture of which so little is left. When the grade of the reservation was raised it covered part of this house, and changed its appearance. The first floor was a foot below the level of the ground, built of stone to about eight feet in height, above which was the frame part of the building. The old officers' quarters at the barracks are of the same style of architecture, and most of the better class of houses in the early days were so constructed, for the protection, then supposed to be necessary, against the high tides which prevail during the passage of a hurricane in this vicinity.

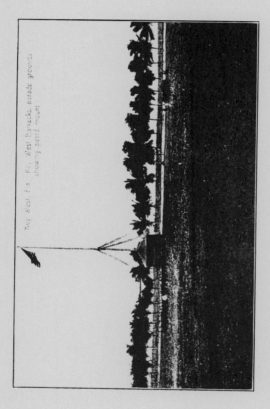

Guard Mount, Parade Ground, United States Army Post

Key West

CHAPTER XII

THE United States government since the first settlement of Key West has recognized the importance of strongly fortifying the island, but progress has been by fits and starts. In 1824 a company of marines was stationed here and barracks erected for them fronting upon the harbor between Duval and Whitehead streets. They were not long occupied and were in a dilapidated condition in 1831, when they were sold and removed.

In February, 1831, Major James M. Glassel arrived with two companies of infantry and established a temporary camp at the present site of the army post on the North Beach.

The proprietors of the island set aside a tract of land for the use of the army embracing all of squares fifty-two, fifty-three and fifty-four, and parts of squares twenty-eight and twenty-nine, fronting on the waters of the bay, on the north side of the island, and in 1833, 1835 and 1837 this and some additional lots were deeded to the United States government, by the original proprietors, and has since been occupied as an army post. By the charter of 1836 all jurisdiction over this property was ceded to the United States government. On May 10, 1836, Lieutenant Benjamin Alvord, afterwards paymaster general of the United States army, came to Key West with Company B, 4th United States Infantry.

Temporary quarters were erected for the accommodation of the troops which were removed in 1844, when six buildings for officers' quarters and two for soldiers' barracks and a guard house were erected. The soldiers' barracks, each one hundred and twenty-five feet long, and twenty feet wide, were about forty feet apart, on the southwest side of the parade ground. Three of the officers' quarters were on the northeast, and three on the southwest side of the parade ground. One of them was destroyed by fire in 1847. The officers' quarters and the soldiers' barracks were of the same style of architecture and admirably suited to this climate. They were built of wood, on stone and brick foundations, seven feet high, with piazzas on all sides. In 1892 three additional sets of officers' quarters were constructed.

In 1906 additional officers' quarters, barracks for the soldiers, and a barracks for the bandsmen, were erected, and three companies of artillery, with a regimental band, under the command of a colonel, garrisoned the post.

In 1909 the old soldiers' quarters, which were built in 1844, were so badly damaged by a hurricane that they were torn down, and two companies, and the band, detached from the post.

There is now only one company stationed at Key West, a force wholly inadequate for the care of the modern guns on the fortifications, and the maintenance of the government property. During the tourist season many representatives of foreign nations visit Key West, and the indifference shown by the War Department for so important a point is a subject of frequent criticism, and ofttimes ridicule.

The fortifications, and the army post are on opposite sides of the island, and squads of troops are marched every day a distance of a mile and a half to the fortifications.

At the time of the Civil War there were no roads or streets directly connecting the army post and Fort Taylor, which could only be reached by marching the troops through the town. In 1861 General John M. Brannan, the commanding officer, cut a road across the island from a point about a thousand feet northeast of the post, so that he could march his troops to the fort without going through the city. For several years this was known as the Brannan Road. As General Brannan only cut away the trees and brush, the road remained full of the coral rock which abounds on the island, and soon became known as the Rocky Road. Later the name was officially changed to Division street, it being the dividing line beyond which on the southeast side there were few, if any, inhabitants. The city has grown far beyond Division street, which is now one of the most populous and best business streets, but is still generally known by the cognomen "Rocky Road." The term, Division street, having lost its significance, it would be historically accurate to change the name to Brannan street.

In 1845 Fort Taylor was commenced, and so much of the work as had been constructed up to October 11, 1846, was by the hurricane of that year destroyed. The work, however, was resumed at once and it was ready for occupancy in 1861. Fort Taylor was a double casemated brick fort of the Bauban plan. Its armament consisted of forty 10-inch Rodmans and ten 24-pounder howitzers on the first tier; thirty 8-inch Columbiads, six 30-pounder Parrott rifles; two 10-inch Rodmans, eighteen 24-pounder howitzers on the second tier, and twenty 10-inch Rodmans, two 15-inch Rodmans, three 300-pounder Parrott rifles, three 100-pounder Parrott rifles, three 30-pounder Parrott rifles, one 10-inch siege mortar, and four 8-inch siege mortars on the parapet.

It was built on a sand spit about a quarter of a mile from shore, and had four bastions and four curtains. Three of the curtains commanded all of the water entrance into Key West. At the breaking out of the Civil War two large sand covert faces were thrown up on the edge of the sand spit towards the town in anticipation of an attack by the Confederates from that direction. Commodious quarters were constructed within the

Ruins of Martello Tower

walls of the fort, but only occupied during the Civil War. In 1899 the parapet and second tier of casemates were demolished, and the gun embrasures in the lower tier built up of solid masonry. Back of this is twenty feet of sand and debris, and back of this twenty feet of concretè. Behind this are two 12-inch guns on barbette carriages; and four 15-pounders for protecting the mine fields in the harbor.

In 1861 the government began the construction of two Martello towers on the water's edge; one near the extreme northeastern end of the island, and the other about two miles nearer town. They consist of a citadel about forty feet high, surrounded by casemates, and a parapet reinforced with sand embankments. When they were built they were capable of withstanding any attack from the land or sea, but with the improvement of ordnance they soon became as useful as paper houses for defense, and have long been abandoned. Their only use now is to gratify the curiosity of tourists, and to adorn postal cards, where they are designated as ancient ruins.

In 1873 a small sand battery was erected on what was once known as Light-house Point, called the South Battery, about a quarter of a mile from Fort Taylor, and another about midway between it and the Marine Hospital, called North Battery, and a few modern guns were mounted upon them.

In 1897 a mortar battery, with two nests of four 12-inch mortars each, was constructed, and the sand battery at Light-house Point enlarged and made into the most modern type of fortification, on which are mounted four 10-inch, and two 8-inch rifles on disappearing carriages, with a small flanking battery on the one hand, mounting two 15-pounder guns, and another mounting two 4.7 Armstrong-Whitworth guns. The old North Battery was replaced in 1904 by a battery of more modern construction, on which are mounted two 6-inch barbette guns. These are flanked on the northeast side by a battery mounting two 15-pounders.

In 1908 the government condemned for military purposes that portion of the water front on the south side of the island lying between the southeast end of the large sand battery and South street, and part of five blocks between the southwest side of South street and the fort reservation. The amount paid for this property was about one hundred thousand dollars. A recommendation has been made by the War Department for the condemnation of the rest of the land in these blocks for the purpose of erecting officers' and soldiers' quarters.

CHAPTER XIII

MAIL AND STEAMSHIP SERVICE

" "THE first post office was established in February, 1829, and the first contract for mail service was awarded to owners of a small sailing vessel called the 'Post Boy' of about ten tons, which was to make monthly trips between Charleston and this city. Captain David Cole, with all the advantages of good seamanship, knowledge of coast, and superior education, was in command of this vessel, but for some very good reason, the monthly trips generally consumed nearer fifty days than thirty. Cape Canaveral was to be doubled in the route, and never did the mariner scan the clouds in the effort to double Cape Horn with more solicitude than did this worthy skipper to effect the same result at Cape Canaveral, but from different motives—the one being proverbial for its storms, and the other for its calms. Fretting did not bring the vessel any sooner than the winds and the current would permit. The mails were brought with regular irregularity. When they did arrive everybody knew it. He who was not certain that his expected letter would be prepaid by his correspondent put a 'quarter' (25 cents) in his pocket to satisfy old Uncle Sam for the cost of transportation (for that was the rate per letter at the time I speak of), and if perchance you subscribed to a newspaper, five cents more would put you all right with the postmaster, for this then enviable means of information that other *Nations* existed besides Key West." (Maloney).

This service proved so unsatisfactory that it was discontinued, and a route established between St. Marks and Key West. In August, 1832, a contract was awarded for the regular transportation of a mail between this place and Charleston, once a month. About 1835 Messrs. Lord and Stocker of Charleston obtained the contract for a semi-monthly mail, and first class sailing vessels were put on the run.

About 1848 Messrs. Mordecai & Co., of Charleston, obtained the mail contract, and the Isabel, a remarkably fast and comfortable steamer of about eleven hundred tons, was put on between Charleston and Key West, which service continued until the commencement of the Civil War. The arrival of the Isabel in port was an important event. When she was sighted the fact was made known by the ringing of a bell on a tower at the agent's wharf. She frequently arrived at night and when that occurred nearly everybody sat up to await her arrival and hear from distant relatives and friends, from whom they had been cut off for two weeks. No family waited alone; those who did not have friends to eat midnight supper with them, went out to the homes of others, and the occasions were ones of jollification and social gathering. Happy, happy days, when all lived together in unity! When the Isabel neared the wharf, the entire adult population would congregate there to get the first news of the outside world, and greet returning relatives and friends.

For some time prior to the Civil War occasional mails were brought to Key West from New Orleans and St. Marks, by a line of steamers owned in New York by Messrs. Morgan & Co. It was from such a modest beginning that the well known Morgan Line developed, which has since passed into the hands of the Southern Pacific Steamship Company, with the largest and fastest coastwise steamships in the United States. Shortly after the Civil War two fine, fast modern steamships—Cuba and Liberty—were put on between Baltimore and Havana, touching at Key West both ways, until 1873, when the line was discontinued.

In 1873 Messrs. Mallory & Company inaugurated their service between New York, Key West and Galveston. They began with a few small steamers, which they replaced from time to time with larger ones, and they now have a fleet of twelve fast, commodious, finely equipped and admirably officered ships. In 1907 they established a line between New York and Mobile, touching at Key West both ways. Four, and frequently six, ships of this line touch at Key West weekly. The Mallory line is now part of that excellent transportation company, the Atlantic, Gulf & West Indies Steamship Lines. Under the management of Mr. H. H. Raymond, vice-president, the line has been brought to a high state of efficiency, and is the leading coastwise steamship organization operating in the Atlantic and gulf.

At the close of the Civil War the regular mail to Key West came via Cedar Keys, the terminus of the Florida, Atlantic & Gulf Central Railroad. For a number of years Miller & Henderson of Tampa, had the contract, and combined bringing the mails, with supplying this and the Havana market with beef cattle. If a drove of cattle was late in reaching Cedar Keys, or an obstreperous steer obstructed the lading, the mails were delayed from twelve to twenty-four hours.

Key West suffered from such irregular and imperfect service until in 1887, when Mr. Henry B. Plant, the pioneer developer of Florida, ran a line of steamers from Port Tampa to Key West and Havana. In the construction of the Mascotte and the Olivette he spared no expense, and the ship builders were instructed to turn out the very best steamships that could be built. After eighteen years constant service, the Olivette retains her supremacy as the fastest coastwise steamship in the United States, and she and the Mascotte can be depended upon, with the certainty of a railroad train, to make their runs within schedule time.

In 1895 Mr. Archer Harmon interested the people of Key West in a project to put a steamer on between Key West and Miami, the then southern terminus of the Florida East Coast Railway. He chartered the fast and commodious river steamer, Shelter Island, but before reaching Key West for her initial trip, she struck on shoals in Hawks Channel, and was a total loss. He next chartered the City of Richmond, a large sidewheel steamer, and changed her name to the City of Key West. She made a few trips under the original management, but the venture proving a failure financially, the stock in the company was taken over by Mr. Henry M. Flagler, who continued to operate the line between Key West and Miami until 1900, when the Peninsular and Occidental Steamship Company was organized, and the Mascotte, Olivette, Miami and City of Key West taken over by it. The principal stockholders in the company are Mr. Morton F. Plant and Mr. Henry M. Flagler. The Mascotte and the Olivette ply between Port Tampa, Key West and Havana, and make three round trips weekly, during the months of January, February and March, and two during the other months of the year.

In 1902 the City of Key West was sold, and the Shinnecock put on the run between Miami and Key West during the winter and the Miami the rest of the year. On the completion of the Florida East Coast Railway to Knights Key, in 1908, the line between Miami and Key West was discontinued, and the Montauk chartered for the run between Miami and Key West, during the winter season. The Miami plys between Miami and Nassau during three months in the winter, and in the summer takes the Knights Key-Key West run.

The Florida East Coast Railway will be completed to Key West January twenty-second, 1912, when mail service by water will be a thing of the past.

The first post-office—if a room where the few letters that were received in Key West at that time, could be called a "post-office"—was in a building that stood on the corner of Caroline and Front streets, and occupied by the family of the postmaster. It was afterwards the home of Mr. Charles Tift, and subsequently occupied by Judge Angel de Lono. Its last tenants were the Misses Higgs, sisters of the Rev. Gilbert Higgs.

When Mr. Hicks was postmaster the office was on the northwest side of Front street, between Duval and Simonton, in the store of Hicks & Dusenbury. Later it was in one end of the stone warehouse on the Tift property on Front street, at the end of Fitzpatrick. When Mr. George Philips was postmaster it was in a room in the Russell House, on Duval street.

Under the administrations of Mr. Eldridge L. Ware, Mr. Joseph B. Browne, and part of that of Nelson F. English, it was in a small building on the southeast side of Front street, about a hundred feet from the corner of Duval. When this building was destroyed by fire in 1886, the post-office was moved tô a small shed-like building on the southwest side of Whitehead street, on the government lot, at the corner of Whitehead and Caroline streets, formerly used as a storeroom by the lampist of the light-house service.

When Mr. Jefferson B. Browne was appointed postmaster in 1886, he erected on the corner of this lot a one-story building with a main office sixteen by thirty-five feet, and a smaller room sixteen feet square. He equipped it at his own expense with two hundred and fifty Yale & Towne lock boxes, the first that were ever used in Key West. This building was used as the post-office during Mr. Browne's term, and part of that of Mr. George Hudson, Mr. Browne's successor. In 1891 it was transferred to the new government building at the foot of Greene street.

CHAPTER XIV

INDIAN HOSTILITIES

IN MARCH, 1836, Secretary of War Lewis Cass requested General Scott, who had charge of the military operations against the Indians in Florida, to detach a garrison from his forces and re-occupy Key West, and directed the ordnance department to forward without delay one hundred and fifty stands of arms, together with the necessary ammunition. to the commanding officer here, and, if there was no army officer, then to the care of Mr. William A. Whitehead, the collector of customs.

On the 15th of December, 1835, Major Dade, who was in command of the army post at Key West, left on the transport Motto for Tampa, with his entire command, where he led an expedition against the Indians in South Florida. On December 28th he attempted to march from Tampa to Fort King, but his command was ambuscaded and one hundred and fifteen officers and men massacred. Only one escaped.

So complete was the ambuscade that all of the officers were killed at the first fire. Among them was Captain Gardener, whose wife and children were in Key West where they had been living during the time that Captain Gardener and Major Dade were stationed here. They were both highly esteemed and had a large social acquaintance, and the news of their death threw the city in mourning. Captain Gardener's wife and children were objects of tender consideration from our people, and every kindness and attention possible was extended to them in their bereavement.

On January 4, 1836, the Indians attacked the family of Mr. William Coolie at New River, murdering his wife and three children, together with Mr. Joseph Flinton, of Maryland, who was employed as instructor for his children.

The inhabitants between New River and Cape Florida, and along the Florida Keys, became justly alarmed, and about two hundred fugitives came to Key West for safety.

There were about three thousand Indians operating in South Florida, and as they carried their hostilities farther south on the East Coast, an attack on Key West was feared. Our citizens chartered a vessel, and sent it to Havana to buy arms and ammunition, and to solicit a visit from any American man-of-war that was then in port. This at once brought Commander Dallas, in the frigate Constitution, and Captain Rosseau in the sloop-of-war St. Louis, to Key West for the protection of our people.

After the massacre of Mr. Coolie's family at New River, several attempts were made by the Indians to attack Cape Florida light-house, and on January 16th it was abandoned by the keepers, and notice of that fact published to the world by the collector of customs at Key West.

About the time of the massacre at Indian Key an attack was made on the light-house at Cape Florida; the keepers and their families abandoned their residences, which were destroyed, and took refuge in the top of the light-house where the Indians were afraid to attack them, the spiral staircase affording excellent facilities for defense. They set fire to the interior of the light-house and destroyed part of the staircase, and but for the timely arrival of a revenue cutter the inmates would have perished.

Among these was the daughter of the light-house keeper, Miss Drucilla Duke, who married Captain Courtland Williams, and was the mother of Mrs. George W. Reynolds and Mrs. H. B. Boyer. At Indian Key the people made ready for an attack by erecting embankments, mounting cannon, etc.

A land patrol of the most prominent citizens was organized at Key West, which kept up until the spring rains set in, when the gentlemen composing the guard abandoned their patrol, and sought shelter on the verandas of the houses, and finally staid at home altogether.

A water patrol was also organized and the island was circumnavigated every night.

An incident, which illustrates the demoralizing effect of fear, is told by Mr. Wm. A. Whitehead. "I was both amused and provoked one night by being summoned by the captain of the watch to leave my family to look after some Indians supposed to be in the woods, saying that 'the sound of a drum had been distinctly heard several times.' The captain was no less a person than Mr. Alden A. M. Jackson. Mrs. Whitehead and I got up, and he marched us all the way to the barracks to see if the drum known to be there was in its place. The ridiculousness of the Indians having gone to the barracks and stolen the drum, and beat an alarm to give notice of their approach, never once occurred to the captain of the watch. It was later discovered that the noise was caused by a dog striking his leg on top of a cistern, while scratching fleas."

This incident found a counterpart in the Spanish American War, when Captain W. H. H. Sutherland of the United States navy, discovered and reported a Spanish fleet in the vicinity of Tampa, just as the transports were about to sail for Cuba. A fog or mist deceived him, as the dog scratching fleas deceived Captain Jackson.

The massacre of a number of Key West citizens on Indian Key was one of the most harrowing events in the history of our people. There were about twenty families living there, all of whom had relatives in Key West. A deputy collector of customs, a postmaster, commission merchant, warehouseman and others,

85

were living on Indian Key. Among them was Dr. Henry Perrine, who had obtained a grant from congress, in 1838, of a township on Biscayne Bay for the purpose of demonstrating the adaptability of that part of South Florida for nearly all tropical and subtropical plants. Dr. Perrine moved to Florida in the winter of that year with his family, and several others who were to form part of the colony which was to develop his grant. On account of the Indian war it was not deemed safe to establish a colony on the mainland, and they took up their residence on Indian Key to wait the termination of hostilities.

Dr. Perrine brought plants and seeds from Mexico, Central and South America, which he planted on Matecumbie and Lignum Vitae Key as nurseries for his mainland colony when the war should end. His massacre by the Indians indefinitely postponed the colonization scheme, but the plants that he set out grew abundantly, and other hands reaped the harvest which the dead had sown. The presence of mahogany and other hard woods on these islands, which do not grow on the other keys, is the result of Dr. Perrine's sojourn there. After his death his family moved to New York, and his son, Mr. Henry Perrine, some years ago married Mrs. Folsom, the mother of Mrs. Grover Cleveland.

Congress lately confirmed the grant made in 1838, and Dr. Perrine's heirs came into possession of a township on Biscayne Bay. His descendants now living in Florida are Mrs. Sarah R. W. Palmer, her sons, T. W. and J. D. Palmer, Jr., two daughters, Misses Jessie and Minnie, who are living in Miami with their mother. Another daughter, Mrs. Sarah Rogers Colmore, is the wife of Rev. Charles D. Colmore, an Episcopal clergyman in Cuba.

INDIAN KEY MASSACRE

For several years people on Indian Key lived in constant dread of an attack from the Indians. At Tea Table Key, about a mile from Indian Key, there was a naval depot and a detachment of United States troops was stationed there. A revenue cutter cruised constantly near Indian Key, making that its principal anchoring place.

Captain Houseman, who owned a large wharf and warehouse, and did a general storekeeping and commission merchant business, had for eighteen months been making preparations to defend the island from an anticipated attack, and spent about $20,000 for that purpose. In the fall of 1838 three hundred Indians congregated on the adjacent keys with a view of attacking the island. They sent a Spaniard, who was living with them, to Indian Key as a spy, but he was taken prisoner by Captain Houseman, who was informed by him that there were two Indians on Lignum Vitae Key. These were also captured, and the Indians realizing that the inhabitants were on the alert, abandoned their plan of an attack at this time. Captain Houseman ascertained from these spies that it was the intention of the Indians, after capturing Indian Key, to proceed to Key Vaccas and thence to Key West. He kept them prisoners for eighteen months, and on the arrival of the revenue cutter, sent for the protection of the people at Indian Key, they were turned over to the captain, from whom they effected their escape.

Captain Houseman and the citizens of Indian Key had repeatedly petitioned the government of Florida and Congress, to furnish troops for their protection. They urged that the troops and the naval depot should be at Indian Key and not at Tea Table Key, but their petitions were ignored. It was believed at the time that Tea Table Key was selected at the instance of certain prominent citizens of Key West who owned that island, and the feeling among the survivors of the massacre was very bitter against some of the people of Key West, whom they felt were to some extent responsible.

A short time before the massacre, Mr. John Whalton, the keeper of the Carysfort Reef lightship, was killed by a party of Indians on one of the keys where he had a garden. Mr. Whalton's family were living in Key West, and he has a number of descendants living here now.

A few days before the attack, Lieut. McLaughline, who had under his command the revenue cutters Flint and Atrego, left the vicinity of Indian Key, and sent one of the cutters to Cape Florida, and the other to Cape Sable. It was while on this trip that the two Indian spies escaped by jumping overboard. They carried the information to the other Indians that the cutters had left the vicinity of the island, and that there was no one on Tea Table Key except one officer and ten sick men. The Indians hastily gathered in force, and between two and three o'clock in the morning of the 7th of August, about three hundred quietly came in their canoes to the island and disembarked, and were proceeding to surround the houses, when they were discovered by Mr. J. Glass, who occupied one of the dwellings on Water street on the south side of the key. Mr. Glass got up, and looking out of his front window, discovered a large number of canoes along the rocks directly in front of his house. He immediately went to the adjoining house occupied by Mr. J. F. Beiglet and called him, and they started to give the information to Captain Houseman and others, but in crossing the public square they were discovered by a large number of Indians who were creeping silently along the fence which led to Captain Houseman's dwelling. As soon as the Indians discovered them, they commenced firing, screaming and yelling, which gave the alarm to another party of Indians coming around by Mr. Howe's house, and they all rushed for Captain Houseman's store and dwelling. Glass and Beiglet escaped, Glass secreting himself under the Second street wharf—Beiglet in a cistern under a large warehouse. They remained there, with James Sturdy and another man, until the building was set on fire. Beiglet and the

87

other man escaped, but Sturdy was burned to death. Beiglet lost about $10,000.00 in gold.

The inhabitants were aroused from their sleep by the blood-curdling yells and war cries of the Indians.

The house occupied by Dr. Perrine belonged to Mr. Howe. It was the largest on the island, being three stories high, with a porch and cupola, and built so close to the water that, during high tide, three sides were surrounded by water. Fronting the porch was a short wharf. Under the wharf was a crawl for turtle. It communicated with the cellar by a narrow passage way walled up above high water mark. The cellar being open to the influx of the sea, was used by the family for bathing, and was entered by a trap door from the dressing room above. It was into this cellar that Dr. Perrine hurried his family when they were awakened by the discharge of guns, crashing of glass and wild yells of the Indians. His family urged him to come into the cellar with them, but he knew that the Indians would discover the trap door, so he remained in the house and closed the opening, and piled upon it bags of grain, etc., so as to completely hide it. He then got his guns ready but discovered that he had no caps. His family heard him parleying with the Indians in Spanish, trying to prevail on them to spare his dwelling. Soon the distressed listeners in the cellar heard the Indians make a furious assault upon the dwelling, and one of them say in English, "All hid; old man upstairs." They heard with terror the rush up the stairs, the heavy blows upon the massive doors which led to the cupola, the terrific crash as it yielded, a single rifle shot, the awful war whoop, and the demoniac yells of the savages; and the family below knew that their father and husband was no more!

Captain John Mott, his wife and two children, and his mother-in-law, were discovered by the Indians about daylight. Mott and his wife were shot. The oldest child, a girl about four years old, was picked up and her brains dashed out against a post. The baby was choked to death and thrown into the sea. Mott and his wife, who were not yet dead, were dragged about fifty yards, and killed with blows from clubs, and their hair and clothes set afire. The mother-in-law escaped and hid under a building until the Indians left.

After the massacre they set fire to houses, and what they did not burn they destroyed. One house alone escaped. It belonged to Mr. Charles Howe. Mr. Howe was a Mason, and when the Indians left the island, his Masonic apron with its all-seeing eye and other mystic symbols, was found spread out on a table. The savages had found it in ransacking the place, and whether they knew anything of Masonry and spared Mr. Howe's house on that account, or whether it appealed to their superstitions and frightened them, will never be known; but it was believed that this home was spared on that account. After his death the apron was presented to Dade Lodge No. 14, F. & A. M., but it was destroyed in 1886, when the Masonic Temple was burned.

Nearly all who escaped massacre did so by secreting themselves in cisterns. Many of them remained in water up to their necks for five or six hours, and where the cisterns were under the houses which were burned, those who escaped, endured frightful tortures.

Captain Elliott Smith's family, consisting of wife and one child and his wife's little brother, who resided on Fourth street, were among those who suffered in this way. The older members of the family managed to escape, but the boy, about twelve years of age, was burned to death.

In addition to burning and destroying property, the Indians carried away all the slaves that they could find. They took three belonging to Mr. Howe and a negro girl from Captain Houseman.

While the Indians were still on the island, the few soldiers who were in the hospital at Tea Table Key, unfit for active service, manned a small boat, in which they placed two four-pound swivels, and put off about daylight to attack the Indians and cut off their retreat. In the hurry of their departure they took six pound bags of powder instead of four. When they came within about two hundred yards of the wharf they opened fire on a number of the Indians, who had congregated on the wharf, but at the first discharge of the swivels, the overloaded guns recoiled overboard, and the Indians fired upon the boat, killing one of the soldiers and they were forced to beat a retreat.

One of the most pathetic incidents of the massacre, which the people of Key West saw the effects of for many years, happened to the family of Mr. Williams, of Key West, who were living at Indian Key. They escaped being massacred, only to find that their young son, James, had been driven insane, and for many years he wandered the streets of Key West uttering harsh cries, and at times screaming "The Indians are coming." "Crazy Jim," as he got to be known, was a pathetic sight in Key West until death gave him relief.

Beiglet afterwards moved to Key West and married the widowed mother of Hon. Peter T. Knight. Mr. Charles Howe also came to Key West, and was afterwards collector of the port for many years. His sons, Charles and Edward, became large land owners and prominent business men of Key West. His daughter, Miss Amelia, married Mr. Horatio Crain, and is living here with her son, St. Clair, who conducts the Key West News Company.

Many years after the massacre Dr. Perrine's remains were taken from lower Matecumbie and interred in the family lot in Palmyra, N. Y. His monument is of granite, representing a cocoanut palm, on which is a tablet with a short narrative of the Indian Key massacre.

CHAPTER XV

THE influence of the cultured Southern men who located in Key West in the early days fostered the spirit of resisting Federal usurpation, and as early as 1832 an editorial appeared in a newspaper then published in Key West, voicing a sentiment which rings true to the Declaration of Independence. Said the writer:

"We have always thought that the value of our Union consisted in affording equal rights and equal protection to every citizen; when, therefore, its objects are so perverted as to become a means of impoverishment to one section, whilst it aggrandizes another, when it becomes necessary to sacrifice one portion of the States for the good of the rest, the Union has lost its value to us; and we are bound, by a recurrence to first principles, to maintain our rights and defend our lives and property. If we are oppressed, it is a matter of perfect indifference whether that oppression be inflicted by a foreign power or our next door neighbor. Upon the same principle we are compelled to resist both—'even unto death.' "

The election of Abraham Lincoln, the first president to be elected upon the sectional issue of antagonism to the South and its institutions, stirred up the people of Key West, in common with the rest of the Southland.

The cultivated and wealthy citizens were nearly all strongly pro-Southern. Among these were Senator Stephen R. Mallory, the elder, Judge Winer Bethel, Mr. Joseph B. Browne, Mr. William Curry, Mr. William Pinckney, Mr. Fernando J. Moreno, Mr. George Bowne, Mr. Asa F. and Mr. Charles Tift, Mr. W. C. Maloney, Jr.; Mr. Peter Crusoe, Mr. William C. Dennis, Mr. John P. Baldwin, Mr. Henry Mulrennan, Mr. Samuel J. Douglass and Mr. William H. Ward, the latter the editor of a newspaper called the *Key of the Gulf*.

Judge Marvin's sympathies were strongly Southern, but he wanted Florida to wait until after the border States had acted, and go out of the Union with them. At the breaking out of the war, he decided to resign, not caring to serve on the bench of a divided country, and so announced his intention, but was prevailed upon by the Federal authorities to withhold his resignation, and he finally accepted the new order of things.

The secession of South Carolina was soon followed by a proclamation from the Governor of Florida for a convention of the people to take into consideration the present and future relations of Florida towards the Federal Union, which brought our people to the question of secession or submission.

A meeting was held on December 12, 1860, at the county court house, for the purpose of nominating delegates to the State convention to assemble in Tallahassee on the third day of January, 1861, for the object of taking into consideration the dangers to this State in remaining in the Federal Union. It was the largest meeting ever held in Key West up to that time. Hon. John P. Baldwin was called to the chair, and Charles Tift and Peter Crusoe, Esqrs., were appointed secretaries. The meeting was in session until after midnight.

Colonel W. C. Maloney, Sr., was the only speaker who favored remaining in the Union. Mr. William H. Ward, Mr. Samuel J. Douglass, Mr. W. C. Dennis, Mr. William Pinckney, Mr. Asa F. Tift, Mr. J. L. Tatum, Mr. Winer Bethel and Mr. Joseph B. Browne spoke in favor of secession. Judge Marvin was not in favor of immediate secession, but desired to wait for the border States and secede with them. The meeting adjourned to the evening of the 13th, and after a few short speeches, Honorables William Marvin, Winer Bethel and William Pinckney were placed in nomination and a vote taken by the holding up of hands, with the following results: Marvin, 33 yeas; 26 nays: Bethel, 66 yeas; 1 nay: Pinckney, 62 yeas; 1 nay. The strong sentiment for secession was manifested by this vote— Judge Winer Bethel and Mr. Pinckney, pronounced secessionists, were elected by an almost unanimous vote, and Judge Marvin, who did not favor immediate secession, received a bare majority.

After the election it was suggested that Judge Marvin's official position as judge of the United States court was incompatible with the duties of a delegate to the convention, and Mr. Asa F. Tift, another avowed secessionist, was elected in his place.

On December 11, the day before this meeting was held, Captain James M. Brannan of the First Artillery, who was stationed at the barracks at Key West, applied to the adjutant general at Washington for instructions whether he should "endeavor at all hazards to prevent Fort Taylor from being taken or allow the State authorities to have possession without any resistance on the part of his command." When Florida seceded, Captain E. B. Hunt of the engineer corps of the army, who was on duty at Fort Taylor, called on Captain Brannan to secure the military custody of Fort Taylor, and asked him to at once assume command of that fort. Captain Brannan on the night of the 13th of January, while the city slept, marched his entire command from the barracks to Fort Taylor, and took possession of it. It was expected that an attack would be made by the citizens of Key West on the fort, and Captain Brannan reported that he had "four months provisions and seventy thousand gallons of water, but that he could not stand a siege unless he was re-inforced immediately."

On January 26th Captain Brannan reported that there had been no demonstration made on the fort to that date, and that he then had no apprehension of an attack from the people of Key West, but he had no doubt that a force would soon appear from the mainland, and urged that reinforcements be sent him, and one or two vessels of war stationed in the harbor.

Captain Hunt, of the engineer corps, threw up sand embank-ments on the shoreward side of the sand spit on which Fort Taylor is situated, and mounted ten 8-inch guns to prevent the establishment of breaching batteries on Key West opposite the fort.

The ordnance stores at Fort Taylor at this time consisted of fifty 8-inch Columbiads; ten 24-pounder flanking howitzers with caissons, and four 12-pounder field howitzers; 4,530 projectiles, 34,459 pounds of powder, 2,826 cartridge bags, 962 priming tubes, and 759 cartridges for small arms.

At the barracks there were four 6-pounder field guns and cartridges, 1,101 rounds of shot and other ammunition for same, 171 pounds of powder, 158 cartridge bags, 538 priming tubes, 7 rifles and 2,000 rifle cartridges.

Key West, the most strategic point within the Southern Confederacy, being in the hands of the Federal government during the entire war and used as a naval base, was one of the determin-ing factors in the result of the war between the States. The senti-ment of Key West was strongly Southern, but with the fortifica-tions in possession of the Federal troops, and no military organiza-tion here sufficient to wrest this control from them, the seces-sionists were deterred from taking any active steps to capture them. Whatever hope the faithful ones may have had that they might ultimately wrest it from Federal control, was destroy-ed on April 6, 1861, when Major French of the Fifth United States Artillery arrived here with his command. He had been stationed in Texas, and in order to avoid surrender, marched his troops down to the Rio Grande to Point Isabel and there embarked for Key West.

Some, who had been wavering in their sentiment towards secession, and who had pretended to be in sympathy with the South, saw on Major French's arrival the destruction of all hope of Key West being a part of the Confederacy, and they became very loud and offensive in their so-called loyalty to the Union. They spied upon the homes of Southern sympathizers and reported to the military authorities every action that their eyes could ferret out, and sought to have them locked up in the fort.

The bulk of the Southerners were firm in their allegiance to the Confederacy, and defiant of the Federal government. Flags of the Southern Confederacy were raised on some of the stores and warehouses, and so strong was the Confederate sentiment, that Captain Brannan reported on March 13th that he "doubted if any resident of Key West would be allowed to hold office under the Federal government unless supported by the military and naval forces."*

The war brought into prominence a number of people who prior to that event were of meager importance, who sought to prejudice the Union officers against those who favored secession, and representations were made which resulted in the suspension by Major French of the writ of habeas corpus. Peremptory orders were also issued by him prohibiting anyone from exhibiting Confederate flags on public buildings.

In May, 1861, Major French refused to permit any judicial or magisterial functions to be exercised, except by persons who would swear allegiance to the United States. Having ascertained, however, that Captain Von Pfister had been elected a magistrate in 1860, but had declined to serve when Florida passed the ordinance of secession, Captain French sent for him and induced him to act.

The time for opening the regular session of the District Court for Florida was on the second Monday in May, and on the 19th of May Judge McQueen McIntosh of that court arrived, intending to hold court under his Confederate States commission. Judge McIntosh was advised that such an attempt on his part might result in a clash with the Federal authorities, and he was persuaded to return without holding court. Major French applied to Captain Craven of the navy to allow the officers of the court to leave the island without applying for a permit to do so. This was necessary, as there was an order in force prohibiting non-residents from going or coming without the authority of the commanding officer, unless they would take the oath of allegiance.

The Union men in Key West could not brook a free discussion of the issues involved in the war. The local newspaper, the *Key of the Gulf*, however, kept up the discussion, and Major French sought to have it suppressed. In his report he says, "I have spoken to several respectable citizens to have the paper suppressed, and had assurances that it would not appear again." The issue of the *Key of the Gulf* on May 4, 1861, contained strong secession arguments and Major French suspending the writ of habeas corpus "in order to arrest without molestation the parties suspected of uttering treasonable sentiments." Mr. Ward, the editor, realizing that he was about to become a victim to persecution, left the island and entered the Confederate service.

Major French further reports: "The Salvor today takes away Mr. Crusoe, the late magistrate of the county, and county clerk; Judge Douglass and family; Mr. Asa Tift and his negroes. Others are preparing to leave, and winding up their affairs."

---

*Appendix N.

93

Matters went from bad to worse, and every act of cruelty towards Southern sympathizers was hailed with ghoulish glee.

On June 17, 1862, the city was shocked to learn that Mr. William Pinckney, the junior member of the firm of Wall & Co., and Judge Winer Bethel had been arrested and held in close confinement in the fort. After several months imprisonment without a trial, they were sent as prisoners to Fortress Monroe, and there kept for nearly a year.

The *New York Herald* of June 29, 1862, contained a most venomous letter from Key West recounting the arrest of these gentlemen, and praying that "there will be no delay in their case, and that they will receive their punishment quickly, and that it will be of a character to strike terror among those who desire to do as these have done." It fairly portrays the feeling of the Northern sympathizers in Key West towards those who were true to their homes and their native Southland.*

Following this came the arrest of Mr. W. D. Cash. An irresponsible negro by the name of Noah Lewis, a drayman of Wall & Company's store, where Mr. Cash was employed, was induced to report that Mr. Cash had made treasonable utterances against the United States government; among them, that he wished every Union officer and soldier would die of yellow fever. Mr. Cash was arrested, and confined in Fort Taylor for about two weeks without a hearing, when he was sent for by Colonel Morgan who offered to release him if he would sign a parole d'honeur. The document contained two clauses to which Mr. Cash objected, and he declined to sign, unless they were eliminated. After some conversation, during which Col. Morgan threatened to send Mr. Cash back to Fort Taylor, the objectionable clauses were stricken out, and the parole signed. Upon his release he was entertained at the quarters of Captain Macfarlane and other officers—an evidence that they gave no credence to the malicious charges which had been made against him.

Facts were distorted or manufactured to curry favor with the Federal army officers. One instance of this was when a young scion of a distinguished family was given a small toy pistol, from which a cork was driven out by compressed air, with a loud "pop." It happened to be about the time that news of a Confederate victory reached Key West, and Union sympathizers carried the report to the Federal commanding officer that Mr. ——————, a rebel, was celebrating the Confederate victory by a champagne party, and that the popping of champagne corks could be plainly heard.

On the 16th of May, 1861, a move was set on foot under the instigation of Thomas J. Boynton, then United States district attorney, and others for the purposes disclosed in the following document:

"We, the undersigned citizens of Key West, believing that the distracted condition of the country demands that our services

*Appendix O.

94

should be offered to her in this hour of need, that we may assist in preserving the honor of our flag, upholding the laws, and quelling rebellion, do hereby agree to form a volunteer company, and hold ourselves subject to the commander of the United States forces at Key West."*

The individuals thus organized on the day named, having assembled in a large room in the building adjacent to the St. James hotel, which stood on the site of the Jefferson, proceeded to Fort Taylor, and Colonel W. C. Maloney, Sr., was made the spokesman for the company. The contents of the paper having been read in the presence of Major French, they were presented with a flag, and mutual assurances of fidelity interchanged. After being hospitably entertained, the members of the company returned to the city and to their several avocations. According to promise they were furnished arms by Major French, and Daniel Davis was elected captain. They drilled regularly and were familiarizing themselves with the manual of arms, when Captain Joseph S. Morgan of the 90th Regiment, N. Y. Volunteers, military commander of the island, disarmed them in 1863, and they disbanded.

About this time an incident occurred which caused Colonel Morgan to be most unjustly execrated by Southerners and Northerners alike.

On January 29, 1863, this order was issued from the headquarters of the Department of the South at Hilton Head:

"HEADQUARTERS DEPARTMENT OF THE SOUTH,
"Hilton Head, Port Royal, S. C.,
"January 29, 1863.
"Col. T. H. Good, 4th Pennsylvania Vols.,
"Commanding Post, Key West, Fla.
"COLONEL: You will immediately send to this post the families (white) of all persons who have husbands, brothers or sons in Rebel employment, and all other persons who have at any time declined to take the oath of allegiance, or who have uttered a single disloyal word, in order that they may be all placed within the Rebel lines. The officer who will hand you this, will take such persons on board the steamer which carries him down to your post.

"By command of Maj. Gen. D. Hunter. Very respectfully,
"Your obedient servant,
"(Record not signed.)
"ASSISTANT ADJUTANT GENERAL."

Before the order was received at Key West Colonel Good had been relieved by Colonel Jos. S. Morgan, and the order being received by the latter, he had no alternative but to obey the instructions contained therein.

This order was of similar character to the reconcentrado

*Appendix P.

policy of General Weyler in Cuba, during the last Cuban insurrection. The Southern army was half starved; farms had been abandoned; many within the Confederate lines were without food, and the enforcement of this order would have resulted in suffering equal to that sustained by the reconcentrados. It was, however, in line with the policy of the United States government towards the South during the entire war.

About six hundred citizens, including some who were recognized as staunch Union men, had been directed to hold themselves in readiness to embark for Hilton Head, thence to be transferred to some Confederate post. "The town," wrote a loyal citizen, "has been in the utmost state of excitement. Men sacrificing their property, selling off their all, getting ready to be shipped off; women and children crying at the thought of being sent off among the Rebels. It was impossible for any good citizen to remain quiet and unconcerned at such a time."

It stirred up the Union citizens to an amazing extent, but instead of placing the blame where it belonged—on the government that issued the order—they made Colonel Morgan the scapegoat for their indignation, and assiduously stirred up a sentiment which caused him to come down in the history of the place as a monster of cruelty.

The order affected Union men as well as Southerners— many of the more prominent of the former having near relatives in the Confederate army. Among these were Colonel W. C. Maloney, Sr., whose son, Walter C. Maloney, Jr., was gallantly fighting for his native Southland, and Mr. Daniel Davis, whose son George had also gone into the Confederacy.

The Union men at Key West, led by United States District Attorney Boynton, sent to Washington a protest against the order. Colonel Good was ordered back to Key West with authority to suspend the operation of the order, if he saw fit, and he arrived in Key West and relieved Colonel Morgan February 22, 1863. His first act before landing from the transport was to suspend the enforcement of the order.

On the day Colonel Good arrived, a transport was about to sail with some of those who were to be forever banished from their homes, and their baggage was on board. Among these were the families of Mr. Fernando J. Moreno, and the venerable Methodist minister, Rev. W. J. McCook, who had gone on board with the few effects they were permitted to carry with them. About four o'clock in the afternoon the first information received by persons living further uptown that the order had been revoked, was seeing Rev. Mr. McCook with his family and their effects, on a dray, waving to all whom he saw, informing them that the order had been countermanded and they were not to leave. It brought great joy to many households, as there was not one of any prominence that had not gone through the sad experience of preparations to abandon their homes. Private residences with handsome old furniture, valuable portraits and silver, were locked up with the hope that they might be secure from vandal hands, but the experience of the rest of the South where the Federal troops were in undisputed possession, shows how vain their hopes would have proved.

The citizens of Key West presented Colonel Good with a gold-hilted sword in appreciation of his action in suspending this order. The presentation was made at Clinton Square by Colonel W. C. Maloney, Sr., as spokesman for the donors. A large concourse of people gathered to witness the presentation, and several companies of troops and squads of marines were drawn up around the square, to add to the impressiveness of the occasion. After the sword had been presented and accepted, the citizens joined hands and sang a paraphrase of the popular song, with the refrain "Bully for that," which ended

> "Colonel Good has got the sword,
> Bully for that! Bully for that!

ROLL OF HONOR

There were a number of our young men who desired to join the Confederate army, but were prevented from doing so by the difficulty of getting away—permits to leave the island being issued only by the army officer in command, to those who would take the oath of allegiance. Too much praise cannot be given to that band of noble men who left Key West under these circumstances to fight for their native Southland. Their names are given to perpetuate the memory of their patriotism.

ALFRED LOWE	MARCUS OLIVERI,
WILLIAM SAWYER,	CHARLES BERRY,
HENRY MULRENNAN,	WALTER C. MALONEY, JR.
G. PACETTI,	JOHN D. SANDS (Bogy)
SAMUEL MORGAN,	MANUEL DIAZ,
JOHN PENT,	JOSEPH FAGAN,
GEORGE ALBERT DAVIS,	ROBERT WATSON,

JOHN T. LOWE.

Mr. Walter Maloney and Mr. Pacetti took a small boat, slipped past the guard boat in the harbor, went to Tampa and there enlisted in the Confederate army.

Mr. Alfred Lowe applied to Major French for a pass, but was refused unless he would take the oath of allegiance, but as that would have thwarted his intention, he with Marcus Oliveri, William Sawyer and Robert Watson stowed away on an English schooner bound for Nassau. After reaching that port they got a vessel to land them at Cape Florida, and walked from there to Jupiter Light, and there got a small boat and went to New Smyrna. Thence they walked to Enterprise where they took the steamer Darlington to Jacksonville, and continued their journey until they reached Tampa, where they joined Company K of the Seventh Florida Regiment under Colonel Madison Perry.

Mr. Joseph Fagan and Mr. John T. Lowe were working in Manatee county and joined their comrades in Tampa. The others were engaged in smack fishing for the Havana market. Their vessels were captured by the Confederates near Tampa, which afforded them an opportunity to give their services to their country.

Mr. William Sawyer, son of Mr. Philip Sawyer, died in camp at Knoxville, Tenn. Mr. Joseph Fagan was captured at Missionary Ridge and kept prisoner until the close of the war. Mr. John Pent was shot in the hand, and draws a pension from the State of Florida as a Confederate veteran.

Mr. Charles Berry, father-in-law of Mr. Joshua Curry, was killed by the explosion of the boiler of the Confederate gunboat Chattahoochee.

Mr. John T. Lowe was a brother of Mrs. Charles Curry and Mrs. John Lowe, Jr.

Mr. Samuel Morgan was an invalid for many years in the Marine Hospital, where he died a few years ago.

All honor to these heroes and may their memories ever be revered in this community!

Of this gallant band the only living are Mr. Alfred Lowe and Mr. John Pent. Long may they live!

CHAPTER XVI

COMMERCIAL

THAT there could be a city of 22,000 population on an island in the gulf, without a railroad or a wagon road connecting it with the county of which it politically forms a part, is the best evidence of the commercial importance of Key West.

No other city in the United States occupies or has òccupied such a unique position. Its harbor, landlocked by keys and reefs, in which the largest ships can float, has four entrances: The southwest passage has thirty-three feet of water on the bar; the main ship channel, thirty feet; the southeast, thirty-two feet, and the northwest, fourteen feet. A vessel leaving the harbor of Key West by the southwest passage has but seven miles to sail before she can shape her course to her port of destination, and through the main ship channel, but five miles.

Ships putting into Key West for stores or repairs add only about ten miles to their voyage—an advantage possessed by no other port in the United States having equal depth of water. At a very little expense the northwest passage can be deepened to twenty-four feet; this would enable the entire commerce of the gulf to pass through the harbor of Key West, and besides saving seventy miles on a voyage between the ocean and the gulf, would avoid the dangerous reefs around the Tortugas Islands, which they must otherwise pass.

By special legislation the president was authorized to establish a custom house at Key West in 1822. A collector of customs—Mr. Joel Yancy, from Glasgow, Ky.—and other officers were appointed, and the following year a revenue cutter was attached to the port. Mr. Yancy did not long remain on the island, but left the office in charge of his deputy, a Mr. Dawley, and Mr. Samuel Ayres, inspector. Mr. Dawley died in June, 1823, and Mr. Ayres having resigned the position of inspector, Key West occupied the unique position of having a custom house with no one to fill the offices. From June, 1823, to January 1, 1824, the custom house was in charge of Mr. Thornton, the purser of the port, a position corresponding to that of naval station paymaster at the present time. On the latter date Mr. Ayres, at the request of the naval officer in command at Key West, again assumed the duties as acting collector, but served only to the 15th day of January of the same year.

No name is found in the records as having filled the office of collector from January 15th to October 5, 1824. It is supposed some revenue cutter officer was detailed to fill it temporarily during this period. Mr. John Whitehead was appointed collector on February 9, 1824, but declined to serve. In July, 1824, Mr. William Pinckney was appointed and took charge on October 5th of the same year, and remained in office until May 27, 1829.*

On September 13, 1833, the government purchased an irregular shaped lot bounded on the north by Whitehead street, on the east by Front street, on the south by Greene street, and on the west by the waters of the harbor. There was a frame building on the end of the lot nearest Greene street, which was used as a custom house until 1876, when a substantial frame addition was made to it. In the early part of 1889 the old part of the building was torn down, and the part built in 1876 was sold and removed, preparatory to constructing the building now used for the United States custom house, post-office and light-house department.

It is an interesting circumstance that the part of the custom house which was built in 1876 was purchased by Colonel Frank N. Wicker, who had, for eleven years, occupied it as collector of customs. He moved it to a lot on Duval street between Front and Greene streets, three doors from the Jefferson hotel, and occupied it as a real estate office. It is now owned by the Key West Investment Company and the lower floor is used for an office by them. After this building was sold, and until the completion of the new building, the custom house business was carried on in a building on Whitehead street, between Caroline and Eaton street, which was erected by Mr. Benjamin Sawyer, and long owned and occupied by Mr. E. L. Ware. It was afterwards torn down, and on the site Mr. W. L. Delaney erected his present residence.

The following sketch of the present government building is from the pen of Mr. Ramon Alvarez, who has been an employee in the customs service since 1873, except for intervals when the country had Democratic administrations; and for fourteen years has held the responsible position of special deputy collector of customs:

"A contract for the erection of the present building was awarded December 15, 1888, and the structure was completed and occupied in the latter part of 1891, the cost of construction, together with building a sea wall, being $107,955.96. It rests on a pile foundation, is constructed of red brick with stone and terra cotta trimmings, and contains an area of 354,634 cubic feet. The building is on a slight elevation facing a small triangular park known as Monument Square (Clinton Place), formed by the intersection of Whitehead, Greene and Front streets. At the rear the ground slopes to the beach. A broad piazza extends around the building at the first floor line, from the rear of which may be seen the shipping as it passes Sand Key Light-House to and from the Gulf of Mexico.

"The first floor is occupied by the postal and customs

*Appendix R.

100

services. On the second story, reached by a broad flight of stairs, are located the court room and court offices, and on the third floor the light-house inspector and other government officials have their offices."

Prior to 1860 Key West was much the most important city in Florida as shown by a table prepared by Mr. William A. Whitehead, collector of customs at Key West, for four years between 1831 and 1835.*

The revenues of the custom house of Key West showed an average of about $45,000.00 annually from 1828 to 1832. In 1874 the amount of dutiable goods imported into this district was $641,335.00, and free of duty $19,077.00, making a total importation of $660,432.00. In 1874 the total amount of duties paid into the customs house was $222,371.35; tonnage dues $2,520.83; hospital dues $2,728.51. In 1875, total $297,238.96. In 1876, total $245,514.73. For decade ending with the fiscal year of 1911 the collections have averaged over $500,000.00 per year.

BOARD OF TRADE

The first commercial body organized in Key West was the Key West Board of Trade on November 30, 1885. The meeting was called to order by Mr. Horatio Crain, and Judge James W. Locke elected temporary chairman, and Mr. R. Alfred Monsalvatge temporary secretary. A committee on organization was appointed who made their report on December 4th, and Mr. John Jay Philbrick was elected president; Mr. E. H. Gato, first vice president; Mr. John J. Delaney, second vice president; Mr. George W. Allen, third vice president, and Mr. Horatio Crain, secretary. Shortly after his election Mr. Philbrick resigned the presidency, and Mr. John J. Delaney was elected in his place, and held the position until the organization died a natural death some years later.

THE MERCHANTS' PROTECTIVE ASSOCIATION

In 1889 the Merchants' Protective Association was organized, largely for the purpose of protecting the old Key West merchants from the competition of the Jew peddlers who had just begun coming to Key West. Mr. William Curry, the first president, resigned after a short time, and Mr. James A. Waddell was elected in his stead. About the only thing that the association accomplished was to have the city charter amended to authorize the imposing of a license tax of one thousand dollars on each peddler. This had the effect of making the Jews quit peddling and open stores. Several of them are now among the most prosperous and progressive citizens of Key West. Of the dry goods merchants who were in business at the time the Merchants' Protective Association was organized, not one has a store today, and of the clothing merchants only one, Mr. George S. Waite.

---

*Appendix S.

101

CHAMBER OF COMMERCE

In 1902 the Key West Chamber of Commerce was organized. Its first president was Mr. W. D. Cash, he holding that position until the consolidation of the Chamber of Commerce with the Commercial Club in 1910.

COMMERCIAL CLUB

The Commercial Club was organized August 1, 1907, and had for its purpose the development of the commerce and industries of Key West. Club rooms were fitted up and the organization was conducted both as a business and social institution. Its first president was Mr. William R. Porter, who was succeeded by Dr. John B. Maloney. In 1910 it was consolidated with the Chamber of Commerce. Under the plan of consolidation the name of the latter was retained, and the officers of the Commercial Club became the officers of the new organization. In November, 1911, in recognition of the valuable services rendered by Mr. W. D. Cash to the commercial organizations of Key West, and his long service as president of the Chamber of Commerce, he was made an honorary life member without dues, a distinction not before conferred on any member.

CHAPTER XVII

A MONG the first of the enterprises which placed Key West on a commercial footing with other cities, was the establishment of a telegraph line by the International ˙Ocean Telegraph Company in 1866.

General W. F. Smith (known as "Baldy Smith"), a retired volunteer officer of the United States army, who was president of the company, had previously obtained from the Spanish government the exclusive privilege for forty years of landing a cable on the coast of Cuba.

He had under consideration two plans for reaching Key West—one contemplated a land line to Punta Rassa, and thence by cable to the island, the other, a continuous land line down the East Coast and over the keys. It was proposed to use iron piles in the water between the keys, and socket them about ten feet above high water mark with wooden poles. It was finally decided, however, to abandon this plan, and adopt the route from Punta Rassa.

The cable came into Key West in front of the United States army barracks on the north side of the island, and was carried underground to a point near the bridge at Fort Taylor, whence it went to Cuba.

GAS COMPANY

In March, 1884, a gas company was incorporated, and a plant erected back of Emma street near what is known as the Fort Pond. The gas furnished was smoky and of inferior lighting power, and the company did not prosper. After a time Mr. John Jay Philbrick acquired a controlling interest in the stock, and on the establishment of his electric lighting plant in 1890, the manufacture of gas was discontinued. In 1911 the circuit court, upon the application of the city, declared the gas franchise forfeited for non-user.

STREET RAILWAY

In 1885 a franchise was granted by the legislature of Florida to Messrs. Walter C. Maloney, Jr., Eduardo H. Gato, Louis W. Pierce, George G. Watson, John White and Charles B. Pendleton, to operate a street car line on any of the roads or streets in that part of the island of Key West lying outside the corporate limits. A charter had previously been obtained from the city council to operate a line within the city of Key West.

The company was financed by Mr. E. H. Gato, who built and operated the road largely as his own private enterprise. The cars were drawn by mules.

In 1894 the company was incorporated under the general laws of Florida, but with the exception of Mr. Gato, the incorporators were nominal stockholders.

One branch extended up Whitehead to Division street, thence along Division to White street, where the car barn was located near the foot of Rawson street; another extended along Front street and proceeded thence on Simonton, Eaton, Margaret, Southard and White streets, to the car barn.

When the road was finished Mrs. Alicia Carey opened an ice cream parlor near the terminus, which became a popular resort for merry-making parties of young people.

In 1896 the street car line was bought by Mr. John Jay Philbrick, who had just perfected arrangements to convert it into an electric line, when his sudden death in 1897 put a stop to the work for a time. His heirs sold it to a corporation composed of New York and Chicago capitalists, who carried out Mr. Philbrick's plans, and in 1900 the electric line was opened for traffic.

In 1906 the Stone & Webster Corporation bought the line, and it is now being operated by this company. Its policy is liberal and its equipment and service of the highest quality.

LA BRISA

When Mr. Philbrick bought the street car line, he erected on the ocean front, at the end of Simonton street, a handsome and commodious pleasure pavilion. It was one hundred and twenty-five feet long, one hundred feet wide, with piazzas twenty-five feet wide on all sides. One room, twenty-five by fifty feet, was used for refreshments, and the other fifty feet square for dancing and concerts. Later, an addition was built on the northeast end, and a commodious stage and dressing rooms added.

For many years it was a favorite pleasure resort for the people of the island, and the principal social functions were held there. Dances were given frequently during the week, and sacred concerts held on Sunday afternoons. These, with occasional private entertainments, made it a center of the general social life of the island. Unlike such resorts in most cities, it was patronized largely by the better classes.

In the hurricane of 1910 it was washed from its pillars and completely destroyed.

In 1909 Mr. A. Louis erected a large two story building on the county road, about a mile out of town, which is now used for social functions.

ELECTRIC LIGHTING

In 1889 Mr. John Jay Philbrick established an electric lighting plant, and discontinued the manufacture of gas. A power house was erected on the site of the old gas plant.

In 1897 William Curry's Sons Company put in a small electric lighting plant for their own use, and furnished a few persons along their line with lights. Gradually the plant was enlarged and it became a formidable rival of the Philbrick plant. After the death of Mr. Philbrick, his nephews, Mr. John P. and Mr. A. F. Laflin, having acquired his interest in the company, incorporated The Key West Electric Company, purchased the Curry plant, and effected a consolidation. This plant was acquired by the Stone & Webster Corporation, when they bought the street car company, in 1906.

ICE PLANTS

Prior to 1890 Key West used natural ice, brought here in sailing vessels from Maine.

The first ice house was owned by Mr. F. A. Browne and in later years the business was conducted by Messrs. Charles and Asa F. Tift and Mr. John Jay Philbrick.

In 1890 John R. Scott and C. J. Huselkamp interested the Sulzer-Vogt Company of Louisville, Ky., in a project to manufacture ice in Key West, and a plant was established on what is now the county road near George street. Shortly afterwards Mr. John Jay Philbrick bought the business, and moved the equipment to the electric lighting plant on Emma street, where he continued the manufacture of ice.

In 1895 William Curry's Sons Company established an ice plant with a daily capacity of fifteen tons, which was enlarged to thirty tons in 1901, and in 1904 was further enlarged to a total capacity of sixty tons.

In 1905 the Consumers' Ice & Cold Storage Company was organized, and began making ice in 1906. The par value of its shares was ten dollars, and its stockholders numbered severa hundred. Its first manager was Mr. E. E. Larkin, and it entered at once upon a successful career. In 1910, on the death of Mr. Louis Mouton, the then manager, who had acquired a large block of the stock, a controlling interest was bought by Wm. Curry's Sons Company, who sold their plant to the Consumers' Ice Company and closed down the Curry plant. The Consumers' Ice plant has a capacity of seventy-five tons per day.

MARINE RAILWAY

Prior to 1835 all large vessels needing repairs or cleaning were hove-down alongside of a wharf. This was done by ropes attached to the top of the masts, and run through heavy blocks on the dock. A strain was then hove on the tackles, and the vessel careened, until one side of the bottom would be out of water. After one side was cleaned or repaired, the vessel was turned around and again hove down, and the other side cleaned. This method was regarded as very hazardous, and was a source of no little uneasiness to the master, inasmuch as tardiness or mischance in righting, or a sudden squall of wind, might endanger the lives of those engaged in the work, or cause injury to the vessel.

Smaller craft were banked on a sand bar at high tide, and when the tide receded the work of cleaning or repairing was done.

The construction of a marine railway in March, 1853, by Messrs. Bowne & Curry, merchants of this city, did away with these practices, except for very large vessels, although it was occasionally practiced as late as 1880.

This railway was the first important public venture by private citizens in Key West. For a number of years it was operated by horse power, but with the spirit of progress which distinguished Mr. Curry and his successors in business, it has been enlarged and kept pace with the march of progress. At first the railway could only take up craft of less than one hundred tons; in 1859 it was enlarged to five hundred tons, and in 1899, another and larger ways was constructed, with a capacity of one thousand tons displacement. Steam power was then installed on both railways.

EXPRESS COMPANIES

In 1876 Mr. J. T. Ball inaugurated what he called "Ball's Express" between New York and Key West. His method was to have packages sent to his agent in New York, who would put as many packages as possible in one case and ship it by freight on Mallory steamship to Mr. Ball. The minimum rate of the steamship company on any package, however small, was two dollars and fifteen cents. Twenty or more small packages could be put in one case, the freight on which would be the same as for a small package. Mr. Ball could thus deliver goods for less than one-half the freight charges per package, and make money from the business.

Later he tried to conduct in the same manner an express business from Cedar Keys, in connection with the Southern Express Company, but it did not work satisfactorily, and in 1890 the Southern Express Company established an office here with Mr. Mason S. Moreno, their first agent.

BANKS

In 1880 Mr. Charles T. Merrill, a son-in-law of W. A. Russell, proprietor of the old Russell House, engaged in the banking business in a small way. He received deposits and advanced cash to cigar manufacturers. He was building up quite a good business, when the failure of Seidenberg & Company, large cigar manufacturers, whose paper Mr. Merrill was carrying, caused him to go under, and Mr. Merrill's brief essay into the banking world came to an end.

In April, 1884, Mr. George Lewis, president of B. C. Lewis & Sons, bankers of Tallahassee, and Mr. George W. Allen, organized the Bank of Key West, with a capital of $50,000.00.

Among the stockholders were Judge James W. Locke, R. Alfred Monsalvatge and several cigar manufacturers.

The bank entered at once upon a remarkably successful career. It was located on the corner of Front and Fitzpatrick streets, in a building belonging to Mr. John W. Sawyer. In 1885 they erected a bank on the corner of Front street and Exchange alley, where Monsalvatge & Reed's store now stands. This building was destroyed by fire in 1886. The day after the fire, when the whole town was panic-stricken, a run on the bank was prevented by the prompt foresight of Mr. Lewis and Mr. Allen. Their books, cash, notes and all valuables were in a fireproof safe, and the second day after the fire, they were taken from the vault and moved to the United States naval station, where permission had been granted to conduct their operations until other quarters could be found. A large table was put out in front of the station, and heaps of silver dollars and packages of currency piled up on it, and bags of silver stacked all around in plain view of the passersby. Behind the table sat Mr. Allen, Mr. Lewis and their clerks. Announcement was made that the bank was ready to transact business. The sight of so much money restored confidence, and the bank was established on a firm basis in the estimation of the people. In a few months they moved into a building erected by Duffy & Williams on the northwest side of Front street, midway between Duval and Simonton streets, where they remained until their new building on the corner of Front street and Exchange alley was finished.

The first year the bank paid ten per cent dividends, which increased each year until 1890, when a stock dividend was declared, thus increasing the capital stock to $100,000.00. The bank was doing a business far beyond its capital, but it was enabled to do this through Mr. Lewis guaranteeing the drafts of the Bank of Key West.

Mr. Allen, Mr. Gato and Mr. Monsalvatge, directors of the bank, repeatedly urged Mr. Lewis to increase the capital stock so that the bank might do business on its own resources. This, however, he refused to do, stating that they could make larger dividends if the stock were not increased.

Mr. Lewis embarked in the banking business in Key West largely because of ill health, having suffered for some time from bronchial troubles, which necessitated him spending his winters in a warm climate. In 1889 his health was so far restored that he was able to continue his residence in Tallahassee during the winter, and he induced Mr. Allen to buy $20,000.00 worth of his stock which he sold to him for $36,000.00. He promised to remain president of the bank and to continue to guarantee its drafts. Shortly after Mr. Allen bought the stock, Mr. Lewis asked to have his remaining hundred shares transferred to his minor children, which request the directors refused. He then resigned from the presidency, but his resignation was not accepted. He was urged to retain the position until such time as the bank could call in some of its loans, and be in a position to take care of itself without his guarantee. When the news of his resignation was made public, a run on the bank started, and nearly $100,000.00 was drawn out in a few days. Matters remained in this condition until Mr. Lewis, over the repeated requests of Mr. Allen, peremptorily resigned as president, and withdrew his support from the institution.

He had committed the bank to its policy of overdrawing with its New York correspondent, in order that it might do a large business on a small capital, and when he withdrew his support, some of the bank's drafts went to protest. Mr. Lewis at once notified the State Comptroller, who on Mr. Lewis' suggestion, instructed State's Attorney Thomas Palmer to apply for a receiver, and the bank's doors were closed.

After a most extravagant administration by the receiver, in which large attorney's fees were paid and other heavy expenses incurred (the bank being in the hands of a receiver for thirteen years), it paid depositors sixty-two and half cents on the dollar. The amount paid to the depositors, and for administration of the several receiverships, amounted to considerably over one hundred per cent. of the bank's liabilities at the time the receiver was appointed.

FIRST NATIONAL BANK

In 1891 when the Bank of Key West closed its doors Mr. George W. Allen was in New York trying to prevent its failure. After the receiver was appointed, his friends in the cigar manufacturing business in New York started a movement to establish another bank in Key West to be managed by Mr. Allen, and subscribed for about $80,000.00 of the stock. With this support he returned to Key West, and in a short time organized the First National Bank of Key West, with a capital stock of $100,000.00. Its officers were George W. Allen, president; August Boesler, of the firm of Wm. Wicke & Co., vice-president; W. W. Flanagan, president of the Southern National Bank of New York, Ferdinand Hirsch, Charles Baker, Remigio Lopez y Trujillo and Oscar Rierson, directors. This institution, starting immediately after the failure of the Bank of Key West, had many obstacles to overcome, but by careful management and excellent business methods, it won the confidence and patronage of the people of Key West, and it is today one of the strongest banking institutions in the State. Its deposits are upwards of seven hundred thousand dollars. The success of the First National Bank is a tribute to Mr. Allen's banking ability, and shows conclusively that had his policies, instead of Mr. Lewis', been adopted in the management of the Bank of Key West, the failure of that institution would not have occurred.

THE UNION BANK

In 1892 the Union Bank opened its doors for business in

the brick building on Front street, which had been erected for the Bank of Key West. Mr. R. Alfred Monsalvatge was president, and Mr. Jeremiah Fogarty cashier. It was an extremely conservative institution, and did not enlarge its business to any extent. After a few years existence, it returned all its deposits and went out of business. It neither made nor lost any money.

THE ISLAND CITY NATIONAL BANK

The Island City National Bank was organized and commenced business on October 16, 1905. Its officers were Mr. George S. Waite, president; Mr. Charles R. Pierce, vice-president; Mr. E. M. Martin, cashier, and Judge Jordan M. Phipps, attorney. It has a capital stock of $100,000.00, and its deposits are over three hundred and fifty thousand dollars.

The first board of directors were Messrs. Geo. S. Waite, Charles R. Pierce, Jordan M. Phipps, John T. Sawyer, Richard Peacon, Theodore A. Sweeting and E. M. Martin.

SPONGE INDUSTRY

For many years the entire sponge industry of the United States was derived from the Mediterranean, although in the early forties a few sponges were shipped to the United States from the Bahamas, but the supply was small, the total imports in 1849 being valued at about $10,000.00. In that year a cargo of sponges was sent to New York from Key West on a venture, which narrowly escaped being thrown away as worthless. Its ultimate sale, however, established a market for this newly discovered product of the keys, and several merchants of Key West began to buy the better grades and take them in trade. The business proved profitable, and a number of sailing craft were fitted out as spongers. The industry increased until the catch was worth over $750,000.00 a year. About one hundred and forty vessels, aggregating two thousand tons, and giving employment to over twelve hundred men, were engaged in the business.

The bulk of the sponges are taken from water averaging twenty feet deep, off the western coast of Florida. The sponge caught near the Florida Keys, taken from shoal water, are of much finer quality.

The Key West spongers retain the primitive method of hooking the sponge with a three pronged hook on the end of a long pole. Each sponging vessel carries a small boat for every two men in the crew; one sculls the boat, while the other, called the "hooker," gathers the sponge.

In 1904 several Greek companies introduced the system of gathering sponge by the use of diving apparatus, and established headquarters at Tarpon Springs in Hillsboro county. This transferred the bulk of the sponge business from Key West, and the value of the catch is now worth only about two hundred thousand dollars a year.

In 1886 a building and loan association was formed with Mr. John Jay Philbrick, president; Mr. D. T. Sweeney, vice-president; Mr. Ramon Alvarez, secretary; Mr. George W. Allen, treasurer, and Mr. Jefferson B. Browne, attorney. It was very prosperous at first, but after a few years gradually ran down, was placed in the hands of a receiver, and went out of business in 1892.

CANNING FACTORY

About 1890 Mr. A. Granday, a celebrated French chef, established a factory for canning turtle soup made from the green turtle which abound in these waters. He accumulated what, to a thrifty Frenchman, is a comfortable fortune, and sold the business in 1904 to Mr. Louis Mouton, who died in 1908, and in 1910 the plant was purchased by Mr. Norberg Thompson.

Its output is about two hundred quart cans per day. It is limited to this quantity, not for lack of demand, but from the difficulty in securing turtle, as only the choice parts are used in making the soup.

A couplet of an old English verse extolling the delicious qualities of green turtle soup, says:

"Land of green turtle, thy very name
Sets the longing alderman aflame."

CIGAR BOX FACTORY

In 1877 a cigar box manufactory was established in Key West, situated on Emma street, southeast of Eaton. It was managed by Mr. A. de Lono, but not being able to cope with the disadvantages of freight rates and lack of transportation facilities, he closed down and the plant was disposed of at the end of about two years.

In 1910 Mr. Norberg Thompson began making plans for the establishment of a plant for cigar box manufacturing. He secured a lot on the water front at the corner of Caroline and William streets, and erected thereon a large one-story building of reinforced concrete, equipped it with the best of modern machinery,and began work in September, 1911. It has a capacity of seven thousand boxes a day; the work turned out equals in quality the output of the best factories of New York.

KEY WEST GAS COMPANY

In the spring of 1911 the city council granted to Messrs. Charles E. Starr and John C. Reed, gas operators of Philadelphia, Pa., a franchise to establish a gas plant in the city of Key West. Work on laying the gas mains was begun in November, 1911, and a plant large enough to serve a population of fifty thousand people will be installed. The Key West Gas Company is incorporated in Delaware and authorized to issue one million dollars' worth of bonds. The contract for the construction of the plant was awarded to Whetstone & Company of Philadelphia. Mr. John Mayer is president and general manager of the company.

THE TROPICAL BUILDING AND INVESTMENT CO.

This company was organized and incorporated in 1892 under the laws of the State of Florida. It commenced business on May 1st of the same year.

The first officers were Messrs. George S. Waite, president; C. B. Adams, vice-president; John T. Sawyer, treasurer; Jefferson B. Browne, attorney; E. M. Martin, secretary and general manager. The company has prospered and is one of the strong financial institutions of the city. Mr. George S. Waite has been president of the company, and Mr. E. M. Martin, secretary and general manager since it was first organized.

CHAPTER XVIII

SALT MANUFACTURING

THE original proprietors and the first settlers of Key West considered the manufacture of salt as the most probable means of making the place known to the commercial world. Small quantities had been gathered from the natural salt ponds in the interior, without any special facilities, and that portion of the island was regarded as destined to be the source of future wealth to any enterprising individuals who might undertake to turn its advantages to account. The resident proprietors, however, were not themselves possessed of sufficient capital beyond the requirements of their commercial undertakings to engage in the business, and the first regular attempt at salt manufacturing was not made until 1830. Mr. Richard Fitzpatrick, of South Carolina, then a resident on the island, leased that year the Whitehead interest in the southeastern end of the island, and constructed the "Salt Ponds."

About one hundred acres of this property were subject to overflow at any ordinary high tide, a large portion being always under water. This was divided into compartments or "pans" one hundred feet long and fifty feet wide, separated by walls two feet high made of coral rock. Small wooden floodgates connected all the pans, and sea water was turned into them from a large canal, in which was a floodgate for regulating the water supply; thus the water could be let into or cut off from all or any of the pans. The pans were then filled with salt water and the floodgate in the canal closed, and as the water was lowered by solar evaporation more salt water was let in. This process was repeated until the approach of the rainy season, when the water was allowed to evaporate, and the salt precipitated into crystals, from an eighth to a quarter of an inch in size.

About the time that Mr. Fitzpatrick began his operations in 1830, a bill was introduced in the territorial council to establish the North American Salt Company here, and the local newspaper estimated that this new company would require five hundred vessels to transport the salt that would be made annually. Mr. Fitzpatrick was a member of the council and opposed the bill and prevented its passage. This gave rise to an attack on him, which became very bitter before the election.

An intelligent negro man named Hart was brought from the Bahamas and placed in charge of the works. Several dry seasons promised favorable results, but they were not realized. In the summer of 1832 the prospect was thought good for

112

sixty thousand bushels, but rains set in early, and the crop was lost. Mr. Fitzpatrick abandoned his works in 1834. The reduction of the duty on salt after he commenced operations had some effect probably in producing this result. At one time he had over thirty hands employed.

The next attempt was made under the auspices of the La Fayette Salt Company, organized through the exertions of Mr. Simonton, the principal stockholders being residents of Mobile and New Orleans. Operations were commenced early in 1835, but success was not achieved, and the work passed in a few years into the hands of another company, Messrs. Adam Gordon, F. A. Browne and William H. Wall being among the stockholders. Subsequently, about 1843, Charles Howe obtained the controlling interest, and after the hurricane of 1846 became the sole proprietor. In 1850 the crop amounted to thirty-five thousand bushels, and Mr. Howe was encouraged to enlarge his works by the purchase of the Whitehead portion of the pond, which had been abandoned by Mr. Fitzpatrick. In 1851 he sold half of his interest to Mr. W. C. Dennis, to whom the management of the works was entrusted. The amount of salt produced annually varied materially, ranging from fifteen or twenty thousand bushels to seventy-five thousand, the largest crop raked in any one year. Mr. Dennis continued the manufacture until his death, which occurred in 1864.

During the Civil War the manufacture of salt on the island was suspended, in consequence of one of the principal sources of demand for salt, the Charlotte Harbor fisheries, having been cut off, the military authorities being apprehensive that the salt furnished would find its way into the Confederacy.

In 1865 Lieutenant W. R. Livermore of the United States army engineer corps, purchased the works and commenced the manufacture of salt. He spent a small fortune in the prosecution of the business, but abandoned it in 1868, after becoming convinced that it could not be profitably produced with inefficient and irresponsible free negro labor.

In 1847 forty thousand bushels were produced, and until 1855 the quantity varied from thirty-five to forty-eight thousand bushels. The banner year was 1855 with seventy-five thousand bushels, and the output until 1861 ranged from sixty to seventy thousand bushels. In 1861 it fell to thirty thousand bushels. Between 1862 and 1865, and 1868 and 1871, no attempt was made to operate the salt ponds. From 1871 to 1875 the output ran from fifteen to twenty-five thousand bushels. In 1876 the hurricane of October 19th washed away about fifteen thousand bushels which was ungathered in the pans, and did considerable injury to the works, which ended all attempts at salt making by solar evaporation in Key West.

In 1871 part of the salt works passed into the hands of Messrs. C. and E. Howe, and was subsequently purchased by Mr. W. D. Cash. In 1906 the entire interest of Mr. Livermore and Mr. Cash was purchased by the Key West Realty Company, who laid it off into town lots.

Remains of the Salt Ponds or "pans," are still to be seen, but in a dilapidated condition.

CHAPTER XIX

CUBAN MIGRATION

A HISTORY of Key West which does not treat of the several revolutionary movements in Cuba, with which Key West was so closely connected, would fail in its purpose of faithfully portraying the events which have shaped or affected its destiny.

In 1843 Narcisso Lopez, formerly a colonel in the Royal Spanish army, went to Cuba with Captain General Valdez. There he saw the oppression of the Cubans and his sympathies were aroused. He was suspected of conspiring against the Spanish government, and came under the surveillance of Captain General O'Donnell, the successor of Valdez, and fled to the United States in 1849. His story of Cuba's oppression raised many sympathizers for the cause, and he found no trouble in recruiting a force of adventurous spirits to join him in an expedition having for its purpose the liberation of Cuba.

His first attempt at invasion, early in 1849, was checked by President Taylor, and the whole expedition captured as it was on the point of departure.

In May, 1850, he organized another expedition, one detachment of which, under the command of Colonel Theodore O'Hara, who wrote "The Bivouac of the Dead," made a rendezvous on the island of Contoy, where they were joined by Lopez on the steamer Creole with four hundred and fifty followers. Matanzas was their destination, but learning that the Spaniards had been advised of their movements, they decided to land at Cardenas. On landing, Major John T. Pickett, with fifty Kentuckians, marched through the city and seized the station of the railroad that connected Cardenas with Matanzas. After a few hours fighting, in which Colonel O'Hara was wounded, the Spanish garrison surrendered and Cardenas was taken. Lopez issued a strong appeal for Cuban followers, but received no response. As he could accomplish nothing without the co-operation of the Cubans he was forced to abandon Cardenas and reimbark, which he finally succeeded in doing after some sharp fighting.

In the meantime the Spaniards had sent the gunboat Pizarro to capture the Creole, and one beautiful May morning the news spread among the citizens of the quiet little town of Key West, that was always alert at daybreak for anything unusual on the water, that the Creole was being chased by a Spanish gunboat, and was in imminent danger of being captured. The people thronged to the wharves and cupolas with which the town was then abundantly supplied (being used as lookouts from which to discover vessels stranded on the reefs).

The Creole was crowding on all steam to reach Key West, and not far behind was the Pizarro belching volumes of smoke, and rapidly closing in on her prey. As the pursued steamer approached Fort Taylor, it was seen that her speed was slackening. A few moments more the guns of the Pizarro would open on the Creole and its gallant band of liberators. Just then black smoke was seen coming from the funnel of the Creole and her wheels revolved rapidly. They had broken open boxes of bacon and were feeding her with this, and parts of the woodwork of the vessel. The Creole maintained her lead, rounded Fort Taylor, and dashed up the harbor to F. A. Browne's wharf (now the Martin Wagner wharf), where the expedition landed.

The Pizarro, without saluting the fort, came on behind her, and "slowed down a few yards away, with port holes open, and broadsides grinning, like the fangs of a bloodhound balked of his prey."

In this expedition Lopez lost fourteen killed and thirty wounded, among whom was the chaplain. The Spaniards had one hundred killed and as many wounded. Lopez was arrested by the United States authorities, and tried for violation of the neutrality law, and acquitted.

He and his party were lionized in Key West. All the best homes were thrown open to them, and they were feted as heroes. He presented to Hon. Joseph Beverly Browne the sword he had worn in the fight at Cardenas.

Their first night at Key West was marked by wild scenes of disorder. Threats were made by some of the more unruly against the Spaniards living here. The saloon of Francisco Cintas on Duval street, and the grocery store of Mr. Arnau on Whitehead street, were broken into and looted, and their stocks thrown into the streets. The old Spanish citizens wisely kept within doors, until Lopez and his captains got the mob under control, which they succeeded in doing about daybreak.

In August, 1851, Lopez landed another expedition at Bahia Honda, and with his little band of two hundred and twenty-three men repulsed a force of thirteen hundred Spaniards, and killed their commander, General Enna.

Cuba, however, was not ripe for revolt, and no recruits came to him. His forces gradually dwindled away and he was captured and carried to Havana, where fifty of his followers were shot, and he was garroted on September 1, 1851.

Colonel W. S. Crittenden, who had served in the Mexican War as an officer of the United States army, was sentenced to be shot, and when commanded to kneel in the customary attitude with his back to the firing party, replied: "A Kentuckian kneels only to his God," and met death facing his executioners.

On October 10, 1868, Carlos M. de Cespedes, a distinguished lawyer and wealthy Cuban planter, gave the cry of "Cuba Libre" on his estate, La Demajagua, near Manzanilla, in the eastern part of Cuba. He was joined by thousands of patriots, and on the 18th took possession of the city of Bayamo, his birthplace, after having subdued the Spanish garrison.

Spain not having on the island sufficient troops to oppose the increasing revolution, raised companies of volunteers from the lowest class of the Spanish population. The cruelties and atrocities of the volunteers was the cause of many Cubans, who were not actively engaged in the revolution, abandoning the island and coming to Key West.

In 1869 a Spanish resident of Havana, a wealthy manufacturer of cigars, Senor Vicente Martinez Ybor, thinking that his business was exposed in Havana to the caprice of the volunteers, who were then committing every sort of depredation, concluded to open a branch factory at Key West. As soon as he commenced making arrangements to do this he was suspected of treachery to the Spanish government, and put under surveillance of the volunteers, who made threats against him and his property.

He then decided to remove his entire business to Key West, and came here with his family. He founded his factory, El Principe de Gales, during the early part of 1869, and thus was laid the foundation of Key West's reputation as the greatest clear-Havana cigar manufacturing place in the United States.

Among the prominent Cubans who early came to Key West, were the Borroto Brothers, Jacinto, Julio and Francisco: J. M. J. Navarro; the Barrancos, Francisco, Augustin and Manuel; Enrique and Esteban Parodi; Mateo and Luis Someillan, and Don Fernando Valdez. Of these only two have any descendants in Key West, Mrs. Robert O. Curry, a daughter of Mr. Valdez, and Mr. Jose M. Navarro, a son of Mr. J. M. J. Navarro, have large and attractive families.

Later came Mr. E. H. Gato, who now has one of the largest clear-Havana cigar factories in the United States, with a reputation second to none.

The continued acts of cruelty by the volunteers, and the establishment of cigar factories at Key West, where labor could be readily obtained, brought an influx of Cubans to our city.

One of the first public acts on their part was to erect a building to be used for the discussion of political matters, for dramatic purposes, and to provide a place for the education of their children. It was dedicated on January 21, 1871, and called San Carlos Hall after Carlos M. de Cespedes.

The chief spirit in this movement was Mr. Martin Herrera, and to his energy and patriotism, the Cubans owe this monument. It is regarded by them as a sanctuary. Many of the leading Cubans of the present generation were there educated, the most distinguished of whom is Hon. Antonio Diaz y Carrasco, the Cuban consul at Key West.

"San Carlos" was destroyed by the fire of 1886—the conflagration is supposed to have originated in the building. It was promptly rebuilt and has had frequent additions. The upper part is used for school rooms, and the lower part as an opera house. It receives annually five hundred dollars from the Monroe county board of public instruction, and twenty-four hundred from the Cuban government.

CUBAN NEWSPAPERS

The first paper in Key West published in the Spanish language was *El Republicano*, edited by Senor Juan M. Reyes in 1870. Several other papers have been published from time to time, most of which were short-lived. The most noted was *El Yara*, edited by Mr. J. D. Poyo, a highly cultured and educated gentleman. For twenty years he upheld and contended for the cause of "Free Cuba." The paper went out of existence in 1898, when Mr. Poyo saw the fruition of his life's work.

A number of Cubans obtained various positions under the city, State and Federal governments, and acquitted themselves with credit. The position of justice of the peace was held by Messrs. Alejandro Gonzales de Mendoza, Diego Andre, Juan M. Reyes, Angel de Lono, and Jose de Lamar. Later Judge de Lono was county judge, which position he held until 1893.

Mr. Diego Andre belonged to a distinguished and cultured family, and was a man of education and refinement, but he knew nothing of our system of jurisprudence. Imbued as he was with the Spanish idea of officialdom, he was keen to secure his costs, and his usual sentence for minor offences was: "I pronounce you guilty and fine you two dollars for me and two dollars for Mr. Williams" (meaning Mr. Joseph P. Williams, the constable of the court).

Mr. Carlos M. de Cespedes, son of the great liberator who started the revolution at Bayamo, was elected Mayor of Key West in 1876.

Mr. Fernando Figueredo was elected a member of the legislature of Florida in 1884, and later was superintendent of public instruction for Monroe county.

Other Cubans who represented Monroe county in the legislature were Hon. Morua P. Delgado, Dr. Manuel R. Moreno, and Hon. J. G. Pompez.

The election of 1892 demonstrated that the Cubans were not only good revolutionists but keen politicians. The Democratic and Republican parties in Monroe county at that time were evenly divided, the Cubans holding the balance of power. A few of these were strong in their party allegiance, but the majority were more or less indifferent, and voted from considerations of friendship or racial pride.

118

Both parties sought to give recognition to the Cubans, and placed a representative on their legislative tickets. The American Democrats voted the straight party ticket, for one American and one Cuban. The American Republicans did the same. The Cubans, however, without regard to politics, voted for their countrymen, who were elected, and Monroe county was represented in the legislature by two Cubans, one a Democrat and one a Republican, Hon. M. P. Delgado and Hon. J. G. Pompez.

In 1870 an unfortunate event occurred in Key West that shocked the community and had direful results. Senor Gonzalo Castanon, a brilliant and intrepid editor of a Spanish newspaper in Havana, became engaged in a controversy with Senor Reyes, editor of *El Republicano* at Key West. It culminated in an editorial attack from Castanon, to which Reyes responded that "Castanon indulged in such language because he knew that Reyes could not go to Havana to hold him to personal account." Castanon at once replied that he would come to Key West, where they could settle their difficulties in mortal combat. Key West at this time was a perfect hornet's nest of revolutionists, and Castanon knew that he took his life in his hands when he came here. After he arrived in Key West, Reyes declined to fight. That afternoon a committee of Cubans waited on Castanon at the Russell House, which stood on the site where the Jefferson hotel now stands. Among them were Mateo Orosco (who, it is said, expressed a desire to meet Castanon in mortal combat), and two brothers, Francisco and Jose B. Botello. High words were indulged in. The parlor and corridors of the hotel were filled with excited people. The street in front of the hotel was thronged with an angry crowd of Cubans. Pistol shots were fired, and Castanon fell mortally wounded. He died a short time afterwards, and his body was carried back to Havana that night. Orosco was concealed in the city by his friends, and escaped later to South America, where he died. The authorities could never get any testimony about the killing, and no one was punished for the crime. The Botello brothers also escaped and were killed in the Cuban army, fighting for their country's freedom.

The peace of Zanjon, which ended the revolutionary movement in Cuba, did not cool the revolutionary spirit of the Cubans in Key West, and this place continued to be the center of the liberation movement in the world, although the junta, the Cuban revolutionary society, had its headquarters in New York. After the treaty of Zanjon some Cubans returned to their homes, but most of them remained in Key West, and adhered to their purpose of keeping the revolutionary spirit alive, and perfecting an organization looking to the ultimate liberation of Cuba from Spanish rule.

There was not a single member of the Cuban community who did not look forward to a new revolutionary movement against Spain, and an organization was maintained for that

119

purpose. Messrs. Lamadriz, Poyo and Figueredo were accepted as the leaders of this idea. They organized themselves into political groups called clubs, which were given patriotic names. Every Cuban was expected to belong to one of these clubs, and men, women and children were enrolled in this singular organization. All the clubs sprang from the central committee of Messrs. Lamadriz, Poyo and Figueredo. Even the manufacturers were organized into a political club. Some of the most noted leaders of the former revolution were ever ready to land an expedition in Cuba and start a new revolution. Bonachea made a movement to this effect, and after a visit to Key West in 1881, where he raised funds for the purpose, embarked from the island of Jamaica, but was captured near Manzanilla by a Spanish man-of-war, and shot, with all his followers, at Santiago de Cuba.

Limbano Sanchez was another unfortunate who landed in Cuba, and after a short fight he and his men were exterminated.

In 1884 Carlos Aguerro, with a band of patriots, most of whom had been in the old army, raised the standard of liberty, and fought for months in the field. The Cubans, however, who had not forgotten the hardships and sufferings of the previous revolution, were not ripe for another revolt, and he had to give up his enterprise.

Aguerro, with Perico Torres, Manuel Aguier and Rosenda Garcia, succeeded in reaching Key West, where they were received with great enthusiasm, and were the recipients of every attention. A monster meeting was held at San Carlos hall, patriotic speeches were made, and the audience requested to subscribe funds to aid Aguerro to fit out another expedition. The first to respond was Colonel Frank N. Wicker, the collector of customs at this port; he contributed one hundred dollars. The Spanish consul telegraphed this to Washington and Colonel Wicker was removed from office.

Colonel Wicker was probably actuated by a desire to serve his political party. He was the leader of the Republicans in Key West, and knew that this act of friendship to the Cuban cause would be remembered by the impulsive patriotic Cubans, and that they would help his party when he should call on them for support. His name should go down in history as the first American martyr to the cause of Cuban liberty, as well as a martyr to his party.

The Spanish government in Cuba charged Aguerro with "rapine, arson, highway robbery and murder," and requested his extradition on those grounds. He was taken in custody by the United States authorities, and the application heard by Judge James W. Locke of the United States district court. It was proven that his so-called offenses had been committed while engaged in a revolutionary movement, and the request for his extradition was therefore refused. The scene in the crowded court house when Judge Locke announced his decision was one of frantic enthusiasm. The audience went wild, cheers and hoarse

120

cries of exultation were mingled with the sobs of strong men as they threw themselves in each others' arms and wept for joy. Aguerro was carried out of the court house on the shoulders of his friends, chief among whom was Miguel Brinas, Sr., an emotional and generous hearted patriot; thousands of Cubans and many Americans formed an impromptu procession, and paraded the streets with Aguerro at their head. It was a scene long to be remembered.

Shortly after this Aguerro equipped and armed a schooner, and with a dozen of his followers, went to Cuba, but the time was not ripe for another revolution, and he and his band were soon exterminated.

Judge Angel de Lono was the hero of a gallant effort to capture a Spanish vessel for the Cuban cause. In 1889 he, with a dozen adventurous spirits, took passage at Santiago de Cuba on the Spanish steamship Commanditario, bound for Porto Plato, Santo Domingo. After they were at sea, Mr. De Lono, having previously instructed his men what to do, went to the captain's cabin with one of his men to act as quarter-master, and placing a pistol to the captain's head informed him that he was a prisoner, and that he had taken possession of the ship. All the crew were put below under arrest and guards kept over them until he got a chance to put them ashore. He took the Commanditario into several ports for coal, but was refused, and received no recognition from any government. The captors soon realized that they were in the anomalous position of sailing without flying the flag of any recognized nation, with no port in which they could get coal and provisions, and that they were in imminent danger of being captured as pirates. In this dilemma they ran the Commanditario ashore near the Bahamas and abandoned her, and her gallant band sought refuge on the friendly shores of the United States.

Key West was always a rich field in which to get money to sustain the revolutionary party in the field of Cuba. The cigar-makers contributed liberally, and the New York junta depended largely on Key West for its maintenance.

General Aguilerra, the millionaire patriot, who sacrificed his time to the cause of his country, was one of the first to call on Key West after leaving the field in 1870.

In 1870 General Melchior Aguerra came to Key West in the Steamer Edgar Stewart, and raised a large fund to organize an expedition. Great excitement prevailed; the Cuban ladies took the rings from their fingers and their jewels from their persons, and donated them to the cause of Cuban liberty.

General Bernabe Verona, Colonel J. L. Pacheco and General Julio Sanguilly were here at various times, to get the "sinews of war," which were freely donated by the Cuban population.

In 1885 General Maximo Gomez and Antonio Maceo came to Key West and sought to fit out an expedition to Cuba. They met with the unanimous support of the Cuban colony, and funds for an expedition were raised. There was at this time a revolution in progress in Santo Domingo, the leaders of which induced General Gomez to postpone his movement on Cuba, promising him aid after their revolution was over. It is worthy of note, as an evidence of man's ingratitude, that the president of the republic of Santo Domingo, after the success of his movement, became one of the most bitter opponents of Cuban liberty.

In 1892 the time and the man seemed to meet in Jose Marti, who came to Key West with perfectly digested plans for the organization of a *Partido Revolucionario Cubano*. He found here an organization ready at his command. Every man, woman and child was in his place. He had nothing to do but to map out to the Cubans his plans of organization. This was patterned after a democratic federal republic. A number of Cubans constituted a club; every club had a representative in a central committee called the Council of Presidents, and the president of each club was a representative. This bound the clubs together in one great organization, and through it they were in touch with the general delegate who was elected by the vote of the councils throughout the entire world. The Cuban revolutionary party conceived by Marti had its ramifications in every country wherever ten or more Cubans were exiled. Marti was the chief of the organization. When he had the expatriated Cubans in all countries completely organized, he commenced work in Cuba, and sent his delegates to all parts of the island to stir up the smoldering embers of revolution. The old generals and officers of the Ten Years War accepted the leadership of Marti. Three years after his appearance in the political field everything was ready for the movement. During these three years he had not rested, but imbued with the great idea of freeing a country, he went from city to city, from continent to continent, always preaching to his people the necessity of revolt. He was a man of delicate frame but was sustained by the thought of the achievement of his ideal. When he had funds sufficient and everything prepared at home, he ordered the revolution to start, and February 24, 1895, saw the beginning of the movement that was to end in the liberation of Cuba.

Marti was distinctively an organizer, and was urged by his friends to remain in this country and raise funds and send over expeditions to keep up the revolutionary movement. He refused to follow their advice, saying that as he had started this revolution, it was his duty to share the fate of those in the field, and on April 1, 1895, he left Monte Cristi, Santo Domingo, accompanied by General Gomez and four companions. After many difficulties he landed on the 11th of April at Playitas in the Province of Baracoa, on the extreme eastern end of the island, and was killed in the battle of *Dos Rios*, in the Province of Santiago, on the 19th of May, 1895, fighting for the cause which was so dear to him, the fruition of which he was never to see.

The revolutionary party now made Key West its base of operations for fitting out and embarking filibustering expeditions. There was always one or more suspicious craft in the harbor, against which it was impossible to get any definite proof. A number of expeditions were fitted out from Key West, or made Key West and the adjacent islands their place of rendezvous.

The collectors of customs at this port were especially charged to prevent any violation of the neutrality laws, and a man-of-war was kept in the harbor with instructions to co-operate with the collector in performing this duty.

In 1895 the tug Geo. W. Childs arrived here, and a rumor soon spread that she had taken an expedition to Cuba. She was kept under surveillance by the collector of customs, Hon. Jefferson B. Browne, and one quiet Sunday in August, 1895, one of her crew made an affidavit before him that the Childs had just returned from a filibustering expedition.

The revenue cutter McLane was under steam ready to start at a moment's notice, and signals were made to her to stop the Childs if she attempted to leave the port, but she was already under way when the message was delivered. The cutter started in chase but the Childs ignored her signals and continued on her way until two shots from the cutter (the last falling very close to her), caused her to stop. She was taken in charge by an officer from the cutter and brought back to Key West, but was finally discharged, her master and owners having previously signed an agreement relieving the government of all claim for her detention.

The Three Friends, Dauntless and Monarch were also in and out of Key West from time to time, and while it was known that they were engaged in filibustering, no conclusive proof could be obtained. The schooner Lark was seized with arms and ammunition on board which could have no destination except Cuba, but no definite proof being obtained she was released.

The Cuban leaders were familiar with our neutrality laws and no expedition of armed men was fitted out on shore—one vessel would take arms and ammunition aboard, and another from a different point would take the men, and the arms and the men would not unite until they were on the high seas.

On May 31, 1897, the U. S. S. Marblehead, commanded by Captain Horace Elmer, under instructions from the collector of customs, intercepted the tug Dauntless while taking on board arms and ammunition off Jupiter Inlet and brought her to Key West. When the Marblehead was sighted, box after box supposed to contain arms and ammunition was thrown overboard. On board her was found rubber spreads, canvas shelter tents, and a seal of the Republic of Cuba. After a hearing before United States Commissioner Julius Otto, the men were discharged "for want of sufficient evidence," and the Dauntless released.

Apart from the sympathies of the citizens of Key West being with the revolutionists, filibustering expeditions were fine revenue producers, so that it was impossible to procure any proof against them.

Many of the Cubans who lived here prior to the establishment of the Cuban republic, have returned to their native home, where they are holding offices of trust and honor. Among these are Hon. Fernando Figueredo, treasurer of the republic, General Alejandro Rodriguez, former mayor of the City of Havana and chief of the rural guards; Hon. Rojelio Castillo, inspector of state prisons; Hon. Francisco J. Diaz Silveria, postmaster general; Mr. Lazan Vila, an employee of the Havana postoffice; Mr. J. D. Poyo, chief of the press bureau of the Interior Department, and Mr. Martin Herrera, chief of the general archives of the republic. "Old Martin" as he is fondly known in Key West, was postmaster of the city of Pinar del Rio, and has recently been elected a member of the legislature of that province. Messrs. Enrique Messonier, Louis Valdez Carrero, Martin Morua Delgado, all former Key Westers, have been members of the Cuban congress. The latter died in 1910, while holding that office. Ambrosia Borges, another former Key Wester, was elected president of the Cuban senate. Last but not least, and one who stands in the very front of the diplomatic and consular officials of the world, in ability, courtesy and high character, is Antonio Diaz y Carrasco, the present Cuban consul of Key West.

CHAPTER XX

NEW-COMERS are prone to imagine that all enterprise in a community dates from their arrival, and that until they came, there was no development. They learn better in time, perhaps.

The cigar industry of Key West dates back to 1831, when Mr. William H. Wall established a factory for the manufacture of cigars. His advertisement, which appeared in the Key West *Gazette*, stated that "he imports the very best tobacco from Havana." This factory employed about fifty workmen. It was located on Front, between Duval and Fitzpatrick streets, and was destroyed in the fire of 1859.

Estava & Williams, in 1837 and 1838, operated a factory in which sixteen men were employed, and made shipments to New York. Communication between New York and this island was exceedingly irregular and uncertain at that date, being dependent chiefly upon vessels going north with cotton from St. Marks and other gulf ports, and the long time elapsing between voyages worked serious injury to the business.

Odet Phillippe and Shubael Brown also engaged in this business with a force of six men, about the same time.

The Arnau Brothers, Francisco and James, as far back as 1834 down to the time of the death of both, were constantly employed in cigar manufacturing, and in 1838 were joined by Albert, another brother.

Messrs. Francisco Sintas, Manuel Farino and E. O. Gwynn, the latter the grandfather of Mr. Gwynn of the Gwynn, Martin & Strauss cigar factory, now operating here, were at different times and for short periods engaged in this business.

Its development, however, into the immense industry which it now is, began in 1868 with the coming of the Cuban population upon the breaking out of the Cuban rebellion that year, as described in the chapter on Cuban Migration.

Among the first of the large factories to come to Key West was "El Principe de Gales" of Vincente Martinez Ybor, followed soon afterwards by Seidenberg & Company with "La Rosa Espaniola." Later came the E. H. Gato Company, Geo. W. Nichols, the Ferdinand Hirsch Company, the Cortez Cigar Company, the Havana-American Company, and Ruy Lopez Ca.

The two first were destroyed by the fire of 1886, but, nothing daunted, Mr. Seidenburg at once found new quarters, and began rebuilding immediately after. Mr. Ybor, induced by a committee which came to Key West from Tampa, after that great fire, moved his factory to that place. This removal, brought about by the solicitations and inducements offered by the committee from Tampa, at a time when our people were nearly all homeless, was the beginning of Tampa's competition with Key West as a cigar manufacturing center.

The next serious blow which the cigar manufacturing industry of Key West sustained, grew out of labor troubles in the Seidenberg factory in 1894. Strikes, which seem to be a part of the cigar manufacturing industry, were constantly occurring therein. The board of trade held almost daily meetings to investigate the labor troubles, but no sooner would one be adjusted than another would crop out. Mr. Seidenberg then decided that he would not work Cuban operatives, and announced his intention to employ Spaniards. He informed the board of trade that threats had been made against the lives of any Spaniards who might come to work in his factory, and asked for protection. He was assured that he would receive not only the protection of the law, but the support of the citizens of Key West, who felt that the right of the people of any nationality to come to the United States to obtain work should not be infringed.

A committee was thereupon appointed to accompany Mr. Seidenberg to Havana, to assure the Captain General that if any Spanish subjects desired to come to Key West to work, they would receive full protection of the law.

Key West at that time was the center of the revolutionary movement, which had for its purpose the ultimate freedom of Cuba, and the Cuban patriots were naturally apprehensive of the effect, the presence of an appreciable number of Spaniards might have, on the secrecy which it was necessary to maintain with respect to their revolutionary plans.

The committee that went to Havana was composed of Hon. George W. Allen, now collector of customs, Judge L. W. Bethel, of the eleventh circuit of Florida, Mr. William H. Williams, Hon. A. J. Kemp, then county judge, Mr. W. R. Kerr, capitalist, Rev. Chas. W. Fraser, a militant Christian with the brains and courage of a Savonarola, and Mr. John F. Horr. When the committee returned, a number of Spanish workmen who had been assured of protection, came with them.

The situation was tense. Reports of threatened violence grew thick and fast, and a large delegation headed by the mayor, met the steamship and escorted the workmen to temporary quarters provided for them.

The Cuban junta sent a lawyer, Horatio Rubens, Esq., to Key West, who collected some ex-parte affidavits, charging Hon. Jefferson B. Browne, collector of customs, Hon. Geo. Bowne Patterson, United States district attorney, and Hon. William Bethel, immigrant inspector, with having abetted the violation of the contract labor laws of the United States. It was also charged that the committee which went to Havana, and other citizens of Key West, had been guilty of violating this law. As soon as it was known that these charges had been made, the board of trade appointed a committee consisting of Hon. Robert J. Perry, mayor, and Hon. Geo. W. Allen, to go to Washington to investigate, and lay the facts before the Treasury Department. They were accompanied by Hon. Jefferson B. Browne. When they arrived in Washington they found that the department was about to make a ruling on an ex-parte hearing. The administration considered the matter of so much importance that the committee was invited to meet with Mr. Gresham, secretary of state, Mr. Olney, Attorney General, and Mr. Carlisle, secretary of the treasury. This interview brought about the exoneration of the three Federal officials concerned, but the cabinet officers were strongly inclined to believe that there had been a violation of the contract labor laws. The committee was furnished with copies of the affidavits against the citizens of Key West, and they asked for time to return to Key West and submit counter affidavits. They left Washington, believing this would be done, but before reaching their destination it was announced in the press that the department had ruled against them, and would order the deportation of the Spaniards, and that any further action would be by the United States court.

The committee thereupon adopted heroic measures, and forestalled the action of the government by lodging complaints against Mr. William Seidenberg, Hon. Geo. W. Allen, Hon. C. B. Pendleton and Mr. Wm. R. Kerr, charging them with violation of the United States alien contract labor laws. Warrants for their arrest were issued, and the charges were heard by United States District Judge Alex Boarman of the Western District of Louisiana, who was holding court in Key West. After a full investigation, Judge Boarman discharged the defendants, and ruled that no contracts, written or verbal, expressed or implied, had been made by the committee or anyone for them.

This decision completely cut the ground from under the attempt of the Treasury Department to deport the Spanish workmen.

Acting under instructions from Washington, however, Immigrant Inspectors Deshler and Bethel arrested ninety-four Spaniards, and charged them with having come into the United States in violation of the alien contract labor laws. Writs of habeas corpus were at once sued out before Judge Boarman, who held that there was no proof to sustain the government's contention. The men were put under bond, pending an appeal to the United States Supreme Court, but the appeal was never taken, and the matter was thus disposed of. The work of the board of trade and the citizens in their effort to keep this factory here, were of no avail, for Mr. Seidenberg soon moved to Tampa.

This move would not have been very serious had it not

127

been for the complications which grew out of it. A spirit of unrest took possession of the Cuban population, who considered the action of the citizens unfriendly to them. This feeling, however, would have soon worn off, and the former friendly relations between the Cubans and the Americans reestablished, had not a committee come from Tampa to take advantage of the delicate situation. They offered attractive inducements to the Cuban manufacturers to abandon Key West and move to Tampa, and succeeded with the factories of O'Halloran, Teodoro Perez & Company and S. & F. Fleitas. The factory of Julius Ellinger was also moved to Tampa at this time.

The change proved of little benefit to the Cuban factories. Mr. Teodoro Perez and Mr. Fleitas returned to Key West after their Tampa contracts expired, and the latter now has one of the largest establishments here. The removal of these factories was heralded all over the country, and the impression created that the cigar business of Key West had been practically removed to Tampa. The largest factories, however, including the E. H. Gato Company, the Geo. W. Nichols Company, the Ferdinand Hirsch Company and the Sol. Falk Company remained here, with forty or fifty smaller ones. Those that remained largely increased their output as the demand was for cigars made in Key West. Discriminating smokers are not satisfied with those made elsewhere and marked "Key West," as they lack the flavor of those made at this place under conditions identical with those of Havana, which conditions do not exist in Tampa or elsewhere in the United States.

The cigar industry of Key West reached its zenith in 1890 when something over one hundred million cigars were made. The output fell off in 1894 but it has gradually and steadily increased, and in 1911 the hundred million mark has again been passed.

Among the large factories in Key West are the E. H. Gato Company, the Ferdinand Hirsch Company, Ruy Lopez Ca, Havana-American Company, the Geo. W. Nichols Company, the Cortez Cigar Company, S. &. F Fleitas, Key West Cigar Factory, Jose Lovera Company, the Martinez Havana company, M. Perez Company, the R. Fernandez Cigar Company, Murias Campana Company, Manuel Cruz, and the Gwynn, Martin & Strauss Company.

CHAPTER XXI

POLITICAL

THE tendency of the American people to divide along political lines was manifest in Key West in the early days of its settlement, notwithstanding the fact that news of the result of a presidential election did not reach the city until six weeks thereafter.

The predominating influence was strongly Southern, and naturally democratic. The islanders, however, were more interested in municipal than national or State politics, and local political battles were waged with as much feeling as if the fate of the nation depended upon the result.

In 1831 Mr. Richard Fitzpatrick and Colonel Lackland M. Stone, then United States marshal, were opposing candidates for representative from Monroe county to the territorial council. Mr. Fitzpatrick was a candidate for re-election; communications signed "Voter," "Honestus," "One of the People," etc., appeared in the *Enquirer* in which the good and bad qualities of the respective candidates were set forth. As both gentlemen were men of culture and high standing, the charges against them were no doubt as false as those promulgated in the primaries of the present day. Among other things, Mr. Fitzpatrick was charged with having traduced and slandered the people of Key West, calling them a "set of dishonest and unprincipled men and that the people of this county were unworthy of trust." He came in for the greater share of the abuse, but was triumphantly elected.

In 1838 the city divided on the matter of paying occupational taxes. Mr. Whitehead resigned the office of mayor and a bitter contest resulted, as is elsewhere set forth.

Hon. Joseph B. Browne and Judge William Marvin were delegates from Monroe county to the St. Joseph's convention in 1838, which framed the constitution under which Florida was admitted into the Union in 1845. It is rather a remarkable circumstance that they were the last two survivors of that historic body.

It was not until 1860 that contests over national politics worked any serious division among the people, but in that year the first rumblings of the cataclysm that was to destroy constitutional guarantees, reached Key West and stirred our people to the depths.

They knew that the great Democratic party which had shaped the destinies of the nation for half a century was menaced with defeat, on account of internal dissensions, and the conservative, constitutional Democrats were anxious that their policies should prevail.

On the 23rd of May, 1860, a mass meeting of Democrats was held in the city hall with Hon. John P. Baldwin as chairman and J. L. Tatum, Esq., secretary. The object of the meeting was explained by Hon. Joseph Beverly Browne, who, after making a forcible address, introduced a resolution on the subject of electing delegates to the State Democratic convention to meet in Quincy, Fla., on the 4th day of June.

The resolution "tendered the thanks of the Democrats of Monroe county to Hon. A. B. Noyes for the manner in which he had represented the Democracy of Monroe and Dade counties, in the convention lately held in Tallahassee."

Hons. Jos. B. Browne, James Filor, Geo. L. Bowne, Asa F. Tift and Wm. H. Ward were appointed delegates to attend the convention at Quincy, and instructed to try and have Monroe county represented in the national Democratic convention to be held at Richmond or Baltimore, or both, on the second day of June. Owing to the difficulties that Key West people had to encounter to reach the mainland, the precaution was taken to name as alternates Hon. A. B. Noyes and Judge R. B. Hilton of Leon county, in case the regular delegates were unable to attend.

The holding of the national Democratic convention at Baltimore in June, its balloting fifty-two times without any result, its adjournment without a nomination, the subsequent nomination of three Democrats for the presidency, with Breckenridge, the candidate of the advocates of the doctrine of the Supreme Court in the Dred Scott case; Douglas, the candidate of the advocates of Kansas-Nebraska legislation, and Bell, the candidate of the Constitutional-Union party, and the consequent election of Abraham Lincoln—who failed by nearly a million votes of being the choice of the people—came with startling celerity, and the Civil War was upon us before we realized it. The political events of that period are set forth in the chapter on Civil War.

The earliest contest after reconstruction, in which the newly enfranchised negroes voted, was the mayoralty election of 1869, when Hon. Joseph Beverly Browne, the Democratic candidate defeated Mr. E. L. Ware, the candidate of the black Republican party, as it was then called.

In 1866 the Democrats, after a hotly contested county election, with Mr. Browne as their candidate for representative in the legislature, carried the county for the first time since 1860.

In 1870 a spirited contest with Col. Walter C. Maloney, Jr., as the Democratic candidate, and James W. Locke, the Republican candidate for the State senate, the Republicans carried the county.

The two parties were very evenly divided in Monroe county

until 1888, since which time the Republican party has been practically without any local organization.

As a result of a split in the Democratic party in 1888 the Republicans elected a negro sheriff and county judge; the latter was removed by the governor for malfeasance in office, but the former served his term. At the same election another Republican, Mr. George Hudson, was elected county clerk.

In 1878 Hon. Geo. W. Allen, a Republican, defeated Col. W. C. Maloney, Jr., Democrat, for the senate by twelve votes.

The most bitter election ever held in Monroe county was that of the senatorial election in 1882. The wing of the Republican party hostile to Mr. Allen, known as the custom house faction, controlled the convention, but even with that advantage they could not have prevented Mr. Allen's nomination, had they not persuaded Mr. John Jay Philbrick to become their standard bearer. Mr. Philbrick was a Republican, but had never taken any active part in politics. He was one of the foremost business men in the city, a college graduate, a man of great versatility of talent, and his liberality and public spirit made him one of the most popular men in the city. Mr. C. B. Pendleton was the Democratic nominee, but certain disclosures in his private life coming shortly after his nomination, caused the Democratic Executive Committee to request him to withdraw from the ticket. The wing of the party that had supported him for the nomination opposed this, and Mr. Pendleton declined to withdraw. Several prominent members of the Democratic Executive Committee, who felt that he was not a proper candidate for their party, resigned their positions and announced that they would oppose his election.

The court house faction, led by Mr. E. O. Locke, clerk of the United States District Court, and Hon. G. Bowne Patterson, United States district attorney, were dissatisfied with the treatment that Mr. Allen had received, and when the split occurred in the Democratic party, they conferred with the Democrats who were opposed to Mr. Pendleton, and induced Mr. Allen to run as an independent candidate.

A campaign committee was organized on which were some of the leading Democrats, including those who had withdrawn from the Democratic Executive Committee, and several of the leading white Republicans, and a systematic campaign for Mr. Allen inaugurated. The Cubans rallied to his support to a man. Political meetings were held once or twice a week, and the county was stirred up to a political frenzy, never witnessed before or since. Families were separated, life-time friends quit speaking to each other, and personal encounters were frequent. Mr. Allen was triumphantly elected, having a clear majority over both the regular Democratic and Republican nominees.

Immediately after the election, the Democratic Executive Committee, which was composed entirely of Pendleton's supporters, submitted to a primary election the question whether

131

the governor should be requested to remove Mr. Peter T. Knight from the office of clerk of the circuit court, and Mr. George W. Demerritt from the office of sheriff, for having supported Mr. Allen. The friends of these gentlemen took no part in the primary and treated the matter as a joke. Several hundred people voted, and the ballot box was stuffed to the extent of several hundred more, and the returns made such a strong showing that Governor Bloxham felt it his duty to accede to the request of the Democrats of the county, and sent their names in to the senate for removal. It was known that Governor Bloxham did not want the senate to confirm his action, and the senate, by a good majority refused to do so, and these officials served out their terms.

Mr. Pendleton contested the senatorial election, and notwithstanding the fact that the senate was almost solidly Democratic, Mr. Allen retained his seat, only two votes being cast for Mr. Pendleton. Mr. Allen served through the session of 1883, but shortly afterwards resigned his seat to accept the position of cashier in the newly established Bank of Key West.

In 1884 a special election was called to fill Mr. Allen's unexpired term. Mr. George B. Phillips was the Republican candidate, Mr. Andrew J. Kemp and Dr. J. V. Harris, the candidates of the two wings of the Democratic party, and Mr. Philips was elected. He had accepted the nomination, however, merely for the influence it would give him in the councils of his party, in the event of the election of a Republican president, a contingency that seemed almost certain of fulfillment. The election of Grover Cleveland destroyed Mr. Phillips' hopes, and rather than give up the important position of head bookkeeper in the E. H. Gato cigar factory, he declined the seat in the senate. Mr. Pendleton, thereupon, went to Tallahassee and had the old contest reopened, and the senate by a majority of one gave him the seat. No one from Key West opposed Mr. Pendleton's claims at this time, and several senators who voted for him did so under the impression that it was the wish of the Democracy of Monroe county that the twenty-fourth senatorial district should have a representative in the senate.

One of the most spirited mayoralty elections was in 1877 when Hon. L. W. Bethel defeated Dr. J. W. V. R. Plummer. There was speech making and torch light processions, and as much if not more interest manifested than in a general election.

In the presidential election of 1876 Monroe county was one of the determining factors. The morning after the election the Republicans realized that Mr. Samuel J. Tilden had defeated the Republican candidate, Mr. Hayes by thirty - three electoral votes, but that by fraudulently changing the result in South Carolina, Florida and Louisiana, they could elect Hayes by one majority. Instructions were sent to the Republican governors of these States to change the Democratic majorities into a majority for the Republican party, and men of great ability, although unscrupulous partisans, were sent to each of them to formulate a plan to carry out the proposed fraud. Monroe county, which had given a large Democratic majority, was one of those selected to be contested. The third ward at that time was almost solidly Democratic, Mr. John T. Barker's family being the only Republicans living therein. The vote of the third ward was four hundred and fifty-seven for the Democratic electors and three for the Republican.

Affidavits were procured to the effect that intimidation had been practiced in this ward, which prevented the negroes from voting. The election was quiet, orderly and practically without fraud on either side. The machinery of the election being in the hands of the Republicans, they alone could have perpetrated any fraud. The third ward was thrown out by the Republican returning board at Tallahassee, and the State was given to the Republican party by a majority less than the Democratic majority in this ward.

The third ward has always been the banner Democratic ward of the county, and its vote, on the side of decency, morality and good government. Until the change in the ward lines of the city, it occupied the same enviable position in city affairs.

In 1887 the county of Lee was created out of part of Monroe county, and the two comprise the twenty-fourth senatorial district. In 1888 Hon. Geo. M. Hendry, of Fort Myers, was elected senator of the new district. Since then Monroe county has furnished the senator, and Lee county has petitioned in vain for the privilege of occasionally being similarly honored.

In 1894 when Hon. J. M. Phipps of Monroe county was nominated, a district convention was held, and Lee county sent her quota of delegates.

In 1898 there was no district convention, and the Monroe county convention nominated Hon. W. Hunt Harris, and the Lee county Democratic convention nominated Mr. Menendez Johnson. Mr. Harris was duly elected.

Since Mr. Hendry's incumbency, Fernando J. Moreno, Hon. Jefferson B. Browne, Hon. J. M. Phipps, Hon. W. Hunt Harris and Hon. W. H. Malone, Jr., the present incumbent, have been successively elected.

Isolated as Monroe county is from the rest of the State, it has been difficult for her to receive the recognition at the hands of the State Democratic party that she is entitled to, although several of her distinguished sons have held State positions. The first was Hon. Richard Fitzpatrick, who was president of the territorial council in 1836. Hon. Stephen R. Mallory was elected to the United States senate while a resident of Key West. Other citizens of Monroe county to be honored were Hon. Livingston W. Bethel, lieutenant-governor from 1880 to 1884, Jefferson B. Browne, president of the senate, from 1891 to 1893 and chairman of the Florida Railroad Commission from 1903

133

to 1907, Hon. W. Hunt Harris, president of the senate from 1907 to 1909.

Since the organization the State Board of Health in 1889, Monroe county's distinguished citizen, who is one of the foremost experts on sanitation and hygiene in the United States, Dr. Joseph Y. Porter, Sr., has held the position of State health officer. Key West has had three delegates to Democratic national conventions; Hon. Joseph Beverly Browne in 1868, Hon. Jephtha V. Harris in 1876, and Hon. Jefferson B. Browne in 1888. From 1904 to 1908 Hon. Jefferson B. Browne was a member of the Democratic National Executive Committee for Florida.

The Republican party has on several occasions nominated distinguished citizens of Monroe county for high offices. Hons. E. O. Locke, Geo. Bowne Patterson and Geo. W. Allen were respectively the nominees for congress in 1884, 1900 and 1908. In 1896 Mr. Allen was nominated for governor but declined the nomination.

In 1900 Captain John F. Horr was the Republican nominee for secretary of state and Hon. Geo. W. Allen in 1904. In 1904 and 1908 Mr. Geo. W. Allen was delegate to the national Republican convention, and Captain John F. Horr in 1892 and 1900. Mr. Ramon Alvarez was alternate to the Republican national convention in 1892.

In 1886 C. B. Pendleton ran as an independent candidate for congress against Col. Robert H. M. Davidson, but did not carry a county in the State, and in the county of Wakulla he failed to receive a vote.

The politics of Key West has not been without its share of excitement. On several occasions during reconstruction, we were on the verge of race riots.

On one election day when the negroes were driving around the city in a wagon with a brass band, shouting and jeering, making themselves generally offensive to the white citizens, they passed the corner of Front and Duval streets, where Captain Phillip Fontaine was standing. Captain Fontaine was a man of quick temper, and unable to submit to their impertinence, drew his pistol and opened fire on them. The rapid report of his pistol and the rattle of the bullets on the brass horns, so frightened the negroes that they jumped out of the wagon and sought refuge in and underneath adjacent buildings. When they discovered that their assailant was attacking them single handed, they emerged from their hiding places, and made a rush for him. He had emptied his pistol, but fearlessly stood his ground, when he was struck down by a stone and would have been killed had not one of the negroes, who was greatly attached to him, dragged him to a place of safety, and concealed him until the authorities got the riotous negroes under control.

Captain Fontaine was a native of Key West and a man of undaunted courage and distinguished bearing. He was an officer in the United States marine corps when the war broke out, and resigned his commission to enter the Confederate service. His daughter married Colonel Samuel J. Wolf of the Florida State Troops, a citizen of Key West.

In 1872 a number of the Republicans who disapproved of the reconstruction policy of their party, and its affiliation with carpet-baggers, negroes and scalawags, sought to purify it by organizing the liberal Republican party, and a meeting was held in the court house for that purpose. The negroes led by the carpet-baggers assembled in force, and attempted to break up the meeting. They became threatening, and a riot was imminent. Several old time Whigs, and some young men, who had never been in politics, attended the meeting in the hope that there might be organized a respectable white Republican party. They soon saw that the hope was futile, and were about to leave the hall when Dr. J. W. V. R. Plummer, the leader of the movement, called upon his friends to stand together and resist the threatened violence of the negroes. There was one young man among them who was just beginning his political career. He had been approached by a distinguished Democrat, who expressed surprise at seeing him in such company, and his allegiance to the movement was already weakened, when Dr. Plummer made his call to his followers to stand their ground. This young man was Mr. Peter T. Knight, who concluding that a riot among negroes and sore-head Republicans was no place for him, jumped out of a window of the court house and landed in the Democratic party, where he has ever since been, a distinguished and active worker.

In the year 1872 the Democrats made their first organized effort to wrest the State from the Republican party, and Colonel John A. Henderson and Hon. W. D. Bloxham made a speaking tour through the State. When they reached Key West a meeting was held at the corner of Front and Duval streets, about where the First National Bank now stands. It was the first big political gathering since 1860, and there was great excitement on both sides. The speaking had not progressed far when someone (said to have been Mr. John H. Gregory, a whole-souled, genial, big-hearted, generous fellow) discharged a pistol in the air. The wildest confusion followed, each side thought they were being attacked; shouts of "Murder!" "O Hell!" "I'm cut!" "Somebody shot me!" were heard on all sides and a stampede began. The women screamed, the white people scurried to the third ward, and the negroes lit out for their homes in the first ward. Whatever slight injuries were sustained were caused by persons running into each other, in their desire to escape the supposed riot. Highly imaginative persons on both sides, for many years, believed that they had witnessed a serious race riot, but it was the source of infinite jest to the distinguished orators whose meeting had been so summarily broken up.

An exciting incident in the Allen-Pendleton campaign occurred at a meeting on the corner of William and Fleming streets opposite Sparks Chapel. It was one of the last meetings

135

of the campaign and statements had been made from the platform, which one of the supporters of Mr. Allen, who was present, felt should be refuted, and he went on the platform intending to address the voters when the Pendleton people got through. On the platform were Col. W. C. Maloney, Jr., Judge Allen E. Curry and Mr. C. B. Pendleton. As soon as the gentleman arrived on the platform, he was courteously offered a seat, and asked his purpose, which he explained. He was told that he would not be allowed to speak. Judge Curry presided, and after a short talk, stated that the meeting was over and the folks could all go home. The crowd, however, saw the prospect of some fun and remained. When the gentleman arose to speak his friends cheered, and his opponents shouted, intending to drown his voice. He made himself heard sufficiently, however, to tell them that he did not intend to attempt to speak while they were holloaing, but would stand there until their voices gave out, and he would then speak. The Pendleton people on the platform, urged their friends to go home, but none moved. Finally someone suggested to tear down the platform. The speaker attempted to draw his pistol to prevent this, but before he got it out, strong hands had grasped the supports and pulled them out. Colonel Maloney, who was sitting with his chair tipped back, his feet on the table, rolled over backwards into the store behind him. The others, who were also sitting down, met with the same castastrophe, but the speaker who was standing, preserved his equilibrium and landed on his feet. A rush was made for him, but having gotten his pistol out by this time, he managed to keep the crowd at a safe distance. The women screamed and rushed for their homes, and wild reports of rioting were scattered throughout the city. The incident, however, amounted to nothing, and the friends of the speaker seeing that he had no opportunity to be heard, abandoned the attempt, and all hands quietly returned home to discuss the incident in a jocular, or angry manner, according to their respective moods.

Presidential elections may be pregnant with hopes of lucrative positions; State elections with matters of polity; city elections with personalities; but it remains for a "wet and dry election" to reach the acme of excitement and interest.

As the women are the greatest sufferers from the open saloon, they take the lead in such movements, and many men rally to their support from a spirit of chivalry.

In 1907 Key West had thirty-eight licensed saloons. One-third of the population belonged to the Latin races who drink mild wines and beer, but rarely to excess. Here the liquor traffic seemed safe from molestation. Suddenly an agitation was begun for a test of strength between the two forces. Rev. E. A. Harrison of the First Methodist church took the lead, heartily supported by Rev. Charles T. Stout, the Episcopal clergyman, Rev. M. A. Clonts of the Baptist church, and all the other Protestant ministers on the island.

Petitions were circulated asking the county commissioners to call an election to determine if the saloon should continue in Key West, and before the whiskey people realized the strength of the movement, the requisite twenty-five per cent of the registered voters had signed the petitions, and the election called for November 4, 1907.

The campaign was a bitter one. Besides the ministers of the gospel, Hons. Jefferson B. Browne, William H. Malone, Jr., Allen E. Curry, and George L. Babcock, took the stump for the anti-saloon side, and Hon. J. N. Fogarty, mayor, George G. Brooks and E. M. Semple, for the wets. Rev. W. J. Carpenter of the Methodist Conference of Florida, and Rev. John A. Wray of the Baptist church, came to Key West and made powerful anti-saloon speeches. A joint debate between Rev. Mr. Carpenter and Hon. Robert McNamee of Tampa, in Jackson Square, was attended by the largest audience ever assembled in Key West.

The "wets" carried the county by forty-eight majority.

Mr. Albert F. Shultz was campaign manager of the anti-saloon campaign, and much credit is due him for his work in that capacity.

The whiskey people did not take out licenses when due on October first, and all saloons were closed during that month and for six days in November. During the period the saloons were closed, there were fifteen cases in the police court; in the month of September there were sixty-two, and for the twenty-four days in November, there were seventy-three.

CHAPTER XXII

BENEVOLENT SOCIETIES

THE numerous benevolent societies which exist in our city are considered one of its marked features.

The first to be established was Dade Lodge No. 14 of the Free and Accepted Masons, chartered January 16, 1845. Its first officers were Mr. O. S. Noyes, Worshipful Master, Mr. Alexander Patterson, Senior Warden, and Mr. Benjamin Sawyer, Junior Warden. It is one of the oldest Masonic lodges in Florida, all but two of those chartered prior to January, 1845, having gone out of existence. Royal Arch Chapter No. 21 was organized in 1868; Monroe Council No. 4 in 1870, and Baron Commandery No. 7 in 1872. In the same year the Cubans organized Dr. Felix Varela Lodge No. 62, F. & A. M. Anchor Lodge No. —, F. & A. M. was organized in 1908; its first officers were Joseph Y. Porter, Worshipful Master; Mr. Julius Otto, Senior Warden, and Mr. Chas. H. Ketcham, Junior Warden.

In 1869 the Masons erected a large two-story building on the northeast side of Simonton street, about midway of the block, between Caroline and Eaton streets. The second floor was used for lodge purposes, the lower floor for entertainments, and subsequently for the first public school conducted in Key West. This building was destroyed by fire in 1886, and a large three story brick one erected in its place, which was completed in 1889.

Second to the Masons in point of time of organization, was the Sons of Temperance, in 1845, which continued in existence until 1862. Captain Francis B. Watlington and Mr. Joseph C. Whalton, Sr., were prominent in bringing this society into existence. It effected much good to its members and society at large.

Key West Lodge No. 13, Independent Order of Odd Fellows, was organized in 1872, Key West Encampment No. 5 on July 4, 1875, and Cuba Lodge No. 15, I. O. O. F., by the Cuban citizens, in the same year. Equity Lodge No. 70, I. O. O. F., was instituted by Grand Master William H. Malone, Jr., on March 4, 1911. The first officers were Ernest P. Roberts, Noble Grand; George A. T. Roberts, Vice Grand; F. J. M. Roberts, Secretary; Marcy B. Darnall, Treasurer. The lodge has doubled its membership in less than a year.

Key West Lodges, I. O. O. F., have furnished to the Grand Lodge five Grand Masters, Dr. Joseph Y. Porter, Judge Angel de Lono, Hon. Eugene O. Locke, Mr. Julius Otto and Hon. William H. Malone, Jr.

In 1874 the Odd Fellows erected a commodious two-story

building on the southeast side of Caroline street, about midway of the block, between Duval and Whitehead streets. The upper floor was used for lodge purposes, and the lower floor, for a time, for balls and receptions, but later was converted into a theatre.

The years of 1874 and 1875 saw the rise and fall in Key West of a benevolent organization which in point of numbers and influence for good, has never been equalled. The Independent Order of Good Templars began by instituting Island City Lodge No. 9, in 1874, and in 1876 reached the crest of the wave of its prosperity with over eight hundred members. In 1874 Unity Lodge No. 11 was organized, and its membership went up to over four hundred; next came Rising Star Lodge No. 13, in 1875, with about one hundred and fifty members.

There was no hall in the city sufficiently large to accommodate them, and Mr. William Curry erected for their use a large two story building just southeast of where the bonded warehouse now stands, on Simonton street, which was known for many years as Good Templars Hall.

The Good Templars was a strictly temperance organization, in which men and women were equally eligible, and as the three lodges in Key West had a majority of women members, the meetings were the most delightful social gatherings. After the regular business was finished, the rest of the evening was spent in music, recitations, addresses, and any other entertainment which conduced to the good of the order. So strong was its influence that there was hardly a man in the city, unless connected with the saloon business, who was not a member. Saloon after saloon closed its doors, and those that kept open barely made expenses. Gradually, however, that State institution, the licensed saloon, resumed its sway, and this organization went out of existence.

The Knights of Jericho, Astral Lodge No. 18, was organized in 1875. Abstinence from the use of intoxicating liquors was one of its teachings, but not the sole purpose of its being. Mr. Allen E. Curry, now police justice of the city, was an active member.

The order of Knights of Pythias is one of the strongest of the benevolent organizations of the city. Island City Lodge No. 14 was organized in 1881, followed by Coral City Lodge No. 53 in 1890. In December, 1907, Isle of the Sea Lodge No. 104 was organized with seventy members. Among its charter members were Hons. William B. Curry and William M. Pinder. Mr. Roger Weatherford is the present Chancellor Commander.

Camp No. 23 Woodmen of the World was organized and instituted by Special Deputy Organizer H. L. Stricker on July 10, 1895, with fifteen charter members. Mr. Benjamin P. Baker was the first Council Commander and Dr. C. F. Kemp its first clerk. It was not a thrifty organization until about 1905, when it commenced to increase its membership, which is now sixty-eight. It is a fraternal, beneficial, insurance organization, with headquarters in Omaha, Nebraska.

On February 14, 1900, Key West Lodge No. 551, Benevolent and Protective Order of Elks, was instituted with forty charter members. Shortly after its organization it rented the second floor of the two-story brick building on the corner of Front and Fitzpatrick streets, from Mr. John W. Sawyer, who used the first floor for a clothing store. A lodge room, reading room, and several club rooms were fitted up, and the organization started at once on a most prosperous career. In 1901 the lodge bought the property known as the Duval House, which was built and used by Mrs. Josephine Bolio as a restaurant. Its present membership is one hundred and thirty. Its successive Exalted Rulers were W. U. Simonds, John B. Maloney, Ramon Alvarez, W. Hunt Harris, George L. Bartlum, William R. Porter, Charles R. Pierce, W. Hunt Harris, Jefferson B. Browne, William L. Bates, Henry H. Taylor, Eugene W. Russell and Charles R. Curry, the present incumbent.

Key West Lodge has been four times honored with the appointment of a District Deputy Grand Exalted Ruler for South Florida. Hon. W. Hunt Harris in 1904; Judge Ramon Alvarez in 1906; Hon. Jefferson B. Browne in 1910, and reappointed in 1911.

On May 8, 1905, Key West Council No. 1015, order of the Knights of Columbus, was organized with thirty-six charter members. The first Grand Knight was Mr. F. C. Brossier. Its meetings are held in St. Joseph's, College on Simonton street. The present membership is sixty-five. The Grand Knights for the successive years were Messrs. P. J. McMahon, A. P. Jerguson, Walter W. Thompson, Henry Haskins and Ulric E. Albury.

The Redmen, Knights of the Golden Eagle, Owls, Eagles and Moose, each have local lodges in the city.

CHAPTER XXIII

NEWSPAPERS

THE first newspaper published in Key West was the *Register* in January, 1829, under the management of Mr. Thomas Eastin, who was subsequently United States marshal. It was published for a very short time, and no copy of it is known to be in existence.

Then came the *Key West Gazette* on March 21, 1831, and lasted until the latter part of 1832.

On October 15, 1834, the *Enquirer* appeared, with Mr. Jesse Atkinson as editor and publisher. The editorials were written chiefly by Mr. William A. Whitehead, assisted by Lieutenant Francis B. Newcomb, Mr. Mallory and others. In December, 1835, the name was changed to *Inquirer*, and it was published until the latter part of 1836.

These papers were well edited and would do credit to the Key West of today. Their ideals were high, their diction pure, their typography excellent, and the literary selections classics. Mr. William A. Whitehead preserved files of these two papers, and in 1869 sent bound volumes here for "preservation in the office of the Clerk of Monroe county," where they are now kept. Since 1838, when Mr. Whitehead left here, there has been no citizen sufficiently interested in the preservation of the records of Key West to keep the files of various newspapers for the benefit of posterity.

The Light of the Reef was started by Messrs. Ware and Scraborough in 1845, but lasted only a few months.

The Key of the Gulf was published for a short period during 1845, and was revived in 1857, and edited by the brilliant Mr. William H. Ward. It was probably the ablest and one of the most fearless papers ever published in Key West. It was suppressed by Major W. H. French, United States army, early in May, 1861, who wrote: "I directed the mayor to inform the editor (a Mr. Ward) that he was under military surveillance, and that the fact of his not being in the cells of this fort for treason was simply a matter as to expediency and proper point of time." Notwithstanding the fact that Key West was under the control of the Northern forces, Mr. Ward continued to advocate in the columns of his paper the constitutional right of secession. After his paper was suppressed he left Key West and cast his fortune with his native Southland. "Laying aside the weapon of the sage for that of the soldier, to try the issues of law and ethics on the field of battle, whence he never returned."

In 1862 and 1863 a paper called the *New Era* was published by Mr. R. B. Locke, an officer of the 90th Regiment, New York Volunteers.

In 1867 the *Key West Dispatch*, published by W. C. Maloney, Jr., and edited by his brilliant father, appeared, and continued to be conducted by him until 1872, when it passed in to the hands of Mr. H. A. Crain as editor and publisher. In 1874 it passed under the editorial guidance of Mr. E. L. Ware, and suspended publication in 1877.

In 1870 *The Key West Guardian*, owned and edited by Mr. R. C. Neeld "arose with porcupine armor to correct the evils of the day." It was a bold, aggressive paper and had a brief existence of about a year.

In 1874 *The Key of the Gulf* made its third entrance into the journalistic field under the editorial charge of Mr. H. A. Crain, who pub ished it until feeble health in 1887 forced him to lay down his pen. On the death of Mr. Crain, Mr. George Eugene Bryson began the publication of a paper, the *New Era*, using the outfit of *The Key of the Gulf*.

In 1880 Mr. William Curry, Mr. Asa Tift and other citizens of means, organized a stock company and founded a paper called *The Democrat*, under the editorial management of Mr. Charles B. Pendleton. Mr. Pendleton was fearless but erratic, and his tendency to attack through the columns of his paper any person or institution that interfered with him, or whom he thought stood in his way politically or otherwise, was most unfortunate. His erratic nature led him to believe that as a Democrat, he should attack the Republicans whether justly or unjustly, and he began a series of articles defamatory of Judge W. James Locke of the United States district court, which led to a libel suit in which Mr. Curry, Mr. Tift, Mr. Moreno and other stockholders were made defendants. The case was amicably adjusted, but resulted in these gentlemen disposing of their stock, and severing their connection with the paper. Mr. Pendleton continued his policy of attack on everyone, and soon included Mr. William Curry, Dr. Porter and others, which brought another suit for libel. He was sued for libel also by Mr. C. T. Merrill, owner of the Russell House. This was the only case that went to trial, and resulted in a verdict against Mr. Pendleton.

Had he been less erratic he might have occupied an influential place in the community for good, but he could see no good in anyone's opinions but his own, and to differ with him in any matter would bring upon the offender the most unreasonable vituperation.

In 1885 he sold the paper to Mr. Philip E. Thompson, who conducted it for a short time, and sold it to Messrs. Peter T. Knight and Mason S. Moreno. It was said that one of these gentlemen wrote the salutatory and the other the valedictory, and that its editorials were written and its policy shaped by Dr. J. V. Harris, then collector of customs.

In May, 1887, Mr. Pendleton again entered the journalistic field with *The Equator-El Equador*, an English and Spanish daily. In 1888 he bought back the *Democrat* and consolidated it with the *Equator*, under the name of the *Equator-Democrat*. In 1894 the paper passed by purchase into the hands of Mr. J. M. Caldwell, who published it for a few months only, when it went back into Mr. Pendleton's control. In 1897, when it was in its death throes, he turned it over to his foreman and printers to run on their own account. They suspended publication after a few issues, and the *Equator-Democrat* went the way of its predecessors.

In 1892 Messrs. William R. Porter and W. H. Hutchinson began the publication of a paper called the *Gulf Pennant*, a name suggested by that distinguished citizen of Florida, Hon. W. D. Chipley. It was edited by Mr. Cassius E. Merrill of Kentucky, who prior to coming to Key West had been editor of the *Jacksonville Times-Union* and *The Standard*. He was one of the most brilliant writers ever connected with Florida journalism, and the *Gulf Pennant* under his leadership was the ablest edited paper ever published in Key West. It suspended publication July 4, 1893.

In 1894 a number of citizens of Key West raised three thousand dollars and bought a newspaper outfit and turned it over to Mr. John Denham of Monticello, Fla., who founded the *Herald*. In 1899 he sold it to Mr. T. J. Appleyard of Lake City, Fla. About this time *The Key of the Gulf* made its fourth appearance. under the management of Mr. Walter W. Thompson, and in 1899 it was bought by Mr. T. J. Appleyard, who suspended publication of the *Herald* and *The Key of the Gulf*, and founded *The Inter-Ocean*. In the latter part of 1900 Mr. Walter W. Thompson bought *The Inter-Ocean* and for four years he edited and published a high class, fearless daily. In 1904 a small weekly paper, *The Citizen*, made its appearance, and after a few months' existence was bought by Mr. Marcy B. Darnall and Mr. Thomas Treason Thompson, and a consolidation effected between *The Citizen* and *The Inter-Ocean*, under the name of the *Key West Citizen*, which is now being issued as an afternoon daily.

In 1908 Mr. Frederick H. Mathews founded a morning daily called *The Journal*, of which he is editor and publisher.

In 1890 Mr. James T. Ball started the publication of a small weekly sheet, *The Advertiser*, which contained a few local advertisements and a little reading matter. It was gradually enlarged and during the last few years of Mr. Ball's life it became quite a good weekly newspaper. Since his death, in 1906, it has been conducted by his son, Mr. Egbert P. Ball.

For several years a discharged Union soldier by the name of Morgan ran a small paper called *The Guardian*. He had no policy except that of abuse and vituperation. He was editor, publisher, printer, and eked out a miserable existence. When he died there was no one to follow him to his grave, and bystanders were called in to assist the undertaker to put his coffin into the hearse. The scene was a pitiful one and made an impression on the writer, who witnessed it.

CHAPTER XXIV

THE SPANISH-AMERICAN WAR

FOR some time before the opening of actual hostilities between the United States and Spain, Key West bore the appearance of a war port.

To conciliate the Spanish authorities, who were constantly protesting against the use of Key West as a base for fitting out and embarking filibustering expeditions, one or more warships were stationed here, as evidence of our government's intention to prevent violations of neutrality laws. The Maine was here for about six months in 1896, and again in 1897; and it was from this port that she sailed on her last voyage. The Cincinnati, Raleigh, Amphitrite, Marblehead and Wilmington, each did its term of duty, assisted by two or more revenue cutters. The officers of these vessels added no little to the social life of the city, and many warm ties of friendship were then formed.

A number of fast tugs, reasonably supposed to be engaged in filibustering, came and went, but no proof could be obtained against them.

In 1896 Mr. Richard Harding Davis and Mr. Frederic Remington, the artist, came to Key West, representing the *New York Journal.*

Mr. W. R. Hearst's power boat, the "Vamoose," then the fleetest in the world, was under their orders to take them to Cuba, where they planned to visit the camps of the revolutionists, and interview the leaders. Mr. Davis was to write the story of their venture, and Mr. Remington to illustrate it with his wonderful sketches.

They fully appreciated the risk they would run, but were keen for the enterprise, and made two attempts to reach Cuba, but the "Vamoose," not able to stand the heavy seas encountered in the gulf, was forced to put back to Key West. Each day the skies were scanned, weather reports studied, and prognostications weighed, in hope of a favorable opportunity to make the run across the gulf, but the fates were against them, and the high winds and heavy seas abated not. The "Vamoose" was a long narrow shell, built solely for speed, and was unfit for a voyage to Cuba except in an unusually smooth sea. After several weeks spent in the vain hope for good weather, the trip was abandoned, and Mr. Davis and Mr. Remington went to Havana by the regular steamship line, hoping to make their way thence to the Cuban camps. In this they were thwarted by the travel regulations, and vigilance of the Spanish authorities, and they returned to Key West, and thence home.

They spent three weeks in Key West—"three years"—as Mr. Remington afterwards facetiously referred to it—and were guests at dinner parties, luncheons and informal receptions ashore and on the war vessels then in port, and their genius and comraderie made them great social favorites.

An incident, which shows Mr. Davis in a light not generally known, transpired when he made his first attempt to reach Cuba. He told a friend that it was probable that after he arrived he would not be heard from for some time, and reports of his death might appear in the papers. In order to spare his parents unnecessary pain, he wrote a telegram to his father, saying: "Reports of your son's death not credited here. He is known to be in another part of the island." This message he asked his friend to sign and transmit, if any bad news was received, adding "if the report proves true, it will be no harder for them to bear later, and if false, it will spare them much unnecessary pain."

The friend has kept the telegram as a memento of a very pleasant epoch. He was also the recipient of several books by these distinguished authors, with autograph inscriptions. In his book, "Pony Tracks," Mr. Remington, wrote "In memory of the nice lunches, the fine dinners, the good times, and other alleviations of my three years in Key West, from the grateful, Frederic Remington."

The explosion of the Maine shocked the people of Key West probably more than any other community, for here the officers and the men had been stationed off and on for over a year, and had many friends.

An accident similar to that on the Maine came very near occurring in Key West harbor, on the Cincinnati in 1895. Spontaneous combustion in her coal bunkers was undiscovered until the fire had been communicated to the magazine, and boxes containing ammunition badly burned. Smoke was seen coming from the magazine, which in a few moments would have exploded. Had it been at night as in the case of the Maine, the smoke would not have been seen, and the tragedy of the Maine in Havana harbor would have had a forerunner on the Cincinnati in the harbor of Key West.*

Not very long before the Maine went to Cuba, she took on soft coal at Key West, which was lightered to her in barges; during the day heavy showers of rain fell, and at least one barge load was thoroughly wet. If any of this was in her bunkers when she again coaled, her disaster is no more of a mystery than the cause of the fire in the magazine of the Cincinnati.

Most of the events of the Spanish-American War, such as the mobilizing at Key West of almost all the ships of our navy, the flotilla of newspaper boats, and war correspondents that gathered here, the military and naval operations carried on from

*Appendix Q.

this point, are matters for the general, rather than the local historian.

Several incidents, however, occurred which have some local flavor. The newspaper correspondents were wont to put on a bulletin board the war news they received, for the benefit of the public; these, the local newspaper, *"The Herald,"* would publish under the heading "Special to the *Herald.*" One day the correspondents put on the board "The American schooner Virginia, loaded with silver bullion and cocoanuts, sunk by a Spanish war ship, off the coast of Spain." In an hour an "Extra" *Herald* was out, with a long "Special to the *Herald,*" telling all about the Virginia and her valuable cargo. The editor was from the mainland, and not familiar with shipping, so did not see the hoax that was apparent, from the incongruity of a cocoanut droger, having silver bullion as part of her cargo; neither did he look in the register of American vessels to ascertain if there was a schooner "Virginia," but swallowed the bait, hook and line, at one gulp.

One wit among the correspondents, who grew weary waiting for orders to go to the coast of Cuba, described his feelings, in a Shakesperian paraphrase, "Cu-be, or not Cu-be; that is the Key Westion."

Among the distinguished newspaper correspondents who were here were Mr. Stephen M. Bonsal, Mr. Ralph Payne and Mr. Harry Brown.

Judge Ramon Alvarez, Special Deputy Collector of Customs, was the local correspondent of the *New York Herald*, and his reports were far more accurate than any sent by the world-famed war correspondents.

CHAPTER XXV

HOSPITALS—MARINE HOSPITAL

THE urgent need for a hospital where sick seamen could be cared for was early manifest in Key West.

The allowances for ports south of the Potomac at that time, were, "for suitable boarding, lodging and nursing three dollars per week; for necessary medicines, the usual apothecary rates; for medical services twenty-five cents for each day, when the aggregate time for which they are rendered shall average less than twenty-five days to each patient. When the average time to each patient amounts to more than twenty-five days, and the number of patients does not exceed ten, six dollars and twenty-five cents for each patient, and when there is a greater number than ten, three dollars and twelve and a half cents for each patient; and for funeral charge six dollars."

This was so inadequate that it was presented by the grand inquest of the county as a grievance demanding redress. In 1835 Mr. William A. Whitehead thus called attention to the urgent need for a marine hospital at this port:

"An object long had in view by the citizens of Key West is the establishment here of a marine hospital, or accommodation for the sick of a more general character than exist at present.

"The want of public institutions, where the destitute and diseased seaman may obtain the relief of which he stands in need, must always be an evil deeply felt in every mercantile community; and our peculiar situation renders it especially necessary that there should be greater comforts within the reach of the sick, than are now to be obtained upon the island under the present administration of the marine hospital fund.

"Situated as Key West is, it is calculated at all times to become a receptacle for the sick of vessels leaving the ports of West Florida, Alabama and Louisiana, and also of those bound to the northward from the coast of Mexico, as there is no port offering equal advantages as a stopping place, and none between Charleston and Pensacola possessing the superior attraction of a hospital. Such being the case, seamen are brought here sick to be left to the care of strangers, dependent upon private charity (there being no municipal regulations for their support), and the hospital fund of the United States for their nursing and subsistence.

"We would therefore recommend an application to congress, through our delegate, for the establishment here of some public accommodations for the sick seaman, whereby his comfort may

be in some measure secured while incapacitated by disease—
to which all are liable—from pursuing his usual avocations."

In February, 1836, the territorial delegate from Florida,
Colonel Joseph M. White, introduced in congress a resolution
inquiring "into the expediency of providing at Key West greater
comforts for the sick and disabled seamen than the present
regulations for the disbursement of the Marine Hospital Funds
will admit of their receiving."

This was a step, but it did not go far enough for our citizens,
who had set out to have an hospital established here, and would
be satisfied with nothing less.

A memorial was prepared and forwarded to congress, setting
forth the many reasons why such an institution was specially
needed here, "not only for our own seamen, but likewise for those
navigating vessels carrying on the trade of St. Marks, Apalachicola" (then two of the principal cotton shipping ports of the
United States), Mobile, New Orleans, and other ports: "Key
West being so situated as to be the most favorable stopping
place for all vessels engaged in the commerce of the gulf, that
may have sickness on board, and for the many shipwrecked
seamen brought into Key West."

After a few years their efforts were rewarded, and in 1844
the Marine Hospital on Emma street, at the foot of Fleming,
was erected. During the Civil War, and again in the Spainsh-
American War, it was used by the navy.

ARMY HOSPITAL

When the army post was established here, a commodious,
well ventilated hospital was erected, which is a model of fitness
and adaptability. Its wide piazzas on all sides protect it from
the rays of the sun, and cool breezes soothe the stricken patient.

CONVENT HOSPITAL

Another hospital, although only a temporary one, will be
remembered as long as there are any survivors of the Spanish-
American War. It was called The Key West Convent Hospital.

Shortly before war was declared, the Sister Superior of
the convent of Mary Immaculate, called on Captain James M.
Forsyth, commandant of the Key West naval station, and offered
the services of herself and her sisters, and the convent and their
two schools for hospitals, in the event of actual hostilities.
Upon this noble offer being communicated to the commander in
chief of the naval forces here, he replied to Captain Forsyth:

> "U. S. Flagship New York,
> "Off Key West, Fla.,
Sir:—   "April 7, 1898.
> "1. Acknowledging your letter of the 5th instant, stating
that the Lady Superior in charge of the schools of the 'Sisters
of the Holy Names, Convent of Mary Immaculate,' at Key

West, has called on you, and offered, in case of war, to place the convent and two school buildings of the order at the disposition of the naval authorities for hospital purposes, and that the Sisters tender their personal services as nurses.

"2. I cordially agree with your opinion expressed, that this is a most generous and patriotic tender, and beg that you will make known to the Lady Superior, and to the Sisters, my appreciation of their offer, and acceptance in case it becomes necessary.

"Very respectfully,

(Signed)   "W. T. SAMPSON,
                    "Captain U. S. N., Commander-in-Chief
                    U. S. Naval Forces, North Atlantic Station."

On April 21st Dr. W. R. Hall, United States navy, arrived to convert the convent into an hospital, and in a short time it was ready for occupancy. The parlor became a drug store; the spacious class rooms of the first floor were converted into wards for the wounded soldiers, and the offices and operating rooms established on the second floor.

Among the first to be treated was Lieutenant John B. Bernadou of the torpedo boat Winslow. Father Chidwick of the Maine was also a patient.

The medical faculty, consisting of nine doctors, under the direction of Major W. R. Hall, were Majors W. C. Borden, S. T. Armstrong, Captain H. A. Shaw, Doctors B. E. Baker, H. P. Jackson, E. G. Ferguson, A. E. DeLipsey, F. M. E. Usher, H. Mann, R. C. Eve, T. A. Clayton and R. G. Plummer.

LOUISE MALONEY HOSPITAL

Early in 1908 Dr. John B. Maloney bought the homestead of Mr. Thomas Curry on Fleming street, near the corner of Simonton. He moved it to the back of the lot, enlarged and remodelled it, and on October 6th, that year, opened the Louise Maloney Hospital, named in honor of his wife.

Proving too small, he bought, in 1911, the residence of Mrs. Affie Sawyer, on Simonton street, remodelled and improved it, and connected it by a covered causeway with the hospital on Fleming street.

The operating room has a cement floor, and all contrivances necessary to preserve a perfectly aseptic condition, and is fully equipped with modern instruments and appliances.

The institution has thirty beds, two of which are maintained by the county of Monroe.

Since the hospital was opened it has treated six hundred and six cases. Mr. Upton Sinclair was a patient, for a short time, and says that it was while there that he adopted the orange and milk diet, which he has since strongly advocated.

CASA DEL POBRE, MERCEDES

In 1904, encouraged and inspired by Mrs. Dolores Mayg, a few philanthropic Cuban citizens, chief among whom was

Don Sr. Antonio Diaz Carrasco, organized the Beneficencia Cubana, for benevolent and charitable work among the poor of their nationality.

In December, 1910, Mrs. Blanca Ferriol de Perez, Mrs. Carlotta Cenarro de Alayeto, Mrs. Maria Gustens, Mrs. Maria Manas de Betancourt, Mrs. Esperanza La Fe, Mrs. Felicia Rodriguez de Rueda, the Misses Caridad Rodriguez, Maria Escalante, Palmenia Hernandez, Maria L. Carrasco, Leopoldina Elizarde, and Ignacia and Angelica Fernandez, conceived the idea of establishing an hospital where the indigent of all nationalities could have the benefit of the best medical care and attention.

To this end they worked diligently for near two years, and on October 10, 1911, the Casa del Pobre, Mercedes hospital was dedicated.

It is situated on the corner of Division street and Salt Pond road, in the former residence of Mr. E. H. Gato, who generously gave it free of rent for a term of years. It is named Mercedes in honor of Mr. Gato's wife.

To Dr. Joseph N. Fogarty is due much credit for the early establishment of this hospital. He contributed liberally in cash; donated all the instruments and equipment for the operating room, and furnished and maintains a room. He is director of the institution, which he visits daily, besides giving, in his turn, his professional services for a month.

Messrs. Pedro Rueda, Benito Betancourt and Delegacion Canaria also furnished rooms in the hospital.

CHAPTER XXVI

FIRE DEPARTMENT AND FIRES

IN OCTOBER, 1834, the first fire department was organized in Key West, and called the LaFayette Fire Department. Mr. Thomas A. Townsend was president; Mr. Asa F. Tift, vice-president; Mr. Joseph A. Thouron, secretary, and Mr. Wm. H. Shaw, treasurer. Messrs. Stephen R. Mallory and Asa F. Tift were members of the election committee.

In January, 1835, a small fire occurred in an out-building in Judge Webb's yard but the fire department failed to put in an appearance. Mr. Mallory then called a meeting to reorganize the company. The meeting was held, at which about twenty-five joined, and Mr. Thouron was made foreman.

A hand engine was purchased by public subscription, but except for parades was seldom used, and was uncared for. In 1843, when the large wooden warehouse of Fielding A. Browne, on the southwest side of Simonton street, below Front street, was destroyed by fire, the engine was brought upon the scene but proved unfit for use, and after the fire the citizens carried it to the end of the wharf and hurled it into the sea.

Key West has been particularly free from great fires, having had only two disastrous ones. In each instance there was no fire engine in the city, otherwise the fires would not have spread beyond the blocks in which they originated.

On the 16th of May, 1859, the first large fire occurred. It began in a warehouse owned by Mr. L. M. Shaefer, whom it was generally believed purposely set fire to the building. It began on Front street, near the corner of Duval, and in the two blocks bounded by Front, Greene, Simonton and Whitehead streets, every house except two was destroyed. No organized body of firemen existed in the city at the time and no fire apparatus adequate for the occasion was on hand. The extensive warehouse and stores of O'Hara & Wells, on Front street, between Simonton and Duval streets; the stores of Fontane & Weaver, P. A. Gandolfo and C. & E. Howe, were among the buildings destroyed.

To Mr. Henry Mulrennon belongs great credit for the preservation of the remaining portion of the city. He procured a keg of gunpowder from Fort Taylor, and entering his own house at the corner of Fitzpatrick and Greene streets, with the fire raging around him, put the keg of powder in place, laid a train, and blew up the house, thus preventing the fire from going any farther.

The *Key of the Gulf*, in an editorial headed "One Year Since," thus describes conditions before and after the fire:

"Wednesday, the 16th instant, was the anniversary day of the great fire in our city. Before that time we were a thriving people; Front street, running parallel to our beautiful harbor, was the scene of busy life; on both sides, built up with large and imposing stores and warehouses, which were filled with expensive stocks of merchandise, arrayed in the most alluring styles of display, while the street itself was peopled with the passing throng, pressing each other, and moved by the impulse of progressive enterprise.

"Then came the fire. The lurid flames spread in serried lines along housetops, streamed their lambent blazes wide from street to street, and rolled their smoky banners all along the sky, for a twelve hours' time, and our city fell. Its fairest proportions were laid level with the earth, and existed only in the smoking banks of ashes which covered all the streets. And, sad to tell, this fearful destruction is supposed to have been the work of an incendiary, who, perhaps, may be even now in our city, with the terrors of an outraged law, like the sword of Damocles, to disturb his midnight dreams while lying upon his downy pillow.

"But with the pliant energies of an elastic genius our people are recovering rapidly. They were 'not broken as the staff, but bent only as the bow.' Soon the recuperative genius of a mercantile community began to repeople the 'burnt district,' and now it is only necessary to visit the splendid edifices which occupy Front and Duval streets, to induce one to come at once to the opinion that the fire was an actual benefit, rather than a permanent injury to our city. Messrs. C. & E. Howe, Wall & Pinckney, James C. Clapp, Carey, Ware & Mulrennon, J. F. Packer, and William A. Russell have each erected elegant structures (the latter a large hotel), which are not only an ornamental embellishment to our city, but give to it that air of permanency and durability, which is the strongest assurance, and the most confident promise of an advancing and growing future which we could possibly have.

"Hon. James Filor has erected a two-story fireproof brick warehouse, and Carey, Ware & Mulrennon have laid the foundation for a three-story building to be finished in the best style of architecture, while in other portions of the town many handsome dwelling houses are being built."

About two o'clock in the morning of April 1, 1886, San Carlos Hall, on Duval street, near the corner of Fleming, was discovered to be on fire. The fire company turned out promptly but the steam fire engine, which had been in use in Key West for about ten years, had been sent to New York for repairs, and there was only a small hand engine with which to fight the fire.

It spread to the buildings of Mrs. Claude Babcock and Mr. John W. Sawyer on the corner of Fleming and Duval streets, and they were soon destroyed. It burned to Whitehead street, where it was stopped by Jackson Square. Meantime it had crossed Duval street, and a small building belonging to the Crusoe estate took fire. It was soon beyond all possibility of control and for twelve hours the fire raged.

The northwest half of the block on Fleming street, between Duval and Bahama streets, was completely destroyed. The fire burned in a northeasterly direction and extended to the corner of Caroline and Elizabeth streets. It then swept along the water front to the naval station, destroying every house northeast of Greene, between Simonton and Whitehead streets, save two.

The loss of property, including Havana tobacco in the United States bonded warehouse, was estimated at over two million dollars, with only about fifty thousand dollars insurance.

A call for aid was sent out, and thirty or forty thousand dollars received, together with a quantity of provisions and clothing. Mayor James G. Jones called a meeting of the citizens, and requested them to appoint a committee to take charge of and expend the funds. An organization was perfected with a finance and a relief committee, who went about the work in a systematic manner, investigating and passing upon all claims for relief. Hon. George W. Allen was chairman of one committee, and Mr. Martin L. Hellings of the other. The relief committee was quite a large one, and for some time they held daily meetings. They received reports of those appointed to investigate claims for relief, and passed upon the claims, which were then referred to the finance committee for further investigation, and upon their being satisfied of the justness thereof, financial relief was granted.

The distribution of food and clothing was done speedily and thoroughly. The work of these committees met with the highest approval of the citizens, and they received general praise from the entire community.

Profiting by this severe lesson, the city bought two powerful steam fire engines, and the county one. Later the city bought another, and these with a new chemical engine, hook and ladder, and hose outfit, comprise a most efficient fire equipment. Since 1886 we have had no serious fires, and it is rare that one spreads beyond the place where it originates.

In 1888 a system of water works for fire purposes was installed, using salt water which is heavier and better adapted than fresh water for extinguishing fires. This accounts largely for the ease with which fires are kept from spreading. In 1910 two new boilers of one hundred horse power each, were installed for pumping water into the stand pipe. Six thousand dollars has just been appropriated to extend the mains to the county road.

Few small places have a more efficient fire department than Key West. It is largely a volunteer one; only the drivers and engineers being salaried men. The companies are well drilled, and on an alarm of fire a full complement is always on hand, nearly all of whom make large personal sacrifices in their efforts to prevent the destruction of property.

For a great many years Key West was without an active fire department, and it remained for Mr. A. H. Dorsett, in 1875, to organize the first efficient one. As chief of the fire department he brought the companies up to a high state of perfection. In 1878 Mr. B. H. F. Bowers was made chief, and held the position until 1890, when he was succeeded by Mr. Hiram G. Fulford, the present chief.

CHAPTER XXVII

EARLY in 1877 a volunteer military company with eighty members, called the Key West Rifles, was organized. Harry W. Hill was the first captain. It was never a crack company on dress parade, but it answered two riot calls (that is, *most* of the company did). The most serious of these was when a mob of about fifteen hundred congregated at the factory of Mr. Francisco Marero, threatening his life. Mr. Marero was suspected of having shot and killed an agitator a few nights before. To appease the mob he was taken to jail, but later in the day the authorities decided to defy them, and take him from the jail and escort him to his apartments in his factory, then at the foot of Duval street. Threats were made that if this were done, he would be shot down in the street, or taken from his home at night and lynched. The military company was called out, and escorted Mr. Marero to his home, and did guard duty for twenty-four hours, until wiser heads calmed the mob, and the incident was closed. The members of the company had been notified to assemble upon the ringing of the fire bell, and about noon on Sunday the town was startled by the violent ringing, calling the company together. Most of the members responded promptly, but it was said that one of the company was met running in an opposite direction, and when asked where he was bound, replied he was going for his tobacco. He was last heard of at the Salt Ponds.

The fire of 1886 destroyed all the equipment, and the company was never reorganized.

On the ninth day of May, 1888, the Island City Guards, a local military company, was organized with thirty-two members. Mr. F. C. Brossier was captain, Mr. Charles S. Williams, first lieutenant, and Mr. George L. Babcock, second lieutenant. On the reorganization of the Florida militia this company became Company I, Second Regiment of Infantry, Florida State Troops, and is now part of the National Guard of Florida.

The captains who succeeded Captain Brossier were Mr. Henry L. Roberts, Mr. Samuel J. Wolfe, Mr. Louis Louis and Mr. Joseph R. Stirrup, who at present commands the company.

NAVAL MILITIA

In 1910 a battalion of naval militia was organized with Mr. N. B. Rhodes as lieutenant commander. It was the first battalion of naval militia organized in Florida. It holds regular drills and has reached a fair state of efficiency.

CHAPTER XXVIII

HURRICANES

THE greatest authority on West Indian hurricanes was Rev. Benito Vines, a Jesuit priest, who was director of the magnetic and meteorological observatory of Belin College, Havana, Cuba. The accuracy of his prognostications is remarkable because he worked with few, if any, of the modern instruments for observing atmospheric conditions. So accurate was he, however, that his warnings of the approach of a hurricane —the signs of which no one else could see—were regarded by the people as supernatural predictions. Mr. E. B. Garriott, professor of Meteorology, in 1900 published a paper on West Indian hurricanes which, on the recommendation of Mr. Willis M. Moore, chief of the United States Weather Bureau, was issued as a bulletin of that bureau. Professor Garriott quotes largely from Father Vines, whose data concerning these storms extended as far back as 1493.

Key West, although in the zone of West Indian cyclones, has rarely been visited by one of first intensity. Father Vines says that cyclones in August have never passed near Havana, and that October cyclones rarely ever passed near Puerto Rico. He says: "The ecclesiastical authorities from time immemorial wisely ordained that priests in Puerto Rico should recite the prayer *Ad Repellendat Tempestates* during the months of August and September, but not in October, and that in Cuba it should be recited in September and October, but not in August. The ecclesiastical authorities knew from experience that the cyclones of September and October are much to be feared in the vicinity of Cuba, but that those of August were not of a nature to cause apprehension."

The history of the three severe cyclones that struck Key West supports this theory. One occurred on October 11, 1846, one on October 11, 1909, and one October 17, 1910.

The first hurricane of any intensity of which there is any record, occurred on the 15th, 16th and 17th of September A. D. 1835. The *Enquirer*, a newspaper published in Key West at that time, in describing it says: "We remember seeing sometime since the prognostications of an officer in the English army or navy who predicted that the visit of Halley's comet now expected, would cause the year 1835 to be remarkable for the frequency of gales and other atmospheric phenomena, and whether it may be considered a strange coincidence or not, we cannot say, but there has certainly been an undue number of severe storms, tornadoes, gales, etc., for the last few years."

In 1909 Halley's comet again visited us, and in 1909 and 1910 two of the severest hurricanes ever experienced, struck the island.

In the hurricane of 1835 the light-ship Florida, stationed near Carysfort Reef, was severely damaged, the wooden covering to her deck was partly demolished, her lanterns stove in, and her boats blown away. Twelve or fourteen large vessels were stranded on the reefs near Key West, and most of our wrecking vessels suffered much damage. An article from the pen of Mr. Stephen R. Mallory tells of the damage done to our home craft, and the courage which their masters and crews showed in the face of their losses. He says: "In considering the extent and violence of the late gale, the severest with which our coast was ever visited, we dwell with satisfaction upon the courage of our people for the preservation of lives and property. In the ordinary course of maritime pursuits the loss of all the masts of a vessel, her boats, anchors, cables, etc., is considered an event of some consequence, and generally claims most of the time and undivided attention of her crew to repair damages, but the rapidity and apparent ease with which much greater disasters were overcome by the wreckers, when upon their celerity depended the fate and property of the shipwrecked, offers us another proof of what man may accomplish when all his energies are brought into action, stimulated by powerful motives and under the guidance of sound judgment. One of the schooners was driven by a gale upon a bank, which, when the wind had somewhat abated, was left high and dry, but her persevering master with eleven men actually cut a canal two hundred yards long, and in twenty-four hours after it was commenced the ship was again at sea and obtained a cargo. Another one lost both her masts, all her anchors, cables, boats and rigging, but the conviction that he had nothing else to lose seems to have aroused her stout-hearted master to greater exertion, and with the aid of two small jury-masts, and an old gun for an anchor, he succeeded in reaching a wreck and relieving her of a large and valuable cargo. Such exertions are worthy of commendation, and verily they will meet with their reward."

At that time there were not over seven or eight hundred people in Key West. They had no telegraphic communication with the outside world, and the mails were about a month apart.

Practically the same conditions prevailed after the hurricane of 1846, and in each instance our people, with prayers to God, but dependence on their own exertions, rallied from the effects of these storms without financial assistance from the outside.

Key West had its severest hurricane in 1846. Colonel Maloney in his history says it was "the most destructive of any that had ever visited these latitudes within the memory of man."

On Saturday, October 9th, there were light squalls of wind

and rain which increased during the night, and on Sunday the wind was blowing fiercely and the rain was almost constant. Sunday night it was blowing a very severe gale, but it was not until Monday morning that the hurricane reached its intensity. It blew all day from the northeast. Trees were uprooted, fences blown down, and houses unroofed. All of the families residing in that part of the city northwest of Eaton street abandoned their homes and sought refuge on higher parts of the island, in the neighborhood of Southard and Simonton streets, which was then thickly wooded. The light-house, which stood on the point where the large sand battery now stands, was washed away and seven persons lost their lives. The residence of Mr. William Curry, which stood near the corner of Caroline and William streets, was washed from its pillars and floated to sea. It carried away with it an old colored servant whose body was never recovered.

Again our people pluckily went to work to overcome their misfortunes. They asked no outside help, and to quote again from Colonel Maloney: "They did not stop to shed tears over their misfortunes. The sun rose the morning after the storm to behold active limbs and stout hearts clearing the ground of the debris, and the waning moon of the next night shone upon the bright hammer of the mechanic as he drove firmly home the nails in the reconstruction of their homes and business houses."

The trees that had been blown down were replanted, and to the energy and indomitable will of those old citizens did we owe the beautiful cocoanut palms and Australian pines that once beckoned a welcome to the coming guest, and waved a farewell to the departing. Most of these were destroyed in the hurricanes of October, 1909 and 1910, and the next generation will best be able to answer the question: How does the new Key West compare with the old?

On October 19 and 20, 1876, another hurricane of minor intensity visited Key West. At one a. m., on the 19th, the barometer stood at 29.55, and continued to fall, until at eight p. m. it registered 28.73. The wind, which reached a velocity of only sixty-six miles an hour, blew from northeast to east until about nine o'clock, the night of the 19th, when it died down to a calm which lasted nearly an hour. It then suddenly sprang up from the southwest, and blew with great intensity until about one o'clock in the morning, when it began to abate. The City of Houston, one of the Mallory steamers, went over the reef without striking, and grounded on the shoals near Saddle Bunches, about twelve miles from Key West.

The damage to the city was slight. A few tin roofs were torn off, fences blown down, and trees uprooted, but again our people pluckily replanted trees and repaired their property, and the effect was soon forgotten.

In September, 1894, the center of another severe hurricane passed over Key West, but the damage was slight.

A number of hurricanes of minor intensity have passed over and near Key West, but it was not until 1909 that a hurricane of first intensity again visited us.

For several days the weather had been threatening, but not until Sunday night did the barometer begin to fall sufficiently to indicate the proximity of a hurricane. This accounts for a great deal of the loss to shipping, as our people had gone to their beds with no warning, and boats were lying at their usual moorings and not secured for a hurricane.

At six a. m., the 11th, the barometer stood at 29.42 and fell rapidly until eleven-thirty a. m. when it reached the minimum, 28.42. During Sunday night the wind was moderate, at about sixteen miles, but at six a. m., Monday, it suddenly increased to a gale and by nine a. m. had reached hurricane force. The wind blew steadily at about seventy-five miles per hour, but in the gusts which are characteristic of West Indian cyclones, it reached a velocity of over one hundred miles. The gusts increased in frequency and force until about noon, when the wind went to the northwest and began to moderate, and by two p. m. the storm was over. The wind blew first from southeast, then went to northeast, at which point we were nearest the center of the storm, which, however, did not pass over Key West.

When the storm first broke over Key West it was traveling north, but before the center reached here it veered to the northeast, which accounts for the three directions of the wind. The rainfall was unprecedented, 8.12 inches in five hours. There were only two lives lost; Frank Gray, a young photographer, who was drowned while trying to save his boat, and Andrew Cooper, second mate on the schooner Medford, who was struck on the head by the falling of the coal hoist at the naval station.

The buildings wholly destroyed were the cigar factories of The Ruy Lopez Company; The Martinez Company; George W. Nichols & Company and Aurelia Torres; St. Paul's Episcopal Church, Sparks Chapel, English Wesleyan Church, Bethel A. M. E. Church, No. 1 Engine Room, Wolfson's building, at the corner of Simonton and Greene streets, Markovitz' five and ten cent store; the city bell tower on Division street, condensing plant and pumping station at the United States army post, and many small structures. Nearly all sheet metal roofs were blown off. Buildings with wooden shingles weathered the storm best, and those with metal shingles next.

The Elks home was blown from its foundations and damaged to the extent of several thousand dollars. The United States army post sustained some damage, the principal injury being the loss of the distilling plant. Every dock in the city was badly damaged, several being almost totally destroyed. Craft of every kind were jammed together or sunken along the water front. Many boats broke from their moorings and went crashing into other boats and docks.

At William Curry's Sons Company the dock was destroyed

and the smokestacks of the ice plant carried away. The schooner Magnolia sunk at the dock.

The Mallory warehouse was badly damaged and much merchandise ruined. The dock was not injured, and the Mallory steamship Lampassas weathered the storm at the dock, and escaped uninjured.

At Taylor's dock the coal runs and warehouses were badly damaged and two launches were lost. The schooner Frontenac, loaded with gravel, dragged her anchor and went ashore on the banks.

The coal conveyors at the naval station broke loose, and plunged through the dock.

The pile driver and plant of the Penn Bridge Company was ruined. The four masted schooner George W. Wilson, loaded with coal, rode out the storm at her anchorage. The schooner Medford, Captain Richardson, loaded with two thousand tons of sand and gravel for the Penn Bridge Company broke away from her moorings at the government wharf and was blown about five miles towards Sand Key, where she sank. The crew abandoned the schooner and were brought in by the Massasoit, having clung to the rigging all night.

The revenue cutter Forward was at the wharf when the barometer began to fall, and her commander, Captain Dodge, undertook to get her into Hurricane harbor. He dropped two anchors, but the cables snapped as soon as they hove taut, and she was blown on one of the banks across from the city, where she stayed nearly a month until the sand was dug out around her, and she was floated into deep water.

HURRICANE 1910

In roulette playing there is what gamblers call a "repeater" —that is that a certain number will come twice in succession. The chances against it are about 1,296 to 1. The chances against a "repeater" of a hurricane of first intensity, while not so great as against one in roulette, are sufficiently so to make the occurrence one of extraordinary import. In 1910 Key West got a "repeater."

For a week prior to October 17th the weather had been threatening, with heavy squalls and rains. Cautionary advice was issued the morning of the 13th by the United States weather bureau, and later in the day storm warnings were issued for South Florida. On the morning of the 14th the storm warnings were changed to hurricane.

On the 15th it was reported that the hurricane, which had been to the south of Cuba, had passed westward through the Yucatan passage. The weather continued threatening, however, and experienced old sailors who had seen many hurricanes, shook their heads in doubt of the weather bureau's statements and did not relax their preparations to meet the blow, should it come.

Sunday, the 16th, was partly clear with light winds. The weather bureau reports that night were quieting and our people went to bed early in fancied security. About ten o'clock the barometer began to fall rapidly and Weather Observer C. J. Doherty sent out bulletins advisory of the rapid approach of the storm.

Northeast winds varying in velocity from thirty to fifty miles with gusts of sixty miles an hour prevailed from midnight to eight a. m. of the 17th, and shifted to the southeast after eight a. m. and increased in velocity from forty-eight to eighty miles an hour. At twelve twenty-five p. m. the wires to the anemometer cups at the weather observer's office were torn down, when the wind had a velocity of seventy-two miles an hour. From three to four p. m. the wind was to the south, and then shifted to the southwest and continued steady on the 17th. The wind reached its greatest force between two-thirty and four-thirty p. m., on the 17th, when it was estimated at over ninety miles an hour, and gusts of one hundred and ten miles an hour were frequent. The wind lessened slightly after five p. m. until three a. m., on the 18th, with a velocity of over sixty miles an hour, after which it gradually diminished. The storm lasted thirty hours. The tide and sea swell were unusually high. At seven a. m. of the 17th the waves were dashing over the southern and western sections of the island.

The rainfall during the storm was estimated at 3.89 inches up to eight p. m. on the 17th. There was no way of knowing exactly, however, as the rain gauge at the observer's office was carried out to sea at one-fifty p. m. The lowest barometer reading was 28.47 at two-thirty p. m. Six miles away, at Sand Key Light the barometer dropped to 28.40, the lowest ever recorded in the United States.

The three-story concrete factory of the Havana-American Company, which had been damaged in the hurricane of 1909, was entirely destroyed. The power plant of the Key West Electric Company was damaged to the extent of about fifty thousand dollars. The United Wireless station was completely destroyed. Seven hundred feet of a new concrete dock, which was being built by the War Department at Fort Taylor was destroyed. The residences of Mr. M. B. Darnall and Mr. N. B. Rhoads, at the southeast end of Duval street, were washed from their pillars and floated about fifteen feet into South street. La Brisa, the pleasure pavilion of the Key West Electric Company at the southeast end of Simonton street, was washed from its pillars and dashed to pieces. The Olivette and the Miami lay at the P. & O. S. S. company dock, and rode through the storm uninjured.

CHAPTER XXIX

N O OCCUPATION is less understood or has been more misrepresented than that of the wreckers of Key West. Mr. Audubon, the great ornithologist, who visited Key West in 1835, thus describes them:

"Long before I reached the lovely islets which border the southeastern shores of the Floridas, the accounts I had heard of 'the wreckers' had deeply prejudiced me against them. Often had I been informed of the cruel and cowardly methods which it was alleged they employed to allure vessels of all nations to the dreaded reefs, that they might plunder their cargoes, and rob their crews and passengers of their effects. I, therefore, could have little desire to meet with such men under any circumstances, much less to become liable to their aid; and with the name of wreckers there were associated in my mind ideas of piratical depredation, barbarous usage, and even murder.

"One fair afternoon, while I was standing on the polished deck of the United States revenue cutter, Marion, a sail hove in sight, bearing in an opposite course, and 'close-hauled' to the wind. The gentle rake of her masts, as she rocked to and fro in the breeze, brought to my mind the wavings of the reeds on the fertile banks of the Mississippi. By-and-by the vessel, altering her course, approached us. The Marion, like a sea-bird, with extended wings, swept through the waters, gently inclining to either side, while the unknown vessel leaped as it were from wave to wave, like a dolphin in eager pursuit of his prey. In a short time, we were gliding side by side, and the commander of the strange schooner saluted our captain who promptly returned the compliment. What a beautiful vessel we all thought; how trim, how clean-rigged, and how well-manned! She swims like a duck; and now with a broad sheer off, she makes for the reefs, a few miles under our lee. There, in that narrow passage, well known to her commander, she rolls, tumbles and dances, like a giddy thing, her copper sheathing now gleaming, and again disappearing under the waves. But the passage is thrid, and now hauling on the wind, she resumes her former course, and gradually recedes from view. Reader, it was a Florida wrecker!

"The duties of the Marion having been performed, intimation of our intended departure reached the wreckers. An invitation was sent to me to go and see them on board their vessels, which I accepted. Their object on this occasion was to present me with some superb corals, shells, live turtles of the hawk-billed species, and a great quantity of eggs. Not a 'picayune' would they receive in return, but putting some letters in my hands, requested me to 'be so good as put them in the mail at Charleston,' and with sincere regret, and a good portion of friendship, I bade these excellent fellows adieu. How different thought I, is often the knowledge of things acquired by personal observation from that obtained by report!"

Those were happy, insouciant days! The wrecker's life, though full of danger and hard toil at times, was jolly and care-free. Their crafts were well victualed and apparelled, and they would lie all night in safe anchorage, but be under way at daylight to cruise along the reef, on the lookout for vessels in distress. When one was found, as was an almost daily occurrence, it was "all hands to work," night and day to relieve the ship, before heavy weather would drive her further on the reef, or cause her to bilge. When that catastrophe occurred, the cargo was saved by men working half the time in water up to their middles, and afterwards by diving. This did not mean going down in a diving suit through which the water could not penetrate, but skin-diving, and generally in water impregnated with the component parts of the cargo; sugar perhaps, mayhap guano.

Prior to the treaty which ceded Florida to the United States salvors from the Bahamas and Cuba would rescue vessels and cargoes from the Florida Reefs, and take them to Nassau and Havana for adjudication of their salvage claims. To prevent this congress on March 3, 1825, passed a law prescribing that all property of any description whatsoever, that should be taken from any wreck in these seas, or from any keys and shoals within the jurisdiction of the United States, on the coast of Florida, should be brought to some port of entry within the jurisdiction of the United States. The act also provided that any vessel which should carry any wrecked property to any foreign port should be forfeited, one moiety of all forfeitures to go to the informer, and the other to the United States. On February 23, 1847, congress further regulated the business of wrecking by providing that no vessel, or the master thereof, should be engaged in wrecking on the coast of Florida, without license from the judge of the district court in the district of Florida, and that before issuing such license the judge should be satisfied that the vessel was seaworthy, and properly and sufficiently equipped for the business of saving property shipwrecked and in distress; and that the master thereof was trustworthy, and innocent of any fraud or misconduct in relation to any property shipwrecked or saved on the coast. This is the only district in the United States where this requirement obtains.

Prior to the establishment of the superior court at Key West, salvages were frequently settled by arbitration and the salvors paid in kind. Their portion and usually the residue of the cargo were sold here.

The richest cargoes of the world, laces, silks, wines, silverware—in fact everything that the commerce of the world afforded—reached Key West in this way. Speculators with capital and underwriters' agents came here to attend the sales, some of whom seeing the opportunity for making money, became residents of Key West.

The wrecks not only threw on these shores rich cargoes, but many valuable citizens were thus furnished to Key West. Several of our prominent families owe their residence here to the fact that their ancestors were wrecked on the Florida Reef. In fact, Key West probably owes its foundation as an American colony to such a circumstance. In 1818 Mr. John Whitehead was shipwrecked in the Bahamas, and on the voyage back to his home, in Mobile, the ship he had taken passage on lay at anchor for several days off Key West. He thus acquired a knowledge of its excellent harbor and other advantages, and it is probable that when he purchased the island from Salas in Havana in 1819, he went there to meet him for that purpose.

One of the earliest settlers, afterwards a large land owner and prominent business man, whose residence in Key West was due to this circumstance, was Mr. Fielding A. Browne. His brother had gone from Virginia to Mexico, and there had been killed. Mr. Browne was on a ship, bound to New Orleans, on his way to Mexico to look after his brother's estate, and was wrecked at Key West, and remained here. In 1830, when his nephew, Mr. Joseph Beverly Browne, was graduated from William and Mary College, he sent for him to come to Key West and go in business with him. Mr. William H. Wall, Mr. ————— Wells, and many of the older citizens were jettisoned on the shores of Key West.

Hon. Peter T. Knight and Hon. George W. Reynolds owe their residence here to the fact that their mothers, who were from the German side of the river Rhine, were wrecked at Key West on their way to New Orleans. Others were Mr. James Filor, Mr. Nicholas Smith, Captain Joseph G. Lester and Mr. James G. Jones.

From December, 1824 to 1825, $293,353.00 worth of wrecked property was sold here, and it is stated on the highest authority that only in one instance did it fail to bring its value, and generally it brought more than was expected. Buyers from Havana usually attended sales of wrecked property, and in the instances of very large cargoes, buyers came from Mobile, Charleston and frequently from New York. In 1824 and 1825 over one hundred thousand dollars was paid to the United States government for duties on wrecked property.

Of the treatment accorded by the Key West wreckers to persons stranded on the Florida Reefs, a passenger on the ship Amulet, that was wrecked here in March, 1831, wrote:

"KEY WEST, March 25, 1831.
"To the Editors:

"GENTLEMEN:—Permit me, through the medium of your paper, to tender my most sincere thanks to Captains Smith and Place, commanding the sloops Splendid and Hydes Ally, for the kind and gentlemanly treatment I received from their hands, whilst on board their vessels. Should it ever be my lot to be cast away again, I hope I may be fortunate enough to fall into the hands of those who have as much honor and fine feelings as the above-named captains.

"JOHN P. DECATUR.
"Passenger on Board Amulet."

After the establishment of the United States court, nearly every salvage case was tried in that tribunal and the conduct of the salvors closely scrutinized. Judge James Webb, in a judicial deliverance from the bench, thus commends the wreckers:

"I am gratified," said the judge, "with the opportunity of expressing on this, as I have done on other occasions, my entire conviction that the course pursued by the individuals now engaged in this occupation on the coast of Florida is as exemplary in regard to the rights of others as that of any other class of this or other communities. They are the instruments of saving an immense amount of property, which without their exertions would be wholly lost, and so far as their conduct in rendering these services has come to the knowledge of this court (and it is often the subject of minute and critical examination) it has, but with few exceptions, been found correct, meritorious and praiseworthy."

How all-absorbing wrecking was in those days may be seen from the following incident. The county court house in Jackson Square was the common place of worship for all denominations. On one occasion Brother Eagan (Squire Eagan as he was called), a good old Methodist, was holding services there, and from his position on the rostrum, which served as a pulpit, he had a clear view of the ocean, whence he saw a brig beating down the gulf dangerously near the Sambos. He saw her miss stays, and drift towards the reef. With cautious eye he watched her until he was certain that she was fast ashore, and then began making his plans. Brother Eagan was the owner and master of a wrecking vessel. The rules of wrecking established by the United States court give the master of the first vessel to reach a ship in distress the right to have charge of the salvage operations, for which he receives extra compensation. He is called the wrecking master.

Brother Eagan knew if he announced from the pulpit that there was a "wreck ashore" his congregation would all get out of the church ahead of him, and the chances were that someone would reach the wreck before him.

His text was from the Ninth Chapter, I Corinthians,

twenty-fourth verse: "Know ye not that they which run in a race run all, but one receiveth the prize? So run, that ye may obtain."

Warming to his subject he came down from the pulpit and exhorted his hearers to equip themselves for the great race for the prize of eternal salvation. Down the aisle he strode, hammering his text into the congregation, with forceful gesture and apt illustration. When he reached the door, he startled his hearers with the cry "Wreck ashore! Now we will all run a race and see who receiveth the prize," and dashed down the steps, and out into the street, with the entire male portion of the congregation at his heels. He had a good start on them, however, and soon got to his schooner, the Godspeed, and with a crew made up of members of his congregation who had overtaken him, set sail and reached the wreck first, and became the wrecking master.

This incident was typical. The cry of "Wreck a-s-h-o-r-e," taken up and repeated, with the last syllable drawn out in a long monotone, was a familiar sound in old Key West, and would empty a church as promptly as a cry of "fire!" It seemed to electrify the slow moving population, and soon the streets would be full of men running to their vessels, carrying small bundles of clothes—for they knew not whether they would be absent a day or a month—and from every quarter of the city, the cry "Wreck a-s-h-o-r-e" would echo and re-echo.

A more thrilling sight cannot be conceived than that of twenty or thirty sailing craft of from ten to fifty tons starting for a wreck. As if upon a preconcerted signal, sails would be hoisted, and as soon as jib and mainsail were up, moorings would be slipped and vessels got under way, crowding on all the sail they could carry. The sight of these, dashing out of the harbor, with a stiff northeast wind, bunched together in groups of threes and fours, jibing with everything standing, as they swung around the bend in the harbor off the foot of Duval street, was a scene never to be forgotten! No regatta could match it.

In 1835 there were twenty good sized vessels regularly engaged in wrecking, in addition to which there were a few of smaller tonnage.*

Wrecking is no longer the important enterprise it once was, but most of the sailing craft hailing from this port carry wrecking licenses, and are equipped to render salvage services. An average of eight or ten vessels a year are stranded on the reefs, and unless driven ashore by the master for the purpose of getting the insurance, are usually rescued by the Key West salvors.

In the case of the Isaac Allerton the largest individual awards were made, which was due to the fact that most of the cargo—an extremely valuable one—had to be dived for and many of the divers' eyes were seriously injured by the water

_____
*Appendix T.

166

which was impregnated with dyes from dry goods and the many other articles which composed the cargo.

From 1900 to 1910, both inclusive, over two hundred and twenty thousand dollars was awarded to Key West salvors by the United States district court. In addition to this amount, over a hundred thousand dollars has been paid salvors for claims settled out of court.

LIGHT-HOUSES

The history of the building of light-houses on the Florida Reef is so closely linked with that of wrecking that it may best be treated under that subject.

A favorite slander against Key West, which has gained some credence, is that the people opposed the erection of light-houses on the reefs. On August 22, 1835, the *Enquirer*, a newspaper published in Key West, contained an extract from a recommendation of the Governor of the Bahamas, acquainting the House of Assembly that "the British government had acquiesced in their request for the erection of a light-house on Key Sal Bank," and said:

"Lights are required not only on Key Sal Bank, but at several other places in these seas, and we are consequently pleased that the British government is showing a disposition to erect them." After they were built, the *Enquirer* said: "Now that the British government has established light-houses on Abaco and Key Sal Bank, it is the duty of the American government to see whether it has not been guilty of equal or greater neglect. From Carysfort Reef to Key West, a distance of one hundred and twenty miles, there is no light. The light at the former place is a floating light, liable to be destroyed or misplaced by gales as was the case last September. This is not relied on by mariners, and it should be replaced by one of solid masonry and steel, and placed on the inner side of the reef. A light is necessary at each of the following places: Key Tavernier, Indian Key, Loo Key, and one in the intermediate space between the two last named places. We are aware that this measure would be attended with great expense, but no greater than is warranted by the magnitude of the object to be affected."

Fully a column is written showing the benefits to be derived from numerous light-houses on the reef, and urges speedy action by congress.

The government, however, did not begin the erection of the magnificent system of reef lights which extend from Fowey Rocks to Tortugas, until 1852, when Carysfort Reef light was established. The other reef lights and the date of their establishment are: Sand Key, 1853; Sombrero, 1858; Alligator Reef, 1870; Fowey Rocks, 1878; Northwest Passage, 1879; American Shoal, 1880, and Rebecca Shoal in 1886.

A light-house was built on Rebecca Shoal in 1838, but in 1879 another light was established in its place. The Sand Key light, and the light-house on Key West, which were built in the early forties, were destroyed in the hurricane of 1846.

Their distinguishing characteristics are thus described in verse by Mr. Kirk Monroe:

LIGHTS ON THE FLORIDA REEF.

The fixed *white* light of Fowey Rocks,
  And Carysfort's *white flash*,
Both may be seen from the middle
  Of a twenty-three mile dash.
Alligator Reef's *red*, *white* and *white*
  Lies thirty miles away.
Log thirty more, Sombrero *white*
  Points to Honda Bay.
Then comes the Shoals American,
  White flashing through the night,
Just fifteen miles from *white* Key West,
  Twenty from Sand Key's *twinkling white*.
The Marquesas are unlighted;
  But on Rebecca's Shoal,
A *white* and *red* is sighted,
  Warning from wreck and dole.
Sixteen miles to Dry Tortugas
  With a *white* light on the fort,
Three more to the *flash* of Loggerhead,
  And all's clear to a western port.

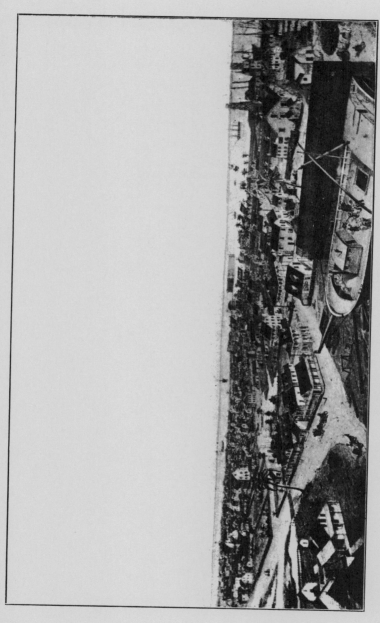

Sketch of Key West Taken in 1855 from Browne & Curry's Cupola.

CHAPTER XXX

POPULATION

IN THE early days of Key West's settlement the population was largely American, with a few Spanish families. South Carolina, Virginia, Connecticut, Alabama, New York and New Jersey furnished their quota.

When congress in 1825 legislated against foreign vessels engaging in salvage operations on this coast, it destroyed a lucrative source of revenue to an element of the Bahama people, and some of them came to Key West to make this the base of their salvage operations. The migration was slow, however, and it was not until a later period that the movement became appreciable.

They were a God-fearing, law-abiding people, industrious and cleanly in their habits, but not progressive, and unfamiliar with the system of American municipal administration. The present generation, however, is imbued with a spirit of progress, which promises well for the future of Key West.

Columbus in one of his letters to Ferdinand and Isabella thus described the inhabitants of the Bahamas: "This country excels all others as far as the day surpasses the night in splendor; the natives love their neighbors as themselves, their conversation is the sweetest imaginable, their faces always smiling, and so gentle and affectionate are they that I swear to your highness that there is not a better people in the world."

This description was written of the aborigines of the Bahamas, most of whom were taken from the islands by Ovando, the governor of Hispaniola, and about forty thousand perished miserably in the mines.

The English, who colonized the Bahamas about the middle of the seventeenth century, intermarried with the few remaining natives, and traces of the attributes narrated by Columbus are yet found among their descendants.

At the outbreak of the Revolutionary War many of the Tories in Georgia and the Carolinas, fearing violence to their persons and property at the hands of the revolutionists, fled to the Bahama Islands. Most of these went thenceto England, but many remained and reared families in the islands. They were a highly cultured and refined people, and it is probably from them that the most intelligent and progressive of the Bahama element are descended. Some of the Curry family have no doubt a common ancestry with Hon. J. L. M. Curry, who was one of the foremost educators of the United States, and at one time minister from the United States to Spain.

The period of the Civil War marks the beginning of the change in the population of Key West. Most of the old settlers were dead, or had removed with their families to their old home States. The cordial relations which existed between the people of the Bahamas and the blockade runners from the south, directed the attention of the former to Key West, and they began to come to our shores in constantly increasing numbers. Thus began the second migration which has so changed the population of Key West, that ninety per cent of the English speaking people are of Bahama ancestry.

In 1868, when the first Cuban revolution of any magnitude began, the vigorous methods adopted by the Spanish government to suppress it, drove many of the Cubans from their homes, who sought protection under the American flag at Key West. The establishment of cigar factories furnished them employment, and since that time there has been a steady influx of Cubans to Key West.

In 1887 a few Jewish peddlers began to ply their trade here, going from house to house with their packs of dry goods, laces, etc. In 1891 the city imposed a license on peddlers of a thousand dollars each, and they gave up that vocation and opened stores. This was the beginning of the Hebrew migration, which has steadily increased, and they now number several hundred.

The first to come to Key West were the Goodman Brothers, Mr. Joe Cupperberg, Mr. A. Zimmdebaum, Mr. A. Louis, Mr. M. Rippa, Mr. Louis Fine, Mr. Abram Wolkowsky, the Wolfsons and the Fischer Brothers. Mr. Louis Fine is agent of the Houston Ice and Brewing Company. Mr. Wolfson has a large up-to-date dry goods store, and Mr. Abram Wolkowsky and Mr. A. Louis are among the principal dry goods and clothing merchants.

The Hebrews take much interest in the improvement and development of the town, and are counted among the most progressive citizens.

As was to be expected of the descendants of a race who preserved through the ages of Greek and Roman pantheism, the belief in one God, their first public act was to organize a Hebrew congregation.

In 1905 they bought the residence of Dr. John B. Maloney, on the corner of Simonton and Southard streets and converted it into a tabernacle. The organization, of which Mr. Joseph Fine was the first president, was known as the Rodof Sholam until recently, when the name was changed to B'nai Zion. The first regularly constituted rabbi was Dr. J. Shapo who officiated for several years.

In 1907 the Young Men's Hebrew Association was organized with Mr. Perry Weinberg as its first president, to which office he was again elected in 1911.

Prior to 1845 the number of negroes in Key West was un-appreciable, being less than two hundred, slave and free. Between 1845 and 1850 they increased to over five hundred and fifty, mostly slaves. This increase was due in part to the govern-ment work on the fortifications, where ready employment was found for slaves at good wages. The general prosperity had some-thing to do with it also, as well-to-do Southern families could not manage with less than six to ten household servants. And such servants! Capable, respectful, neat, trustworthy, affec-tionate, and honest where money was concerned; is it a cause for marvel that family servants were held in the most affectionate regard? And woe betide the outsider who interfered with one of them! The institution of slavery took savages from Africa, and made of them a most docile, capable, respectful, honest and religious people. The contrast between what this institution produced, and what the period since 1865 has brought forth, is a study for the ethnologist.

Among the old colored citizens of the island who came to Key West about the year 1846 were Hannah Brooks and Petrona Alvarez—"Aunt Hannah" and "Aunt Petrona" as they were universally designated. As they were the only trained nurses of that day whose services were for hire, they ministered in almost every family on the island, and won the affection of all.

Other well known and respected colored people were James D. English, who was a member of the Monroe County Board of Public Instruction after the war. Pablo Rogers for many years was the principal colored musician on the island, and no social gathering was complete without the strains of Pablo's fiddle, and the belles and beaus of the old days grew to mature woman-hood and manhood, firm in the belief that neither Strauss nor Sousa could produce such rythmical dance music as Pablo. When he died his mantle fell on "Mony" Sevelle.

The Fish and Clarke families were fine seamstresses, and no New York or London haberdasher or tailor could equal them in making the linen shirts and white duck suits worn by the elegant gentlemen of that day. Descendants of these families are still living in Key West, and maintain the reputation of their ancestors in this respect.

George Garvin, the Roberts family, Peter A. and Samuel Welters, pilots, Jesse and William Williams, William Martinelly, James Rubeo and John Cornell came from St. Augustine, where they or their ancestors resided before the change from the Spanish flag.

Theresa Darley claimed the distinction of being the daughter of an African king, but was deserving of more consideration as the mother of Thomas Darley, who became the minister of the African Methodist church, and quite an able preacher, notwith-standing his limited education. He was always respectful and deferential, and exerted a good influence on his race, at a time when wise leaders were needed to offset the pernicious teachings of the carpet-baggers.

Sandy Cornish, known only as "Uncle Sandy," had the best fruit grove and garden on the island. In his later years he became almost a hermit, and adventurous boys who robbed other groves and gardens with impunity gave Sandy's place a wide berth. When Hon. Salmon P. Chase visited Key West he went to see Sandy, who presented him with the choicest fruits and flowers from his grove and garden. On being asked by Mr. Chase what he could do for him, Sandy requested a picture of his distinguished guest, whereupon Mr. Chase handed him a dollar treasury note on which was a vignette of the distinguished visitor. To "Sandy" is due largely the establishment of the African Methodist church, where he frequently preached, in a voice that could be heard for blocks.

Old "Uncle Tom Romer" came from the Bahamas, and as bumboat-man was known to every officer and man in the navy of the old days. He lived to be something over a hundred years old, and as he added five or six years to his age every few months, he would in a short time have rivalled Methuselah, but his demise at about a hundred and ten deprived him of that distinction.

Most of the St. Augustine colored people were members of the Catholic church, and they and their descendants are still firm in the faith. Some were Episcopalians, and a few Baptists and Methodists, and all attended the white churches, where separate space was set apart for them. The African Methodist Episcopal church, built in 1865, with Wilbur G. Strong as preacher, was the first colored church built in Key West; others have followed, and the Baptists, Wesleyan Methodists and the Episcopalians have churches for the exclusive use of the colored people. The Catholics continue to worship in St. Mary's Star of the Sea.

Hannah, Barry and William Hart and John Delancey were among the first colored people to come from the Bahamas.

Many of the old negro families were free when they came here, but slave or free, the old time Key West colored people belong to a fast vanishing type.

The population of Key West is now composed of forty per cent. white Bahamans, thirty per cent Cubans, twenty per cent negroes, and ten per cent who do not derive their ancestry from any of these sources.

The government census separates the population into whites and blacks, but prior to the 1910 census, which is not yet complete, did not record the place of nativity of the inhabitants.

POPULATION OF KEY WEST BY DECADES FROM 1830 TO 1910

	White	Free Negro	Slaves	Total
1830	368	83	66	517
1840	516	76	96	688
1850	2,088	126	431	2,645
1860	2,302	160	451	2,913
1870	4,631	1,026	All Other	5,657
1880	6,746	3,132	12	9,890
1890	12,390	5,654	36	18,080
1900	11,526	5,562	26	17,114
1910	14,410	5,515		19,945

CHAPTER XXXI

" *TEMPORA mutantur, et nos in illis mutamur"*—and Key West, too, has changed with the times! The island in the early days had a great many persons among its inhabitants who would have been noticeable in any community. It was a cosmopolitan population; Bahama wreckers and immigrants, small fishermen from Noank and Mystic, Conn., refugees from the mainland, gentlemen from Virginia, Georgia and the Gulf States, business men, commercial adventurers and mechanics from the Northern States, and world wanderers from every portion of the globe, brought to Key West by chance or inclination, and held here by her lotus charms. Englishmen, Bahamans, Irish, Dutch, Swedes, Norwegians, Hindoos, Russians, Italians, Spaniards, Cubans, Canary Islanders, South Americans, Canadians, Scotch, French, shipwrecked sailors, deserters and discharged men from the army, navy and marine corps; men who had knocked about all over the world and developed personalities of their own, which they retained, were indeed a rare aggregation.

One of the first things to impress the visitor to Key West, who expected to find uncouth pioneers at this out-of-the-way place, isolated from the rest of the world and inhabited with less than a thousand persons, was the scrupulous elegance of the dress of its men of affairs. In summer all wore white linen duck of the finest quality, perfectly laundered; during the winter, and always on Sundays and festal occasions, frock coats and silk hats. This particularity in dress was accompanied by a dignity of deportment, and elegance of demeanor, rarely elsewhere found in so small a community, and neglected in the New Key West.

Mr. William H. Wall, a tall, slender, graceful Englishman, with the perfect diction of the cultured men of that nation; Colonel Oliver O'Hara, a giant in height and physique, a ruddy faced Irishman with snow white hair, a voice rich in the music of the Irish brogue, but modulated like the typical Irish gentleman; his partner, Mr. Charles M. Wells, equally tall but slim as a bean pole, soft-voiced and suave; Judge William Marvin, in mind, body and appearance the perfect type of the old statesman and jurist; Mr. Peter Gandolpho, who had sufficient native shrewdness and industry to accumulate a comfortable fortune, but whose knowledge of mathematics was limited, as he himself expressed it, to knowing "If I buy a thing for one dollar and sell it for two dollars, I make one per cent;" Mr. Fielding A. Browne, the typical Virginia gentleman, with the manners and pronunciation which distinguished them; were men to do honor to the most cultured community.

In later years passengers from the Mallory steamships landed, then as now, at the dock then owned by the Tift brothers, Asa and Charles—two brainy, cultured, suave gentlemen of New England origin from Georgia.

Passing from their premises one came first to the general mercantile store of White & Ferguson, situated on the corner of Front street, where there is a vacant lot. Old John White was then one of the notable men of Key West, and one of the wealthiest. Keen eyes, beneath bushy brows, nose projecting like a beak, from above a bushy, rather short grizzled beard, head always drawn down between his shoulders, garbed in clothes that when new—long ago—must have cost at least twelve dollars; he was always found humped up in his store, or being hauled slowly around the streets at a snail's pace in an old buggy drawn by an old horse. He managed a large business, bought real estate, built and rented houses and accumulated a fortune. He commenced his rent-collecting rounds at an early hour, and his morning salutation to dilatory tenants, "You're sleeping on your rent" became a local by-word.

His partner, Mr. George W. Ferguson, tall, lean, with high forehead, acquiline nose, long coat, and equally long gait, was also a person to impress on first appearance.

A little way along Front street was Wall & Company's store, presided over by Mr. Fernando J. Moreno, who was also underwriter's agent. Mr. Moreno was a thorough American, though of foreign descent. Courtly, polite, with distinguished manners, he was to be seen each afternoon taking his constitutional on a pacing pony, out to the bush and South Beach. He was slightly deaf, and carried a silver ear trumpet gracefully suspended from his left arm, which strangers often took for a cornet, and a wag was once known to stop him with the question, "Old man, when are you going to give your concert?" Needless to say the question was not heard, for no man was familiar with Mr. Moreno with impunity. His chief assistant at that time was Mr. William McClintock, afterwards mayor of the city; a large, portly, powerful ex-man-of-war's-man from Philadelphia, who had had among other vicissitudes the experience of going down with the United States steamship Congress when she was sunk by the Merrimac.

Across Duval street was the "Gem" saloon, presided over by "Captain Jack," as its owner George Alderslade was known. He was a man of medium height, but built on the lines of "Tony Weller;" was an Englishman, and once a sailor, and could neither read nor write. It was told of him that on one occasion he picked up an illustrated newspaper which had pictures of some ships, and holding it upside down, exclaimed "There's been a hell of

175

a hurricane somewhere—five ships capsized." He was a man of good judgment, fine mind, and a heart of size proportionate with his body. He was the best yellow fever nurse in Key West, and gave his time freely to those afflicted with that dread disease. His place was a favorite resort of the officers of the navy and army, who met him as an equal, as indeed he was.

Back of his place, near where the P. & O. Steamship Company's approach now is, "Old Man Dixon" had a curio store. He was small, dark, long haired and bearded, shaggy and wild looking. He made it a point to hoist a flag when a steamer was coming in, and fire salutes from a little cannon on holidays or whenever the spirit moved him.

Across from him, where Waite's store now is, was Roger Gordon. He kept a news stand and general store—or he had it—it kept itself! Irish, short, with a large head like a billet of wood, hair close cropped and standing erect, usually with several days' growth of beard over his jaws, he would sit out in front of his door, part of the time asleep in his chair, dressed in shirt, trousers and brogans (soldier) shoes, which latter articles he often dispensed with, no socks, and if a customer wanted anything, he was as likely to say "Go in, boy, and see if you can find what you want," as to get it for him—and perhaps more so. And if a customer worried him too much he would swear at him and run him away. He was a discharged soldier who had made some money while in the service by lending his savings at usury, and after his discharge continued so doing until he accumulated a tidy fortune. One of his peculiar ideas at first was that a debtor's title deed was sufficient security for a loan, as long as the creditor had it locked up in his safe. He learned better!

Across from the "Gem" was the store of Allen Brothers, of whom there were in Key West William S. and George D. William S.*was of medium height, broad, genial, brainy and under military rule had been, as was popularly said, "the best mayor Key West ever had." He had a hearty, impulsive manner, and a geniality that attracted strangers, and made them acquaintances. From his brisk, Rooseveltian manner of butting in, and personally directing or doing things, he won the sobriquet of "Buffalo" Allen. If he saw the peace and dignity of the city disturbed, he would rush in and perform the functions of the police. On one occasion a well known character about town who was frequently too full, but not for utterance, was singing and swearing alternately, when Mr. Allen came along. Failing to quiet him, he took him in custody, and carried him to the "Sweat Box," as the city lockup—the caboose of a wrecked ship, which had been converted into a place of confinement, at the foot of Duval street—was called. By the time he had turned the key on him, the brother of the prisoner, himself a character of those days, came along, and being in his cups, began abusing the mayor for having locked up his brother. It took "Buffalo"

*Appendix U.

Allen but a few minutes to have both of the brothers locked up together, where they remained until they got sober.

Mr. George D. Allen was short, with a large head, usually surmounted by a silk hat, worn tipped back. He was full of energy, with a finger in everything that was going, or at least, comments to make on them. He had been a druggist, clerk of the United States court, merchant, United States marshal, member of the school board that instituted the first public or "free" school, tax collector and warden of St. Paul's church. His speech while voluble, was accompanied by a kind of hesitating pause in the middle of his sentences and accentuated by a peculiar motion of the lower jaw, as if chewing, from which he acquired the nickname "Gum Drops." For many years he was superintendent of the Episcopal Sunday school, where he had a class of probably the most mischievous boys that ever saw the inside of a church. Disorder reigned in his class, and it was the envy of the boys who were afflicted with sterner teachers. A favorite prank of his scholars was to put a lot of tamarind seeds in his silk hat, and when he would put it on, they would scatter with rattling noise over the pews and aisles—to his discomfiture and the boys' happiness. He was a man of great and varied information, good ideas as to every one's business but his own; he was always trotting up and down the streets at something; was always most decidedly in evidence.

He had an old saddle horse, with a peculiar gallop, whose rythmical hoof beats suggested the name of the drugs Mr. Allen usually prescribed for all ailments, which caused the old plug to be nicknamed Calomel-Jalap, a crude reminder of Virgil's *Quadrupedante putrem sonitu quatit ungula campum.*

Mr. W. A. Russell, proprietor of the only hotel in the place, was a tall, handsome man, slightly stooped, with a curly beard, always garbed in a long frock coat and silk hat. He ran his hotel much as Roger Gordon ran his store. It was reported of him that one time, when a guest wanted a "shine" he called out to "Toby" (his factotum Toby Collins was somewhat of a character, too): "Here Toby, here's a d—d fool wants his boots blacked!" And other things were according.

On Front street, opposite Wall & Co.'s, was the Louvre, in which were several clothing stores, barrooms, etc. Its owner was Mr. Henry Mulrennan, a tall, once handsome gentleman, who was born in Paisley, Scotland, of Scotch-Irish ancestry. He came to this country when eleven years old, was a compositor on the *New York Herald,* a volunteer in the Mexican War when only eighteen years old, and came to Key West with his regiment, where he was mustered out and went in business with Mr. E. L. Ware and Mr. Geo. H. Carey. At the commencement of the Civil War he hoisted the secession flag on his building, and sent a written message to Major French, who was in command of Fort Taylor, demanding the surrender of the fort within an hour, or he would come down and capture it. Thereupon

177

Major French, who was his friend, advised him to leave the island, or he would be compelled to make him a prisoner. He then left Key West, joined the Confederate army, was captured running the blockade between Tampa and Havana in 1864, where he was kept imprisoned at Fort La-Fayette, New York harbor, in the same cell with General Roger A. Pryor for seven months after the war ended. He came near being hanged on a charge of having disguised a squad of men as negro contrabands, and enticing the Yankee gunboats in Tampa Bay to send ashore to get them, and when the boats were close in shore, turned loose a masked battery and blew them out of the water. Through the intercession of Fernando Wood, James Gordon Bennett and Robert Bonner, he was finally exonerated and released. On his return to Key West after the war, he was elected mayor, and died February 15, 1872, at the age of forty-four years. A short life to have passed through so many vicissitudes! He was a witty, rollicksome, boisterous person, such as Lever so successfully portrays.

George Carey kept a barroom next his place. He too, wore a silk hat and generally no coat. (Silk hats were common in those days). He was a handsome, ruddy, white bearded Englishman, an ex-sailor, and said to be of a good family; in his cups he was wont to boast that his "ancestors could write on paper without lines on it."

Another roaring Irishman was Jack Gallagher who kept a bar down beyond where the foundry now is. Always happy, always noisy, and sometimes sober, he was prominent among the frequenters of Front street. Pat McKeown, too, was Irish, and a barkeeper. His advent, however, was not until about 1870. He was discharged from the marine corps, and started business with a keg of beer and a jug of whiskey, sleeping at first under his counter, till times mended. Small, sandy, with a large head, Pat was a man of brains, and despite the sprees which he indulged in at stated intervals, he acquired a large property.

An old timer whose career lasted down into modern times, was James G., or Jim Jones. Of medium height, he was strongly built and powerful, with a round head and broad face, large mouth, with white teeth that he was always showing in a broad smile, or gritting in an attack of temper! He was a French Canadian, had been railroad builder, gas plant installer, sailor, shipmaster and had travelled all over the world. He located at last in Key West because his ship was wrecked on the reef near here. In time he was justice of the peace, tax collector, sheriff, mayor, United States marshal, and finished his days as deputy clerk of the United States court and United States commissioner. In his old age he was quieter, but in his early days he was full of vitality, with a new story every time he met one, and a big laugh to accompany its telling; always in good humor until something or some one disagreed with him, when a cyclone succeeded the sunburst! Raving like a maniac, he would grit his teeth, shake his fists, and rising on his toes come down on his heels, and out—Ajax, Ajax! On one occasion while sheriff he got into an altercation with Captain Joe Lester, a shipmaster and pilot, of Scotch ancestry, and no mean antagonist for the most powerful. After some hot words Captain Lester threatened to strike him, and Mr. Jones responded, "When you strike me, you strike the State of Florida." "Well, down goes the State of Florida," said Captain Lester, and down went "Jim Jones."

There were many other Key Westers who became residents, as he did, by being wrecked on the reef. There was old Peter Smith, a Hollander, broad shouldered, powerful, who testified in the United States court to having worked in the hold of a wrecked vessel, at the age of eighty-two. Jack Gaze, an Englishman, small, natty, elegant, no one's enemy but his own, celebrating each trip from the Light by treating everybody, and, if he had any money unspent when his time was up, throwing it away, so if he "got drowned on his passage back, it wouldn't be lost! Some one would have the good of it." Other notables there were. Old man Jaycox, seaman and wrecker, of whom it was told that he could seat a man on each hand, and with arms extended, walk the length of a schooner. "Bull" Weatherford, and Tom Johnson, divers, who were noted for their ability as bare-back divers to go under a vessel, stop a leak, and cut out damaged parts of keel, and bolt on new pieces. It is told of Weatherford that he sculled the Hannah, a six ton schooner, from the Dog Rocks to Key West, during a calm, when Colonel Maloney was with him and anxious to get home!

Captain Jack Buckley, smack fisherman, and incidental wrecker, a lean sailor man such as Cooper used to depict, was also a well known character; and there was "Chief" or Calvin Nedson, the last of the Pequots, who came out from Connecticut as a boy on a fishing smack, and spent the rest of his life at Tortugas; coming to Key West, when he chanced in a wreck, to get his money—and a good time with it! Slender, dark, taciturn, he was known as an expert with the grains and cast net.

The king of the wreckers of that time, however, was "Old Ben Baker". He owned and lived in the large two-story house at the corner of Whitehead and Caroline streets, diagonally across from the Stone building, where the United States court tried his salvage cases. He also owned a plantation on Key Largo, where he raised pineapples, in the intervals between wrecking in his fourteen-ton schooner the Rapid. Tall, gaunt, shrill-voiced, hook-nosed, hawk-eyed, he was in those days nearly always master wrecker at every wreck upon the reef.

In later years Sylvanus Pinder succeeded to his mantle. Large, robust, handsome, jolly, the pride of "up-town", perhaps with the greatest personal following of any man in the third ward.

Old Captain Geiger must not be overlooked, a master wrecker and the most skilful of pilots, in his later years he pass-

ed most of his time up in his "buffalo"—as he called his cupola—
with his glass, watching passing vessels, or down along the beach,
superintending his pet schooner, the "Nonpareil" in which he
claimed to have beaten up Nassau harbor under jib alone "to
show the Conchs what an American vessel could do".   Dutch
built, portly, large blue eyes and thin white hair, he was a relic
of older than old times. It was said that as a boy he was captured by pirates, but he would not talk of that experience. He was
pilot for Commodore Porter, and for all naval vessels since 1830,
until age and infirmity compelled him to stop on shore. He
was best known from his reputation as being able to surpass
Mrs. Malaprop, in the use of the vernacular, so that a "Geiger-
ism" when mentioned needed no explanation. A sad commentary
on public opinion, that in his last days, a man of sterling character,
adventurous life, and even heroic deeds, should be known to
and by later generations, only by reason of a trifling deficiency,
and the exploitation of the same!

Old Nicholas Smith, "Long Smith," as he was called, from
his great height, was also a man who wore a tall hat. He was a
Swede and owned the Stone building, the ground floor at one
time occupied, by W. D. Cash, as a grocery store, with Jerry
Fogarty as clerk, and the second and third stories by the United
States court which paid him twelve hundred dollars a year rent.
It is said he never cashed his government checks, but had them
all when he died. He was over six feet in height, with white
hair, and a nose that was large, pendulous and inflamed. He
lived in a back room on the ground floor, cooking for himself
and living a hermit's life. At times after protracted drinking
bouts with himself, he would get to imagining things, and go
hunting over his building to find who was trying to ruin it.

Fred Filer was another unique specimen of former days.
Broad, fat and Dutchy, and hardly able to speak English, he
was still a power as a vessel owner and lumber dealer. And there
was Jacob Rain, a Russian, with a little cobbler's store on Duval
street. Hardly ever speaking unless spoken to, but when one
penetrated the crust he was genial, and proved to be an estimable
character. His knowledge of English was not sufficient, however,
to understand all that was meant, and when John Boyle with
Irish wit one day threatened to "beat his brains out with a
sponge" he did not get mad until the next day, when he saw the
implication.

"Old Tinker Bill" was also one who added to the gaiety
of life in those days, especially when "inspired." There are many
who recall when lower Duval and Front streets would resound
with his voice as he sang in stentorian tones, "Home again, home
again from a foreign shore" to be suddenly broken into with
"Who the hell's that?" or "Where the hell are you going?"
shouted to some midnight passer-by.

John Baptiste Grillon, French, was also a well known

character on the street—the first peddler of ice cream; bent, broad, bearded, with a skew eye.

And Marcus Oliveri, known as Mr. "Marcus" only; the tall handsome Italian, who kept the only restaurant up-town, where Yankees could have pie eating contests, and the hungry could get (canned) oyster stews. He was another of the independent type of merchant, which were common in Key West, and when complaint was made of careless treatment or inefficient service, and loss of patronage intimated, he would reply, "Go somewhere else, I don't care shucks for your patronage."

There was Manuel Acosta, ex-wrecker and master of the United States quartermaster's schooner the Matchless. A Spaniard, large, full-chested, keen eyes, with a grip like a vice and a heart like a baby's.

At that time, also, there were some prominent young men, who were coming "on deck," and occupied among the younger generation the place like the old fellows did with the preceding generations. Among the champion disturbers of the peace and quiet of up-town, there flourished Edgar Baker, the bully of the Key, and Lassy Pent, whose name was associated with every deviltry upon the Beach. George Demerritt (Rabbitt) was just becoming prominent from having whipped three brothers, all larger than he, one after the other. He was a ship carpenter and caulker, boatman and wrecker, small but with a vitality that carried him to the front. He was afterwards the most prominent wrecker of his day, with his schooner the Ida McKay. He became sheriff, and died in 1903, captain of the night force of inspectors in the custom house. George Dillon, afterwards a P. & O. steamboat captain, and his brother Charlie (Bluey), were leaders among the young men. "Young" Lewy Pierce was an accepted champion with his fists, and is now a sedate retired capitalist at Miami.

Among the professional, official and business men, in addition to those mentioned, were a number of distinguished and notable characters. Mr. Eldridge L. Ware from the north, was postmaster from 1872 to 1876. He lived in a large stone house which stood on the lot where Mr. W. J. Delaney now lives, built by Mr. Benjamin Sawyer in 1842. Of medium height, thick, with large head, and full but close-trimmed beard, he could be seen daily perambulating the markets, ancient beaver hat on head, cane in hand, and a market basket on his arm, picking out what looked good to him.

Mr. Samuel C. Craft, clerk of the circuit court, was a marked individuality. Cruikshank has depicted him often. Tall, lean, thin and long faced, thin grey hair and beard, and always clothed in a suit of sepulchral black, he looked indeed as the old time English "clark" was supposed to look. He officiated on the Sabbath as pastor of the Baptist congregation.

Another was old Judge Charles S. Baron. A little old man with white hair and long thick flowing white beard; a mild, lovable character, doing as little law work as possible, and interesting himself with his flowers and his home. He was one of the oldest and most faithful members of Dade lodge of Masons, and a portrait of him, which is a speaking likeness, now adorns the walls of the Masonic Temple.

Colonel Walter C. Maloney, Sr., was one of the earliest settlers, who lived to an advanced age; white hair and beard, acquiline nose and fierce blue eyes, that glared from a rubicund face, with his ancient beaver, long coat and cane, and dignified walk, he bore on first appearance the demeanor of a most irascible old gentleman, and when his temper was aroused he justified his appearance; but when not spurred to action by some, as he deemed, unwarranted aggression, he was geniality itself, polite, witty, a "real old Irish gentleman," and a most lovable companion. He had a spark of genius, that often irradiated the dullness of pending legal business, and was a sure guarantee against any stagnation of affairs when he was present. In one of his last appearances in the court house as counsel, a characteristic incident occurred. It was in the trial of a salvage case in which Colonel Maloney was one of the proctors for the libellants, and Mr. Treadwell Cleveland, a young but brilliant member of the New York bar, was leading counsel for the underwriters. In the progress of the trial, Mr. Cleveland was not observant of the amenities which distinguished the bar of Key West at that time, and of the South generally, and was discourteous to Colonel Maloney. At last, upon Mr. Cleveland becoming more offensive, Colonel Maloney rose from his seat, and with flashing eyes, and thin form trembling with just anger, he shook his long, bony finger in Mr. Cleveland's face and said: "If the gentleman will do me the courtesy to step outside the court house and repeat the words he has used within, I will put a button-hole in his waistcoat which no seamstress (semstress as he correctly pronounced it) can sew up." It is needless to say that Mr. Cleveland did not accept the invitation.

Circuit Judge Winer Bethel was a large, portly, handsome man, with full curly beard, and dignified demeanor, whose appearance was always calculated to impress. He came to Key West from Nassau, N. P., in 1847, and has many descendants here, among whom is Judge Livingston W. Bethel, who now wears the judicial ermine, which fell from his father's shoulders on his death in 1877.

Dr. Daniel W. Whitehurst, both physician and attorney, was a quiet, cultured, lovable gentleman of the old school, a man of education, travel and experience.

Dr. Joseph Otto, who at that time was in active practice, was a figure often seen upon the streets. He was a fugitive from Prussia at the time of the student's revolution, escaped in a load of hay, reached New York, became attached to the army in the medical corps during the Seminole war, and was afterwards contract surgeon for the post at Key West. His drug store was a popular place of resort for officers and citizens, who found no other place to sit and discuss the matters of the day.

The list of notables would be incomplete without reference to the "Spanish Doctor"—so called, though he was a photographer, dentist, artist and general Jack-of-all-trades, except "doctor." Neither was he Spanish, but Venezuelan. He had a studio in a ramshackle building next to John Sawyer's store, where he took photographs, and did anything his genius suggested. He was tall, but did not look so, as he was so fat and barrel-shaped. And his fat was not all fat, but muscle. With his big arms and legs, he was immensely powerful, and with his broad shoulders, the little head, with smooth sallow face, ornamented with mustachios, that seemed but exaggerated eyebrows, he had an uncanny appearance. Always dirty—being large he could carry more dirt than most—and stained with chemicals, he was far from attractive, until he commenced to talk. Educated, travelled, with ideas on all subjects, a linguist, a musician, he was, as Dr. Mason Whitehurst said, a second "Count Fosco." But he could not make a living for himself and "my Mary," as he called the beautiful daughter who lived with him. All his talents did not avail to make money. He complained that fate was against him. "If I went to make shoes, all the children would be born without feet" he said. Governor Perry appointed him assistant adjutant general on his staff, in return for his supposed influence with the Cuban voters, which it is needless to say he never possessed. This gave him of right the title of colonel, which he had occasionally used prior to this, but which he insisted on being called ever afterwards. On one occasion when the local company of militia responded to a riot call, the spectacle of the "Spanish Doctor" marching ahead of the company, in a uniform coat that he had worn in some South American revolution twenty years before, which lacked about four inches of meeting across his aldermanic waist, a belt which refused to reach farther around than the coat; holding his scabbard in one hand, and his sword perfectly upright in the other—as a drum major holds his baton when he is not tossing it in the air— was a sight ever to be remembered. He was one of the best known characters in Key West, and occupied a noticeable place for a time, but finally disappeared. And "my Mary," the beautiful girl that always represented the Goddess of Liberty in the numerous patriotic parades of those days! Where is she? Where have her lines fallen? Let us hope in happy places, and where life has been more for her than it was in Key West!

A mechanical genius who would have acquired a world wide reputation as a ship builder, had his field of operations been larger, was Mr. John Bartlum, who came to Key West in the early days from the Bahamas. With the bare rudiments of an education, he constantly sought knowledge from books on mechanism and ship building, and soon acquired a local reputation for building small vessels of most beautiful models and remarkable for their sailing qualities.

He built a large schooner, named the *Euphemia*, after Mr. William Curry's wife. Later she was sold to a party who used her in the slave trade, for which she was admirably adapted on account of her remarkable speed.

Messrs. Bowne and Curry, who were quick to recognize genius, entrusted him with the construction of a clipper ship, a venture which had never before been attempted in a Southern shipyard. The ship, named the Stephen R. Mallory, launched in 1856, was one thousand tons burden and cost eighty thousand dollars. On her bow she carried a life size figurehead of the distinguished man for whom she was named. Under the command of Captain Graham J. Lester she made voyages to all parts of the world, and was sold in 1866 to Nova Scotia parties.

The Mallory was rated "A1" in New York, and Bartlum's fame spread through the great commercial cities of the country. He was offered some very attractive inducements by large ship building firms in the North, all of which he declined, and ended his days in Key West. He left a large family of distinguished descendants. One of his sons, Mr. George L. Bartlum, was mayor of the city for three terms.

MR. WILLIAM CURRY.

There came to Key West on March 3, 1847, from the Bahamas, a small boy whose imagination had been fired by the reports of the wealth to be acquired in this place, and who achieved a success far beyond his early imagination. He went to work as an office boy in the store of Weaver & Baldwin. His hours were from six in the morning until eight at night, for which he received at first one dollar a week, a small room over the store, and board with Mr. Baldwin's family. Although engaged to work only fourteen hours a day, he crowded into that time the work which most boys accomplish in twenty-four, and steadily rose from office boy, to clerk in the office of the United States quartermaster, and later chief clerk for Messrs. Wall & Company.

Subsequently he established the firm of Bowne & Curry. In 1861 Mr. Bowne retired from the firm, and Mr. Curry carried on the business alone until 1891, when he established the firm of William Curry's Sons. He died on January 23, 1896, the richest man in Florida.

He was a man of medium height, stockily built, with short whiskers beneath his chin, and eyes that indicated unusual intelligence. His voice was low and well modulated. He was dignified yet gentle. His apparel of the finest, yet so modest in hue and cut that its elegance was apparent only to the critical few. His capacity for making safe and lucrative investments amounted to genius. What subconscious ability was it, that enabled the proprietor of a general store in a country town, to know that the stocks and bonds of the Chicago, Burlington & Quincy, Rock Island, Milwaukee and St. Paul railroads; New Orleans street railway stocks, mining stocks in Colorado, and many others which were then selling below par, would some day sell far above par?

He claimed that one of the causes of his success was his early resolution not to spend money for anything until he had given it long and mature consideration. He liked to tell of an incident which led him to form this resolution. Once as a boy he went with a party in a small boat to one of the uninhabited Bahama islands to gather native wild fruits and berries. The party separated and he became lost in the thick undergrowth. He shouted, but no response came, and his youthful imagination pictured with horror a night alone on an uninhabited island, which his fancy filled with wild beasts. After wandering about for a time, he finally speed the boat, and waited on the shore until the rest of the party returned. Shortly after this he came to Key West, and one day he noticed in a show case a small pocket compass, valued at a dollar. It occurred to him that if he had had a compass the time he got lost, he could easily have found his way to the boat. He concluded to save up his money and buy it. In five or six weeks he had saved a dollar, and hastened to the store, fearful lest someone had already secured the treasure. It was still there, however, and he bought it and carried it up to his little room. He said, it never occurred to him that he would have no occasion to use it, as he was too constantly employed on week days for frolics in the woods, and such practices on Sundays was not countenanced in the old Key West. Day after day the compass rested on a dry goods box which served for a bureau, and he gradually became impressed with its uselessness, and that his dollar had been thrown away. It began to get on his nerves. He thought of the many things he might have done with that dollar if he had not bought the useless compass. He hid it in a tin box, where he could not see it, thinking he might forget it, but it preyed on him more and more.

"I got up one morning," said he, "before it was time to go to the store; I took that compass out of the box, went down on the dock, and threw it as far as I could out into the stream, and for all I know it is there yet."

This characteristic incident deserves a place alongside of Benjamin Franklin's story of the boy who paid too dear for his whistle.

MR. JOSEPH BEVERLY BROWNE*

I refrain from writing of another who deserves a place in a history of Key West, preferring to give what was said of him by others when he laid down his earthly burden.*

---

*Appendix V.

CHAPTER XXXII

THE WOMEN OF KEY WEST

IN WRITING of the men of a nation or city, conflicts and strife, both personal and political, must needs fill a large part of the record, but to write of woman, is to enter a more delectable field, where love and beauty sing their rhapsodies, and the *Miserere* of the afflicted in soul or body, is changed to a *Te Deum*, by her gentle ministrations.

First in point of time as well as in affection and esteem of her contemporaries, was Mrs. Ellen Mallory. Two distinguished men have told of her virtues, and they can best be recorded by quoting them. Judge Marvin, writing of her, says, "I mention Mrs. Mallory last because she is the last to be forgotten—not because she was the mother of an United States senator and secretary of the navy of the Confederacy, but because she was situated where she could do good and she did it. Left a widow in early womanhood, she bravely fought the battle of life alone, and supported herself by her labor in respectful independence. She kept the principal boarding-house in town. She was intelligent, possessed of ready Irish wit, was kind, gentle, charitable, sympathetic and considerate of the wants of the sick and the poor. She nursed the writer through an attack of yellow fever and was always as good to him as his own mother could have been."

Colonel Maloney says of her, "Let me therefore be permitted (with feelings akin to filial regard and devotion) to place upon the canvas which is intended to represent your city, one portrait, one name, without which the picture would be more incomplete than it is—that of Mrs. Ellen Mallory, one of the earliest female settlers upon our island, one whose residence antedates the existence of our chartered rights as citizens of Key West.

"Methinks I hear her musical voice today, as she was wont to speak, standing at the bedside of the sick and dying, in days gone by. Catholic by rites of baptism, Oh! how truly catholic, in the better and non-sectarian use of that term, was her life, devoted as it was to acts of kindness. Her husband having died shortly after their arrival, she kept for many years the only comfortable boarding house on the island, located first on the north side of Fitzpatrick street, and subsequently, after the proprietors had expressed their appreciation of her character and usefulness by a donation of a lot of ground, on her own premises, on the south side of Duval street, near Front.

"With many opportunities of becoming rich, she died

comparatively poor. Next to her God, her devotion centered in her son, Stephen R. Mallory, whom she brought to this island a child of tender age, and lived to see occupying a seat in the senate of the United States as one of the senators from Florida.

"Twice, as I remember, I had the pleasure of receiving the proffered hand of this lady. First, with words of 'welcome' to your city, when as a poor young man I became one of your number. Second, on the occasion of a sore affliction, when the balm of consolation gratefully reached my ears, and pointed my mind to contemplations of future usefulness. She died in 1855. Her mortal remains lie in yonder cemetery, respected of all men. She left no enemy on earth."

Such was the woman who founded the family of Mallory in Florida; is it any marvel that she was the mother and grandmother of United States senators, and that her great-grandchildren are among the most cultured and distinguished citizens of Pensacola?

Soon after Fielding A. Browne came to Key West his sister, Miss Susan, paid him a visit. Beautiful and accomplished, she was one of the belles of James City county, Virginia. Here, she was wooed by many, and won by Captain Thomas Mann Randolph, who commanded the United States revenue cutter Washington. They were married in one of the old family places, in Ashland, Virginia, and returned to Key West, where she made her home.

Captain Randolph died of yellow fever in 1836. He left two children, William B., who adopted his father's profession, and became a captain in the United States revenue cutter service, and a daughter, Miss Mary Ann, who married Mr. Joseph Y. Porter of Charleston, S. C.

On Captain Randolph's death the officers of his service placed a tablet to his memory in St. Paul's Episcopal churchyard.

Mrs. Joseph Ximenez, Mrs. Whalton and Mrs. William H. Wall were women of Spanish descent who came here in the early days. During yellow fever epidemics which were then of frequent occurrences, these good women would give all of their time to nursing the sick, and ministering to the afflicted. They would leave home and family and devote themselves to the stricken stranger, never leaving his bedside until he recovered or went to his last home. They soothed the fevered brows of hundreds, and saved many stricken ones by their careful attentions. The succeeding generation of women followed in their footsteps, and freely ministered to the sick and afflicted, and it was not until after the Civil War that a paid white nurse was known in Key West.

One of the clever women of those days was Miss Evie Spencer. For several years her father lived at Indian Key, whence he came to Key West shortly before the massacre. Miss Spencer was a brilliant and intellectual young woman. She married Mr. L. Windsor Smith, a leading business man of

Key West, and a talented lawyer and writer. He wrote in 1835 a series of articles on the flora and fauna of South Florida, and the agricultural possibilities of that section. He was the first to advocate the reclamation of the rich alluvial lands of the Everglades by cutting canals into Lake Okeechobee.

Mrs. Adam Gordon, whose husband was collector of customs and a prominent lawyer, was a woman of sterling qualities. They had one daughter, Miss Eliza. She was only a girl when her father left Key West, but her sweet disposition caused her to be much loved, and her intercourse with her girl friends kept up until separated by the Civil War. The family moved to New Haven, Conn., and thence to New Brunswick, N. J., where Miss Gordon still lives.

Miss Mary Nieves Ximenez and her sister Miss Frederica, daughters of Mr. and Mrs. Joseph Ximenez, were dark-eyed beauties of much charm and vivacity. Their mother was a di Borgo from the island of Corsica; a granddaughter of the statesman Pozzo di Borgo, who was a companion of Napoleon. When the latter left Corsica, the di Borgo family went to Spain, and married into the family of Cardinal Ximenez, whence they went to St. Augustine, and from there came to Key West.

Miss Mary Nieves married Mr. Joseph Beverly Browne, and raised four children: Miss Ann Elizabeth, who married Dr. Robert Jasper Perry of Tennessee; Miss Mary Nieves, who married Hon. L. W. Bethel; Miss Leonor Ximenez, who married Hon. Geo. W. Allen; and Jefferson B. Browne.

Mrs. Browne was distinguished for her zeal in church work, and all public enterprises in which the women of her day took part. She was treasurer of the Ladies' Missionary Society of St. Paul's church in 1851, president of the Confederate Memorial Association in 1867, the first president of the Daughters of the King, which position she filled for many years, until failing health required her to give up active work.

During yellow fever epidemics she, like her mother, gave her time to ministering to the sick. She lived to be eighty-seven years of age, and passed away on April 14, 1911, loved, honored and respected by all.

Miss Frederica Ximenez married Captain Osmond Peters of the revenue cutter service, and moved to his home in Portsmouth, Virginia, where three of their children, Osmond, William H, and Miss Mattie are living. Her youngest daughter, Miss Josephine, married Hartman Henry Rohland, and lives in Brooklyn, N. Y.

Miss Mary Ann Randolph, the daughter of Mrs. Susan Randolph, of whom mention has been made, was a young woman of rare qualities. Beautiful and accomplished, she had a disposition of unusual sweetness, which won for her the love of all who knew her. She was the first organist of St. Paul's church, which position she filled without compensation until her death in 1860. She married Mr. Joseph Y. Porter, and died at the early age of thirty-two, leaving one child Dr. Joseph Y. Porter, Sr., now State health officer of Florida, who resides in Key West.

Miss Lizzie Wall, daughter of Mr. and Mrs. William H. Wall, the first merchant to accumulate a fortune in Key West, married Lieutenant Julian Myers, United States navy, who resigned his position when the war broke out, and went with his native Southland. After the war they lived for a time in Savannah, Mr. Myers' native place. They afterwards moved to New York, where she died in 1907.

The Misses Hortensia and Louisa Tatine, half sisters of Misses Petrona and Mary Martinelli, were four bright, vivacious and attractive belles of their day. Like Mrs. Ximenez, they were descended from Pozzo di Borgo. Miss Hortensia married Lieutenant Mayo Carrington Watkins of the United States navy. He, too, resigned his position when the Civil War broke out, and cast his fortune with his native land. Mrs. Watkins is living in Washington, D. C., where she has made her home for many years—a charming and delightful woman, who embellishes her conversation with the flavor of the old regime.

Miss Louisa Tatine married Mr. Fernando J. Moreno. She lived in Pensacola for many years and died in 1909. She left four children, Mrs. W. A. Blount, Mrs. W. H. Hunt, Miss Louise, and Fernando, who live in Pensacola, and Mason S. Moreno of Key West.

Miss Petrona Martinelli married Mr. James D. Hicks of New York, and shortly after the Civil War they moved to that State and never returned.

Miss Mary Martinelli married Mr. Salisbury Haley and died a few years after her marriage. She left a daughter, Miss Ellen. After his wife's death Mr. Haley went to California with the forty-niners where he afterwards made his home.

Mrs. Alexander Patterson was one of the coterie of good women who adorned Key West by her Christian virtues and great charity. She left two sons, George Bowne and Fielding Alexander, and four daughters, Misses Aletta, Dora, Susan and Mary. Miss Aletta married Dr. William Cornick of the army, and after spending many years of her married life in Key West, moved to Portsmouth, Virginia, where she died. Miss Dora married Mr. W. A. Wright of Savannah, Georgia, and moved away from Key West soon after her marriage. Miss Susan married Mr. Edwin Folker, and is living in Key West. Miss Mary lives here with her brother, and is a type of the dear old maiden lady that is fast passing away.

There was born on Turks Island, B. W. I., in 1815, a child who was destined to leave her impress on the minds and characters of the young women of Key West, and to shed joy and happiness on all around her; Miss Euphemia Lightbourne, who came to Key West with her brother-in-law, Judge Winer Bethel, in 1847.

She at once opened a private school and began active work

189

as a member of St. Paul's church. Every moment of her time out of school hours, was devoted to her church and to visiting the sick and afflicted. She confined her ministrations to no class; it was enough for her to know that a fellow being was sick or afflicted, and she hastened to help him or give consolation to the family. She died on September 18, 1887, never having married. A memorial tablet to her was placed in St. Paul's church by the members of the Sunday school, on which it was well said of her: "A life of noble self-sacrifice is ended. A golden record is closed. A vacancy is left that cannot be filled. Charity, religion, education have lost a model representative, a devoted follower, and mankind a faithful friend."

One of the most beautiful and accomplished women that grew up in Key West was Miss Ellen Haley, whose mother before her marriage was Miss Mary Martinelli. After completing her education at Bishop Doane's school, St. Mary's Hall, Burlington, New Jersey, Miss Haley returned to Key West, and lived for a short time with her aunt, Mrs. Hicks, and then went to California to join her father. There she met and married Lieutenant Yates Sterling, United States navy. Admiral and Mrs. Sterling are living in Baltimore, where Mrs. Sterling by her birth and intellect, occupies the highest social position in that intellectual and aristocratic community. They have five children, Lieutenant Commander Yates Sterling, Jr., of the navy; Miss Maria, who married Mr. Lee Tailer, lives in New York; Miss Helen, Miss Margaret and a son Archibald, live in Baltimore with their parents.

Another cultured and beautiful woman, who combined with these qualities the desire for a useful life, was Miss Josephine Ximinez. On her return from the Misses Edwards' school in New Haven, Conn., where she was educated, she took an active part in church and Sunday school work, became assistant to Mrs. Mary Ann Porter, as organist of St. Paul's church, and on the death of Mrs. Porter in 1860 took her place, and rendered faithful service for a quarter of a century. Like Mrs. Porter, she gave her services as organist of the church and Sunday school without compensation. She taught for many years a school for young ladies, which was one of the foremost educational institutions in the city. She was married in 1875 to Mr. E. B. Rawson, who died in Key West in 1900. Mrs. Rawson is still living here, and although time has whitened her hair, she remains with us as a type of the cultured, accomplished and beautiful women of the old Key West.

Judge Marvin had one daughter, Miss Kitty. She married Lieutenant Luddington, who rose to the rank of brigadier general in the army. Mrs. Luddington died in 1910. She always retained her love for Key West, and visited here a few years before her death.

Mr. William Pinckney had two beautiful and accomplished daughters, Misses Hattie and Dora. Miss Hattie married

Lieutenant Caleb Huse, United States army, who resigned his commission and cast his lot with his native Southland when the Civil War began. He rose to a high station in the Confederacy and was commissioner to Europe to procure vessels for the government. After the Civil War he devoted his life to educating young men and fitting them for West Point. He established at Highland Falls, N. Y., one of the best schools in the country for that purpose. One of their sons, Henry L., is a captain in the United States navy.

One of the most highly educated and accomplished women raised in Key West was Miss Ann Elizabeth Browne, who married Dr. Robert Jasper Perry. Miss Lizzie, as she was affectionately called, was born October 18, 1841, and died July 24, 1891.

In 1854 she entered Bishop Doane's school, St. Mary's Hall, Burlington, N. J., and was graduated in 1858. The same year she entered Spingler Institute, New York city, of which the distinguished Gorham D. Abbott was president, where she was graduated in 1861. She was accomplished in music, both vocal and instrumental, and a fluent French scholar.

On her death it was said of her: "Thus passed away one of Key West's noblest women, who had by her varied accomplishments and natural attainments done much for the education of the youth of her sex. Returning to her native city she did not waste her talents in idleness; being a highly accomplished musician and possessing a powerful and sweet voice, she gave the young the benefit of her acquirements. For several years she taught a select school for young ladies in this place, many of whom today bless her for her instruction. She was a devout member of St. Paul's Episcopal church and for many years the leader of its choir. Always at her post of duty and ever among the foremost in church work, she lived as she died, a Christian woman. Of a lively buoyant disposition, a face always covered with smiles, and a heart sympathetic and kind, such a character as she, taken out of any community must cast a gloom over it, and the long and sorrowful cortege that followed her remains to the cemetery showed that no ordinary one had passed away."

She left two children, William Y., who is in business in Chicago; Sidney R., an attorney in New York, and an adopted daughter, Rose Forbes, who married Mr. Albert R. Erskine of Tennessee, now living in East Aurora, N. Y.

The record of the good Christian women who made Key West better for having lived in it would be incomplete without mention of Mrs. George Bowne Patterson.

Born in the Bahamas, she came to Key West with her father Judge Winer Bethel. She was a bright, beautiful and accomplished young woman, and like the other members of her family was an ardent church worker. On her death on May 5, 1906, it was appropriately said of her: "In her daily life, her God and her church came first and above all other considerations, nor was anything allowed to interfere with her religious obligations. Unless prevented by sickness she was ever in her seat whenever the doors of St. Paul's church were opened for service, and her Sunday school class, to which she was devotedly attached, had her unremitted attention. As wife and mother, she was devotion in every act. Her husband and her children came next to her church and her God, in loving and self-sacrificing attachment to their wants and requirements."

She was married to George Bowne Patterson, Esq., on January 27, 1876, and left six children: Mrs. Clifford Oakley, Mrs. Jacquelin Marshall Braxton of Jacksonville, Fla; Mrs. Henry Prindle, and Mr. Elliott Patterson of New York, and the Misses Etta and Aletta, who live with their father in Key West.

Miss Bettie Douglass, daughter of Judge Samuel J. Douglass married Mr. George Lewis, a banker of Tallahassee, where she now resides with her husband and an interesting family of children. One of her daughters, Miss Sadie, married Senator John W. Henderson, a distinguished citizen of Florida. Mrs. Henderson is a very superior woman, "a worthy daughter of a worthy mother." Another, Miss Evelyn, married Dr. Manning and resides in Jacksonville. Her son, George, and one daughter, Miss Mary, reside with their parents in Tallahassee. A daughter, Miss Bessie, named for her mother, was a young woman of rare beauty and accomplishments. Her sprightly temperament shed sunshine wherever she went, and her cordial disposition won her friends alike with old and young. Her early death, at sixteen, was a severe blow to her family, and left a void in the young social life of Tallahassee.

Captain Francis B. Watlington's home was for many years one of the social centers of Key West. Built in 1832, it still stands on Duval street, adjoining the residence of Mr. William R. Porter. He had six accomplished daughters. The eldest, Miss Hannah, married Mr. Ed. Howe, and lives at Newton Center, Mass. Miss Sarah married Judge Joseph B. Wall, of Tampa, and died a few years ago. Miss Emeline married Mr. Joseph P. Roberts, the well known merchant (Joe Pilot), whose store for many years stood at the corner of Caroline and Elizabeth streets. Miss Maria married Chief Engineer King of the navy, and died in 1910. Miss Mary, who married Dr. Charles S. Johnson, lives in Key West. Miss Florence married Judge Ramon Alvarez, special deputy collector of customs at this port. She died in 1910 and left several children. Miss Lillie never married and resides in the old home place.

Mr. and Mrs. Charles Johnson lived for many years in a quaint old house on Whitehead, between Greene and Caroline streets. They had three attractive daughters. Miss Emma married Dr. Sweet, Miss Louisa married Dr. Armstrong and Miss Ophelia married Dr. Pickering, all of the United States marine hospital service. The family moved from Key West many years ago.

Mr. James Carey had three beautiful daughters. Miss Jane married Paymaster W. C. Blackwell, United States navy. On his death she married Chief Engineer Mortimer Kellogg of the navy, who was shot and killed by a brother officer, Dr. King, on Duval street, near where the Jefferson Hotel stands. The killing was one of the great sensations of Key West. Much feeling was aroused and the case was taken to Manatee county on a change of venue. Dr. King was defended by Senator Mallory, Mr. Henry L. Mitchell, afterwards circuit judge and Judge James W. Locke, and acquitted on the grounds of self defense. Mrs. Kellogg afterwards married Mr. John Hartman of Bristol, England, where she now lives. Miss Emma died without having married. Miss Annie died in the bloom of her young life, and a portrait of her in existence shows her to have been a young woman of rare beauty.

Captain John Geiger raised a large family of beautiful and attractive daughters, and their home which stands on the corner of Whitehead and Greene streets was for many years the center of a joyous social life. As his daughters grew older and retired from society their children easily took their places as beautiful and accomplished young women; one, Miss Urania Neal, married Mr. George H. Glassier of New York, and lives at Dania, Fla. She too, has a beautiful and accomplished daughter, the third generation to be thus distinguished.

The truthful historian when describing individuals must needs feel some hesitation about approaching the realm of the present. Where so many women are beautiful, so many wise and witty, so many have led faithful Christian lives, and devoted themselves to doing good; who shall select those to describe, and those to leave unsung? I have therefore refrained from sketching living persons as much as possible, and have only transgressed in exceptional instances.

It is natural that people of means should devote a large part of their time to benevolent enterprises, but it is rare that a woman poor in this world's goods, who has to devote herself to her household and family duties, can find time to keep alive the spark of an almost extinguished church organization. Such a woman was Mrs. Jonathan Cates, affectionately known as "Sister Cates." For years the Baptist church struggled along, pastorless most of the time, and but for her persistence in raising funds to bring a preacher to Key West occasionally, and keep the little organization together, this church would have closed its doors as a place of worship. To her belongs the credit and the honor for keeping the little congregation together, until it came under the jurisdiction of the Home Mission Board of the Southern Baptist Convention.

CHAPTER XXXIII

FLORIDA EAST COAST RAILWAY

K EY WEST is alert for the era of prosperity to be ushered in on the completion of the Florida East Coast Railway, and a renaissance, not of physical well being only, but a moral and intellectual one as well, is a consummation most earnestly desired.

Claimants are not lacking for the honor of having been first to advocate the building of a railroad to Key West, for as far back as there are any records, some dreamer or optimist was giving expression to his hope. The Key West *Gazette* in 1831 pictured it, the *Inquirer* in 1835 advocated it, and Senator Stephen R. Mallory, chairman of the Senate Naval Committee, crystallized into a masterful report, what was a general topic of conversation in Key West at that time—the great advantage the United States would derive from a railroad to Key West, from a strategic point of view.

The first survey of a railroad route to Key West was made by Civil Engineer J. C. Bailey in 1866. He was employed by the International Ocean Telegraph Company to make a survey of a route over the keys to Key West, when they were considering the feasibility of running their telegraph line to Key West in that way.

In 1883 General John B. Gordon of Georgia obtained from the legislature of Florida a franchise for a railroad to Key West. Work on this road was commenced, and fifty or sixty miles completed on the mainland, but he was unable to finance the company, and it passed into other hands, who abandoned the project of building to Key West.

Several other promoters obtained franchises with large land grants, by which they hoped to induce capitalists to carry out the project. The charters required work to be commenced within stated periods, but each succeeding legislature extended the time. In 1891 the senator from Monroe county opposed all such extensions, for the reason that the existence of speculative franchises would deter responsible parties from considering the project, and defeated them. This cleared the way for new legislation along these lines.

The Jacksonville, St. Augustine & Indian River Railway in 1893 was operating a railroad from Jacksonville to Rockledge, in Brevard county, under a charter which authorized it to build through the counties of Duval, St. Johns, Putnam, Volusia, Brevard, Orange, Osceola, Dade, Polk and Hillsboro.

In that year Senator Browne, of Monroe county, at the request of one of the officials of this road, introduced a bill, which became a law April 29, 1893, with this preamble:

"Whereas, The said Jacksonville, St. Augustine & Indian River Railway Company has filed a certificate, as required by law, *changing and extending its lines on and across the Florida Keys to Key West* in Monroe county, Florida; Therefore, Be it enacted by the legislature of the State of Florida; etc."

This charter contained a land grant of eight thousand acres for each mile of road constructed south of Daytona. This was the beginning of the legislation which culminated in the extension of the Florida East Coast Railway to Key West.

In 1905 Senator E. C. Crill, of Palatka, introduced senate bill number eleven, granting certain rights and privileges to the Florida East Coast Railway, which became a law May 3, 1905. Mr. Flagler then announced his intention to extend his railroad to Key West at once.

In 1896 there was published in the *National Geographical Magazine*, Washington, D. C., an article entitled "Across the Gulf by Rail to Key West," which gave a fairly accurate forecast of this great work. The article closed with this tribute to its probable builder:

"A railroad to Key West will assuredly be built. While the fact that it has no exact counterpart among the great achievements of modern engineering may make it, like all other great enterprises, a subject for a time of incredulity and distrust, it presents, as has been shown, no difficulties that are insurmountable. It is, however, a magnificent enterprise, and one the execution of which will call for the exercise of qualities of the very highest order. Who will be its Cyrus W. Field? The hopes of the people of Key West are centered in Henry M. Flagler, whose financial genius and public spirit have opened up to the tourist and health seeker three hundred miles of the beautiful East Coast of the State. The building of a railroad to Key West would be a fitting consummation of Mr. Flagler's remarkable career, and his name would be handed down to posterity linked to one of the grandest achievements of modern times."

The writer of that article in hazarding the opinion that the intervening channels would be crossed by bridges constructed of steel piling such as are used in the light-houses on the Florida Reef, underestimated the magnificent genius and Roman courage of Henry M. Flagler, who in building this road has made use of a construction rivalling that of the aqueducts of ancient Rome, which will last long after the accretions of centuries shall have filled the space between the islands, and in the aeons to come, the archaeologist will marvel as he uncovers these remains of a vanished and forgotten civilization.

When Mr. Flagler announced his intention to build this road, engineers and capitalists stood aghast. The light that showed him the way to Key West, dazzled the brightest and appalled the strongest intellects. Who can describe the construction? Why attempt it? The wonderful aqueducts at Segovia, the Porta Maggiore, the Aqua Claudia, the Port du Gard were man's first message in arch building. Henry M. Flagler's railroad in the construction of which he enlarged, extended, amplified that message, is man's last word on that marvelous style of construction, and will echo and re-echo through the ages to come.

Where the Romans built one arch, he constructed a score; where they crossed streams, he bridged arms of the ocean; where they went over valleys, he covered surging waters; where they encountered hills, he found channels; where they met with barriers, he came to quicksands; where the precipice halted them, the quagmire threatened him; they cut through rocks, he filled chasms; the obstacles that barred their way they gripped with iron claws, and made them do the work of the master; his obstacles—the bog, the quagmire, the quicksands—evaded, eluded, shifted, swallowed up tons of concrete with their capacious maws and ravenous stomachs.

To conquer these obstacles it required twenty-five thousand men, fleets of sail vessels, naphtha launches, barges, house-boats, dredges, steamboats, monster pile drivers, stupendous rock-crushers, intricate concrete-mixers!

Why attempt to give in detail the history of the building of this road? Only in an epic poem may it be adequately described. The Greeks before Troy suffered no greater hardships, exhibited no greater heroism, practiced no greater self-denial, endured no more discomforts, met with no greater terrors, experienced no more annoyances, bore no greater burdens, showed no greater courage, than the men who built this road. Its story is told in deaths from drowning, lives crushed out by masses of iron and concrete, bodies blown to atoms by dynamite, swept away by hurricanes, engulfed in surging waters. Everything claimed its tribute, the sea, the wind, disease, exposure to burning suns and drenching rains, and more ravaging than all—rum—liquid drops of Hell—destroyed body and soul alike!

And through it all one master mind planned, directed, controlled! Everything that went into the construction of this work obeyed his will, and took its place by his command in the grand scheme which culminated in a feat of engineering which has seldom been equalled, and will never be excelled.

Every pile that was driven, every foot of water covered, every concrete column that reared its head from its coral foundation forty feet below the sea, obeyed the will of one man, who was thinking only of how mankind was to be benefited, and his country saved in some great foreign war, through his achievement.

He was humanity crystallized, patriotism embodied! As Henry M. Flagler was the brain, Joseph R. Parrott was the arm, Meredith, the hand, and Krome, Wilson, Coe, Cotton, Smiley and Cook the fingers, that did the work the brain conceived.

The work is done! Let it speak for itself, now and forever!

196

CHAPTER XXXIV

A S I CLOSE this history and bid good-bye to the early settlers of Key West, it is as if I had known them all. Those who are phantoms to others are living people to me. For nearly a year I have thought of them, studied them, lived with them; goodly company indeed!

Mr. Whitehead, Dr. Waterhouse, Dr. Strobel, Major Glassel, Mr. Fielding A. Browne, Mr. Arnau, Colonel Stone, Mr. Newcombe, Judge Webb, are actual acquaintances. I am saddened at the tragic drowning of Dr. Waterhouse and his son at Indian Key. I share with my Aunt Susan her grief at the death of her husband, Captain Thomas Mann Randolph, in September, 1836, and her long years of lonely widowhood.

I see Miss Mary Nieves Ximenez, and Miss Mary Martinelli, those rosy-cheeked elfins, and hear their voices ring in merry laughter. I listen to the rich brogue of Mrs. Ellen Mallory, sometimes in harsh admonition, ofttimes in gentle kindness.

I share with the cultured Mr. Whitehead, who gave the best years of his life to Key West's development and progress, the humiliation that was cruelly put upon him by his fellow citizens, when they elected a vulgar, illiterate grog-shop keeper to the office of mayor, from which Mr. Whitehead had resigned rather than stultify himself by a non-enforcement of the law; and left Key West never to return!

I am shocked and saddened at the news of the massacre of Major Dade and Captain Gardener, whom we all liked and admired, and I join in the offers of help and sympathy to Mrs. Gardener and her fatherless children.

I sit around the festive board with the happy care-free people, who wait until midnight and later, for the ringing of the bell that tells us "the Isabel is in sight." I join in the greetings, and the good natured badinage at the wharf, as we watch her dock, and get the first news from the outside world in two weeks.

I drop in at Mr. Scarrett's for an afternoon game of loto with Mrs. Lancaster and Mrs. Douglas, and partake of the delicious coffee and wafers that were ever ready when callers came to the hospitable homes of the old time women of Key West.

I worship in the old court house before the cornerstone of any church is laid, and ask not of which denomination is the preacher, so long as he preaches "Peace on earth and goodwill towards all mankind," and "Love thy neighbor as thyself."

Hope springs up in me at the expectation of the great prosperity that is to come to Key West with the hundreds of thousands of bushels of salt, that will be made at the new salt works, which will require five hundred vessels a year to transport.

I attend the sale of the cargo of the Isaac Allerton, and purchase massive solid silver, suited to the then every known use for table ware, marked "Hubbard" which none of that name will ever use.

I hear the bell ringing at nine o'clock that tells all negroes without a permit, to get home before it finishes, and hear the cry, "Run nigger, run, the patrol'll catch you" chanted to some belated slave running for the shelter of his master's house.

I join in the jollification in December over the news just received, that Polk and Dallas were elected president and vice-president on the fourth of November.

And the old order, old ideas, old customs, old beliefs, old ideals—and the old people who cherished them, all, all are gone, and soon all the present order—men and women who are here today—will be gone into the desolate land of the forgotten! Sadder still, however, is the fact, that the *noblesse oblige* of the Old Key West, has been supplanted by the *sauve qui peut* of the New.

Nevertheless, there are features of Key West which change not with the onward progress of development, and attract new-comers as they fascinated the pioneers. The wonderful water with its varied hues showing a different color every day, and never the same tint in different localities, that no brush can paint or pen describe; here a light shade of olivine runs into indigo blue, which in turn fades into almost milky whiteness from the sand stirred up by the storm; now a patch of seagrass produces a moss-agate coloring, and light winds cause the surface to ripple and glisten like a flowing stream of precious stones, and reflecting all their hues. The starlit nights are so bright as to cast vague shadows, and the moonlight on the white coral streets resembles the frost and the newly fallen snow. The heavens, like an inverted bowl of sapphire, across which flits occasionally a diaphanous cloud of white, are as pure as the world that lies beyond them.

The sun that rises from the bosom of the waters with a burst of glory, flashes on the soul "the idea of the power which called into existence so magnificent an object," and when the day is done, he sinks back into the western deep, attended by a pageantry of color that can be produced only by the Master Artist; streaks of red across cerulean blue, fade to delicate pinks and greens and soft tones of gray, whilst the sun from his place below the horizon sends his rays through the clouds, till they resemble mountains of molten gold.

Come weal, come woe; come progress, come decay; come nature with her beauty, come man with his mistakes; nothing can mar the sky, the water, the sunrise and the sunset, which make the unchanging and unchangeable Key West!

THE END

APPENDICES

APPENDIX A

JOHN WATSON SIMONTON

Mr. Simonton was a native of New Jersey, but his business connections were with several Southern cities and Cuba. After the settlement of Key West, his winters for several years were generally spent here, his Northern residence being Washington, D. C. He had an extensive acquaintance among the members of congress, and was on intimate terms with several prominent men of the then administration, his influences always being exerted for the best interests of the island. After the location here of the United States troops in 1831, he was for some time sutler of the post, and was subsequently interested in the manufacture of salt, as the representative of a company whose stock was principally held in Mobile and New Orleans. He afterwards engaged in business in the latter city and died in· Washington in May, 1854. His social qualities, amiability of temper, energetic business habits, and various places of residence, caused him to have an extensive circle of friends and acquaintances.

APPENDIX B

JOHN WHITEHEAD

Mr. John Whitehead was the son of Mr. William Whitehead, cashier of the Newark Banking and Insurance Company, the first bank chartered in New Jersey, and his early years were spent as a clerk in that institution. He subsequently entered a mercantile establishment in New York, and was among the first to organize a partnership and emigrate to Mobile. His first acquaintance with the island was in 1818. Having been shipwrecked on the Bahama Banks, on his way to Mobile from New York, the vessel in which his voyage was continued put into Key West harbor, giving him an opportunity to observe its peculiar adaptation for the purposes to which it was soon after applied. He was consequently prepared to enter with alacrity into the arrangements of his friend, Mr. Simonton, for its settlement, so soon as they were made known to him. His business relations at the island were, at first, on his own individual account, but from September, 1824, to April, 1827, he was one of the firm of P. C. Greene & Company. Although that partnership was dissolved, he continued, with some intermissions, to regard the island as his residence until about the year 1832, when he established himself at New Orleans in the insurance business; and thence, a few years thereafter, removed to New York, where he died August 29, 1864, while holding the vice-presidency of one of the leading insurance companies of that city. He visited the island for a short time during the winter of 1863, when on a voyage for his health, accompanied by a nephew (a son of his brother, Mr. William A.), whose early childhood had been spent on the island. This visit enabled him to renew his acquaintance with several whom he had been associated when a resident. Mr. Whitehead was a very accomplished merchant. He left no children.

APPENDIX C

JOHN WILLIAM CHARLES FLEEMING

Mr. Fleeming, like Mr. Whitehead, was a personal friend of Mr. Simonton, and engaged in a mercantile business at Mobile when the purchase and settlement of Key West were first thought of. He accompanied the first party to the island in 1822, but left before the end of the year for New Bedford, Mass., where he married. Taking a warm interest in the projected salt works, he came to Key West in the autumn of 1832, expecting, ultimately, to make arrangements for the manufacture on his own portion of the Salt Pond, but died on the 19th of December of that year, and his remains were deposited in St. Paul's churchyard. Mr. Fleeming was a gentleman of culture and of refined taste, and Mr. W. A. Whitehead, then collector of the customs, with whom he resided, in a letter written at the time, thus expressed his own and the public's estimation of their loss:

"On depositing in their last resting place the remains of him who had for a short month added so much to my pleasure and comfort, I bade adieu to many fond anticipations of enjoyment which I had expected to realize, not only during the present winter, but for many years to come. There was hardly a subject in literature, the arts or the sciences, on which he could not converse and give information, and yet unpretending in his manners, mild and amiable to an extent seldom met with in men of his age and standing.

"Everything I do reminds me of him, for his habits and pursuits were so similar to my own, notwithstanding the difference in our ages, that he seemed to be connected with me in all my desultory pursuits. Many delightful plans for amusement and instruction during the winter in which we were to be partners—our drawing—our music—in fact every employment that could tend to while away agreeably the hours not required for our daily duties—has by this blow been so entirely demolished that it will be long ere my feelings will resume their wonted elasticity. My private loss is great, but never has Key West experienced before a calamity to be compared with his death. Many years will pass away before our island will have on it a man so able to bring to light the capabilities of the natural Salt Ponds, to which we look for the ultimate prosperity of the place, as he had for many years made the manufacture of salt his study; and probably there is not a man in the United States who understood it as thoroughly as he did."

Mr. Fleeming left one daughter. His widow became the wife of Mr. George B. Emerson, of Massachusetts.

APPENDIX D

WILLIAM ADEE WHITEHEAD

Mr. Whitehead came to the island in October, 1828, while yet in his minority, with the intention of acting as an assistant to his brother, one of the original proprietors, in his commercial pursuits.

In 1830 Mr. Whitehead was appointed collector of customs and entered upon his duties before he was of age, and during his residence here filled several other local offices. He resigned his office on July 1, 1838, to engage in business in New York, was for several years in Wall street, and subsequently connected with the New York and Harlem and New Jersey Railroads. In 1876 he was treasurer of a financial institution at Newark, N. J., the place of his birth, his leisure hours being principally employed in illustrating the history of his native State, with whose Historical Society he had been associated since its organization, and in observing and recording meteorological phenomena for monthly reports to the *New York Daily Advertiser* and Smithsonian Institution at Washington. His observations, which covered a period of over thirty years, embody much valuable information. Having always taken a warm interest in the cause of education, he filled several important trusts in connection therewith, and for a number of years before his death was president of the board of trustees of the State normal school, and vice-president of the state board of education. His historical memoranda are principally embodied in a communication to a gentleman in St. Augustine, made early in 1836, a copy of which is in the office of the clerk of Monroe county, bound in one of the volumes of newspapers on file there. Mr. Whitehead, when transmitting these papers to be deposited in the clerk's office, gave some advice which is worthy of being followed:

"I hope my former suggestions have been carried out in relation to the preservation of files of your newspapers in some one of the public offices.

We are too apt to underrate the importance of the events of today, forgetful that their results constitute the history of tomorrow. Without the preservation of papers, your changing population will soon be at a loss for the connecting links between Key West of the present and the Key West of the future." There now adorns the wall of the City Hall a fine portrait of Mr. Whitehead, presented shortly before his death in 18—.

APPENDIX E

PARDON C. GREENE

Mr. Greene had been for several years master of a vessel in the merchant service, trading between Northern and Southern ports and Cuba. As stated in the text, he personally took up his permanent abode on the island soon after its first settlement, but the residence of his family continued to be in Rhode Island. He died in the autumn of 1838, having for several years been in ill health from inflammatory rheumatism. "Green's wharf" and "warehouses" were for many years the only ones of any prominence. His only child, William C. Greene, died at Fort Jefferson, Tortugas, in October, 1860.

APPENDIX F

1. The Memory of General Washington. May his example be the star that guides our destiny. (Drank standing and in silence.)

2. The Day We Celebrate. May our remotest posterity hail its approach as did the shepherds of old the Star in the East.

3. Our Country. The independence guaranteed to us by the blood of our ancestors, should never be forgotten by their descendants. (Three cheers.)

4. The Union. An inheritance to us from Washington and his associates. Let no trifling cause burst the holy band. (Three cheers.)

5. Patrick Henry. His doctrines he left as a legacy to his country. May these times find them as fearlessly and as eloquently supported.

6. Our Statesmen. May they remember the principles of '76—think less of self and more of country.

7. The President of the United States. (Six cheers.)

8. The Army and Navy of the United States. Ever ready in the cause of freedom. (Three cheers.)

9. Charles Carrol of Carrolton. The associate of our Washington. He reaps the reward of his labors. (Nine cheers.)

10. LaFayette. The hero of three revolutions in two hemispheres. May his last exertions in the cause of liberty be as successful as his first. (Nine cheers.)

11. One Hundred Years Ago! A period from which to date a nation's gratitude. May the next centennial recurrence of this anniversary find our countrymen in the enjoyment of the privileges secured by our fathers—found wise by the experience of more than fifty years' trial, and rendered sacred by the association therewith of the name of George Washington. (Nine cheers.)

12. The People. May posterity never blight the fair fruits of their virtue and intelligence.

13. The American Fair. (Twelve cheers.)

VOLUNTEER TOASTS

By O. O'Hara, Esq., the president of the day: Henry Brougham. The fearless advocate of civil and religious liberty. (Three cheers.)

By F. A. Browne, Esq., vice-president: The Place of Our Nativity. The parted bosom clings unto its home.

A letter was read from Major J. M. Glassell, United States army, regretting his inability to attend, and offering the following sentiment:

Andrew Jackson. Envy pursues the living—the same man, when dead, will be revered. (Nine cheers.)

General D. Parker of Philadelphia, an invited guest, who was not able to attend, sent the following:

The City of Key West: No section of the United States has so delightful a winter climate and no city so great a proportion of intelligence and hospitality in its population.

By the Hon. James Webb: Washington—May those principles of heroism, patriotism and virtue, which have rendered him immortal, be ever diffused through our land.

By E. Chandler: The Book of Life. Like the book presented to the apostle by the angel—sweet to the taste but bitter in digestion.

By P. B. Prior: Liberty. Secured to us by our forefathers; may we always maintain, uninfringed, that sacred right.

By W. A. Whitehead: Our National Flag. May the stars that compose its union forever remain united and as brilliant as they are now.

By Geo. E. Weaver: The United States of America. Liberty their boast—a legacy bequeathed by Washington. May we ever be a free, united and happy people.

By B. B. Strobel: The Union. Its best safeguard—the virtue, intelligence and patriotism of the people.

By Hez. R. Wood: Jos. M. White, Our Honorable and Faithful Representative—May his services be appreciated. (Six cheers.)

By Wm. H. Shaw: The Memory of General Warren—who gloriously fell in bravely defending the first rampart ever reared in defence of American liberty.

By Alexander Patterson: The Hero of South Carolina, General Francis Marion—His camp, the swamp; his table, the pine log; his rations, roots and sweet potatoes; his pay, nothing; his reward—*freedom and independence!*

By Joseph Cottrell: LaFayette and DeKalb. Though foreigners, their arms were devoted to the American cause—their motto—"Liberty or Death!"

By Captain James J. Board: The American Eagle. May she never want a Hickory upon which to perch.

By O. O'Hara, Esq.: Major J. M. Glassell. His amiable and gentlemanly deportment has secured him the good wishes and approbation of the community.

By S. R. Mallory: Daniel Webster. Changeless as the Northern Star of whose true, fixed and resting quality there is no fellow in the firmament.

By E. Bunce: Our Commerce. Its white wings waft the rich productions of the country over every sea.

By Antonio Giraldo: Love for Our Country and Confusion to Our Enemies.

By T. A. Townsend: The Twenty-second of February, 1732. May it never be forgotten by those who succeed us.

By R. W. Cussans: Marriage—the first best blessing enjoined by the Great Creator.

By P. Gandolph: The Progress of Improvement. The womb of time is pregnant with events beyond conception great.

APPENDIX G

To the Right Reverend Benjamin T. Onderdonk, Bishop of the Protestant Episcopal Church, New York.

SIR: The undersigned having been deputed by the citizens of Key West to address you on the subjects embraced in the second resolution herein enclosed, and to solicit your attention to them so soon as your convenience will permit. They have also been directed to state that should the objects contemplated in that resolution, be attained, it will be in their power to advance to the gentleman who shall undertake the duties therein specified at least five hundred dollars for his support during the first year of his ministry, and to furnish him with schools, the proceeds of which, during the same period, will add to his income at least five hundred dollars more and to assure him that a reasonable belief is entertained of the gradual increase of both sums, as society advances, and the benefits expected to be derived from his labors shall be developed. The citizens of Key West heretofore have had to submit to all the inconveniences resulting from the want of an enlightened minister

202

of the gospel, permanently located with them and a well organized school. The transient character of a large portion of the population, and other circumstances beyond their control, have until now prevented their making any successful attempt to administer to these wants but late accessions of much worth to their permanent society, and a general state of improvement which has commenced, and is now progressing on the island, give them assurance that these conditions have, in a great measure ceased to operate and they feel it due to themselves, to their posterity, and to the respectability of their community, that they should avail themselves of the earliest opportunity of taking such measures as will prevent their being longer deprived of the advantages which they know must flow from a better system of religious, moral and scientific instruction than they now possess.

The undersigned have also been instructed to say that a gentleman with a family would be preferred, if one such, possessing equal qualifications in other respects, could be induced to reside here upon the terms proposed. So far as regards the health, enjoyment and comfort of his family, the undersigned do not hesitate in saying that he has little to apprehend. The society, both male and female, is rapidly improving and at this time affords the material for rendering pleasant the time of a gentleman or lady of refinement, taste and education. Should a married gentleman determine to come, it would not be expected of him to remove to the island before the month of October, and in that event, he will avoid the exposure which persons of a habit formed in a northern climate might experience on removing to a southern one in the summer season; nor will it be required in any year that he shall spend a greater portion of the months of August and September here than will be entirely agreeable to himself.

The undersigned respectfully beg leave to request an answer at the earliest date convenient to you, in order that they may be enabled to communicate to those whom they represent the result of this application in time to take such other steps as shall be found necessary. They also avail themselves of this opportunity of tendering to you their high consideration and respect.

(Signed)   JAMES WEBB,
            DAVID COFFIN PINKHAM,
            W. A. WHITEHEAD,
            L. M. STONE,
            B. B. STROBEL,
            N. S. WATERHOUSE,
                        Committee.

APPENDIX H

KEY WEST, March 5, 1838.

Messrs. J. P. Baldwin, G. E. Weaver, J. H. Sawyer, P. J. Fontaine, W. H. Wall.

GENTLEMEN: Your communication of the third inst. I have received.

You state that the tenth section of the city charter was intended to make perpetual the licenses to be issued to those engaged in certain employments—that any other construction would compel those individuals to take out licenses daily or hourly at the pleasure of the common council and, secondly, that several individuals have not paid their taxes for the last year.

The object had in view in furnishing me with this information is, I presume (though not stated in the communication), to make me aware of the reasons that actuate you in refusing to renew the licenses you held, and which expired on the twenty-eighth of February last.

I shall answer your communication at length, without reference to the official relation which I hold to the matter, with a hope that on more mature reflection you may be convinced of the unsoundness of your views and concede the authority, which I hold the common council possesses, to enforce the payment of the city taxes under the recent ordinance. The office of mayor must forever be a disagreeable one if the incumbent has to support himself in the exercise of his legal duties, against the combined efforts of those, whose standing in the community gives to their acts and opinions that weight which renders them examples of a prejudicial tendency; and it is for the purpose of avoiding any disagreeable collision with my fellow citizens that I postpone taking such steps as will give to the matter a legal character, until I have endeavored to present it to them through you in the same light in which it is presented to me.

Your first objection is that the present common council has no right to levy a tax upon retailers of spirituous liquors, dry goods and groceries, auctioneers, keepers of billiard tables and nine or ten pin allies, previous councils having already assessed and collected from those residing here the amounts specified in the tenth section of the charter as the appropriate tax for each (I do not presume that "commission merchants" are included in this objection as they are not mentioned in the section referred to).

This objection can only be raised on the ground that the common council of the city possesses a charmed life—that once in existence it must necessarily exist so long as the charter of the city continues in force; an argument, the truth of which I deny, and with all due respect for the opinion of the learned gentlemen who I understand have countenanced an opposite doctrine, I will endeavor to prove its fallacy.

The first question that arises is what constitutes the body corporate? or who compose the component parts of the "city of Key West," the name and style by which this corporation is known? Is it the common council of the city? No! The charter expressly declares "that all the free white inhabitants of that part of the island of Key West, etc., be and they are hereby constituted a body corporate," etc. The city of Key West then, which is the enduring substance, consists of the free white inhabitants within the limits, and the common council for the time being is merely an agent chosen in a certain way for the management of the body corporate for a limited time— viz.: one year. The charter itself recognizes the transient existence of the city officers; in the fifth section it contains the expressions "new council" and "preceding" (or old) "council," and it is my opinion, in consequence of the loose manner in which it is put together, that the charter actually presents a case in which though the body corporate continues there shall be no common council. The fifth section says that if from sundry causes mentioned there should be a default in choosing the city officers at the regular period, "the corporation for said cause shall not become void, but another election shall take place within five days thereafter, until which election the preceding common council shall continue their duties until others are elected and qualified to fill their places." From this it appears plainly that there is no provision made for any subsequent election and consequently there would be no common council in existence if from any untoward circumstance an election did not take place within the five days.

I do not consider any further arguments necessary to convince any one of the transitory nature of the common council, and, consequently, whenever the words "the common council" are used in the charter one meaning only can be attached to them, which is that they designate the city authorities for the time being, and having, as I think, established this point I conceive the matter to be rendered perfectly plain and divested of all its difficulties.

The ninth section of the charter specifies all the powers of the common council. Do you think or believe, gentlemen, that "the power and authority to prevent and remove nuisances, to regulate and fix the assessments of bread, to restrain and prohibit all sorts of gambling, to establish and regulate markets, etc., were intended to be given to any particular common council, that if once exercised they are at an end? That the same power and authority are not vested in the present common council as well as in the first? You certainly cannot entertain such a strange idea! Of course the power and authority thus vested in the common council for the time being in the first part of the section will apply also to the common council for the time being in the last part of the section. They are authorized "to license, tax or restrain billiard tables, nine or ten pin alleys and all public games or amusements, to license and tax bankers, peddlers, transient traders, retailers of dry goods and groceries, commission merchants and auctioneers, etc. Here, then, the common council of the city for the time being derive all their powers, and among them the right of taxing certain individuals and professions. What follows? The tenth section, which

204

says that "The said common council"—in other words the common council which has been invested with the powers enumerated in the foregoing section, the common council for the time being shall not exceed certain rates, specified, when levying the taxes required for the financial affairs of the city. This is the only obvious construction to be placed upon the section. If the right to tax is given to the council for the time being, the right to collect the rates specified in the section is also vested in the council for the time being, and if not, then is the whole corporation a nullity and the common council possesses no powers whatever—for from the commencement to the end of the charter the common council alluded to as possessing powers or performing duties is the same; if the council for the time being is meant in one place it is meant in all.

You speak of the intention of the section—I must differ from you in opinion that it was ever intended by the framers of the charter to have the construction what you represent it to be. That section was framed on the island, was embodied into a draft of a charter here, and that draft went to Tallahassee signed by a vast majority of the citizens (conflicting interests having been consulted to such an extent that a most lame and impotent instrument was the result), and I have my doubts if one solitary individual can be found who attached his name to the paper who will say he ever conceived the idea that such a construction as you name was his intention at the time he signed it.

But, gentlemen, you say that unless this construction obtains those persons who must have licenses for their business are at the mercy of the council and may be required to take them out "daily or hourly"—this conclusion is as erroneous as your construction of the section. The council for the time being having only one year's duration, the licenses issued, and taxes levied under limitations, must necessarily be annual—or in other words the specified rates must not be exceeded in any one year; but I have been told my doctrine would give this authority of taxing and collecting to the mayor and aldermen however frequently they may be changed, and I presume it is upon the same supposition that you have arrived at the conclusion stated—but the assertion is incorrect. I say that though the common council of the city is reviewed annually and consequently obtains annually a grant of the powers contained in that charter, yet all elections that take place to fill vacancies do not change the identity of the council. The members thus elected hold their offices only the balance of the year. They, as well as those already in office, must give way to another board at the termination of the regular period and though the members of the council may be changed entirely in the course of the year, the fact cannot in the least affect the soundness of the doctrine. The introduction of the words "per annum" in the latter part of the tenth section was, I have no doubt, entirely accidental.

Your second objection is that several individuals have not paid any taxes for the last year. Is that any reason for refusing to pay yours this year? If your neighbor committed murder would it be justifiable for you to do the same? "Two wrongs never make one right" is a proverb which though hackneyed I cannot help introducing as appropriate. Were each individual to do what his own conscience tells him is his duty there would not be much occasion for any laws, but as all men do not wish to adopt this mode of concluding upon what is right and what is wrong, it should be the province of him who is satisfied as to the performance of his own duties to see that his neighbors do theirs should the good of the community require it. There is a clause in the ordinance recently passed providing for an examination by the mayor and council of any complaints made, relative to the non-payment of any license tax, for a compliance with which I trust my character will be a sufficient guarantee. Your complaint, however, refers to the last year and would have been more properly addressed to the last council, for if they failed to assess any tax it cannot be remedied by the present one. All the taxes that, from any official record handed to the present city officers appeared to be due and uncollected have been received with the exception of a small sum, which the collecting officers say may in their opinion yet be collected, no one having refused to pay any legally due according to their list, excepting Mr.

P. J. Fontaine, whose name I find appended to the complaint before me. The present council had no way of ascertaining what taxes were due and unpaid save from the documents transferred to them, which I have endeavored to render available and the filling up of Front street and the bridge on Simonton street are the fruits of the taxes collected from the information thus derived and the present council cannot justly be censured for not doing what was only in the power of their predecessors.

I have thus, gentlemen, answered your communication with a view of having the matter fully understood by my fellow citizens, and that such may be the result I have to ask, as an act of justice to the members of the present common council, that you call a meeting of all those interested in the payment of a license tax, at which meeting this communication may be read without curtailment, and that it then be determined whether or not it is advisable to support the common council in the exercise of their functions by adopting the interpretation I have given the charter or at once dissolve all the power of the city government (which must be the effect if the contrary construction prevails) and return to the primitive authority of physical force. It has been truly said by an eminent statesman of our own day that, although it was a boast of freemen that they lived under a government of laws—not of men—yet unless they obeyed those laws the boast was empty and unmeaning.

Should my fellow citizens disapprove of the course which I have pursued since they, unsolicited, conferred upon me the office which I now hold I will cheerfully resign it into the hands of a successor who may possess more of their confidence, satisfied, however, that my duties have been performed to the best of my abilities and with a single eye to the good of the city and the community generally.

Requesting that the meeting alluded to may be called without delay,

I remain, gentlemen, yours,

(Signed)   W. A. WHITEHEAD,

Mayor.

APPENDIX I

TABLE SHOWING ASSESSED VALUE OF PROPERTY AND AMOUNT OF TAXES COLLECTED IN MONROE COUNTY

1850

Value of real estate and wharfs	$ 340,135.00	
State taxes assessed		$ 1,452.75
County taxes assessed		726.37
Total		$ 2,179.12

1860

Value of real estate and wharfs	$ 413,301.00	
State taxes assessed		$ 1,885.01
County taxes assessed		941.81
Total		$ 2,826.82

1869

Value of real estate and wharfs	$ 382,112.00	
State taxes assessed		$ 5,324.46
County taxes assessed		2,551.64
Total		$ 7,876.10

(1870 missing)

1880

Value real estate and improvements	$ 830,616.00	
Value of personal property	419,991.00	
State taxes assessed		$ 9,078.74
County taxes assessed		5,952.23
Licenses collected for State	4,590.00	
Total		$15,030.97

1890

Value real estate and improvements	$2,150,225.00	
State taxes assessed on real estate		$13,171.18
County taxes assessed on real estate		21,635.20
Value of personal property	658,400.00	
State taxes on personal property		4,034.92
County taxes on personal property		7,912.33
Licenses collected for State	16,515.49	
Total		$46,753.63

1900

Value real estate and improvements	$1,474,205.00	
State taxes assessed on real estate		$ 7,371.08
County taxes assessed on real estate		19,904.78
Value of personal property	310,450.00	
State taxes on personal property		1,551.25
County taxes on personal property		5,053.48
Value railroad and telegraph lines	24,000.00	
State taxes on railroad and telegraph lines		120.00
County taxes on railroad and telegraph lines		324.00
State licenses collected	11,936.23	
County licenses collected	5,629.00	
Total		$34,324.59

1910

Value real estate and improvements	$1,803,524.00	
Value of personal property	312,800.00	
Value of railroad and telegraph lines	401,362.00	
State taxes on real estate		$13,532.00
County taxes on real estate		32,022.00
State taxes on personal property		2,346.00
County taxes on personal property		5,552.00
State taxes on railroad and telegraph lines		3,010.00
County taxes on railroad and telegraph lines		7,124.00
State license taxes collected	37,936.50	
County license taxes collected	13,936.75	
Total		$63,586.00

APPENDIX J

MEMORIAL TO CONGRESS

To the Members of Both Houses of Congress:

The establishing of a court at the island of Key West is founded on a necessity so strong that little need be said to prove its propriety. The senate have thought proper to sanction a bill for that purpose; it is presumed the reason which induced it, when properly presented, will claim an equal force before the house of representatives to whom the bill from the senate has been referred.

The population of the island is at present nothing short of three hundred souls, while the county of Monroe, of which this key is the capital, amounts to seven hundred, which is daily and rapidly increasing. It must hence result, as matter of course. that differences and disputes of a civil, and charges too of a criminal nature, must occasionally arise, requiring the interposition of the judiciary. Protection and allegiance are reciprocal terms. It is a principal for which the United States have always contended, and which, even in their colonial state, they boldly asserted. But when it is borne in mind that the population of this island, being citizens of the States, are at a distance of four hundred miles from Pensacola, which is the nearest point to which a judicial reference can be had, the trouble, expense and difficulty to which they must and will be subjected must at once be obvious. If a civil suit shall arise, thither, or to St. Augustine, which is a hundred miles more distant

207

must the parties proceed, to obtain a decision of the difference; while, should it be a criminal matter, the accused, contrary to that leniency and indulgence which other citizens of the United States are possessed of, must necessarily be carried to a distance from his friends and home, put upon his trial, remotely from the point where his witnesses are; and, if a poor and humble man, be greatly without the means of enforcing their attendance. The affluent and the wealthy are never without the means of sustaining and defending themselves, and derive other facilities than those which the law itself extends. Legal interposition in their behalf is, perhaps, not a matter of such great necessity, although it is still right and proper, that even for them proper tribunals should by the government be established. But with the man who is without property and without friends, whose life and liberty alike deserve to claim protection from his country, the thing is different. Charge him with an offence, and without a court to hear him, he must be seized and carried to Pensacola or St. Augustine for trial, where to be confronted with witnesses will be difficult, and where the appearance of his own for the purpose of defence and acquittal, will be rendered by the distance impracticable, if not impossible. Difficulty of prosecution will exist on the one side, while on the other the means of defence will be procured at great expense and at still greater hazard.

Considered in this point of view only, it would seem that enough is urged to induce a belief that the measure proposed is correct and right. A reference to our former history will show that in our list of grievances pressed against the mother country was the sending our citizens abroad for trial; and certainly it was strongly urged. It was decried as a grievous and heavy imposition, and one altogether contrary to the rights of the governed. But in what consisted the difference, in the cases then complained of, and in the present? To be sure, the distance was greater from America to England, than from Key West to the United States. Yet in the principle there was no difference. In both there is perfect identity. The complaints then urged was the inconvenience to which the accused was subjected, the increased hazard necessarily to be met—the injury done to the unoffending, in forcing them to appear as witnesses on the prosecution, and the unavoidable consequent, and increased dangers to which the accused was exposed by being dragged to a distance from his home and friends, where character might aid him, and from witnesses whose attendance might not be in his power to procure. The government of the United States, it is respectfully conceived, ought not, in cases of such strong resemblance, so soon to forget the strenuousness with which the right now asked for was by them so fearlessly urged and maintained. Were the citizens of Key West within any reasonable distance of a court, where judicial investigation could be had, the cases would be different; but surely it cannot be considered other than a grievance, when it is apparent that no remedy is presented, short of proceeding four or five hundred miles to obtain it, at great cost, and at an imminent risk both to life and liberty.

Nor·are the people of the island alone interested in this business. The frequent wrecks which take place along the reef of Florida makes it matter of interest to the citizens of our commercial towns, who of course are in want of some tribunal competent and independent, which, in reference to all the circumstances, may decide upon the amount of salvage, properly chargeable on the various shipwrecks that take place. The property when abandoned must in some way or other be disposed of. The wrecker, with a view to his own interest, will carry it to that point, where least hazard from the dangers of the sea will be encountered, and where on its arrival it may most speedily be decided on. Heretofore, for the want of a court, the parties interested have consented to refer the matter to arbitration, and thereby to have the salvage ascertained; this most certainly they had not merely the power, but the right to do. If, as is alleged to be the case, higher rates of allowance have been made, than was required by the risks and labor encountered in rescuing the property, it only proves the necessity of creating a tribunal clothed with government sanction, that thereby such errors may for the future be prevented or avoided.

Previous to the treaty which ceded Florida, persons engaged in wrecking were in the habit of carrying property thus obtained to New Providence or to Cuba. They were points which could most easily be reached—at less expense and at less hazard; and, of course, were resorted to, in preference to those which were more distant. The consequence was, that the revenue of the United States was thereby impaired. To prevent this, congress early after the cession of Florida passed a law, requiring that all wrecked property should be brought to the United States, and denouncing against those who should attempt to carry it beyond our limits severe forfeitures. The provisions of this law were doubtless more readily complied with, for the reason that the port of Key West, being contiguous to the point where the wrecks took place, induced no great advantage in taking cargoes there; but let congress by an embarrassment thrown in the way impose the necessity of their proceeding to a more distant port, or to one where an adjudication cannot readily be had, and forthwith, with all the property found there be carried to ports beyond the limits of the United States, to New Providence or Cuba, to the injury of the revenue, and certainly not to the benefit of the owners. To prevent this, laws may be passed; but to enforce and render them effectual will require all the energies of the government. Over and above this, by a transfer of the cargoes to Nassau an additional injury will be sustained to the commercial interest, by diverting the Spanish trade entirely from this section of the country.

Capital and capitalists will always go where profit is to be found; a law established then, which shall recognize Key West as the point of resort for the various wrecks that take place along the coast, will so attract public attention, as that property will always bring its fair and proper value; and thus everything of suspected injustice to owners be avoided. Already considerable capital is centered on the island, in addition to which, merchants from Havana, only about nine hours sail, will, as they have usually done, resort there when sales are about to take place.

In a single year, from December, 1824, to December, 1825, $293,353.00 of wrecked property was sold there and never but in one instance did it fail to bring nearly its value, some of it going even beyond its value. Since December the amount has greatly exceeded the proportion of the previous year, nor have the sales been of less value to the owners. During this time, or rather since October, 1824, the duties accruing to the government at Key West, as I have been informed, have exceeded a hundred thousand dollars, most of which would have been lost to the United States, if by any embarrassments thrown in the way the wrecks had been carried to Nassau; and this indeed would have been the case, if, under the provisions of our law, the wreckers had been required to proceed to any remote or inconvenient post.

The case alluded to, where the property did not bring its full value, is that of the brig, Hercules, Captain Seaman of New York. Of this I speak with confidence, having been at the island at the time this cargo was sold. Respecting this brig, incorrect representations have been made. She had been wrecked and her cargo brought something less than a hundred thousand dollars. Insurance had been made upon her cargo for two hundred and eight thousand dollars. It does not, however, follow that it was in fact worth that sum. Be that as it may, owing to the circumstance of her having heeled and received a considerable quantity of water in her hold, some of the most valuable goods on board were materially damaged. Upon this vessel it is alleged, seventy-two thousand and five hundred dollars was paid for salvage; this is not true. The amount received by the wreckers was twenty-five thousand and eight hundred dollars or thereabouts. Thus, instead of seventy-two thousand and five hundred dollars, as has been represented, a much less sum was paid, making a difference between the amount imputed, and that actually paid, of forty-six thousand and seven hundred dollars.

Shortly after the sale Mr. John Searle, agent of the underwriters, arrived at the island, and proposed to pay seventy-two thousand and five hundred dollars to have returned to him the vessel and cargo as it was when wrecked. P. C. Greene & Company acceded to the proposal, and set about to re-purchase the goods, although they were in the hands of the various purchasers, and actually paid forty to fifty per cent advance, in some cases, to obtain them. Some of them, however, could not be procured, and for this deficiency a deduction proportional to the sum first offered was made, and the contract was thus concluded. It is from this circumstance that the imputation has obtained currency that seventy-two thousand and five hundred dollars was allowed for salvage, when, in fact, and in truth, it was the result of arrangement, and compromise.

One objection to the establishment of a court is found in letters insidiously pressed upon members of congress from St. Augustine. Who, let me ask, are the persons who urge these objections? Have the people met and presented any memorial? Have the merchants there, who understand the nature and force of business, come forward? Not at all. It proceeds altogether from one, two or three emigrant lawyers, who have gone to Florida in quest of better prospects than they could find in a fair competition of talents in the States where they resided. They have discovered, forsooth, that the island is sickly, that designing men live there, and that the commercial interest of the country materially demands a change of places for the sale of wrecked property—and that place is *St. Augustine.* Now, is it not obvious to every one who will reflect for a moment, that interested and selfish considerations alone must influence the writers of those letters? Bring, if it were possible, the wrecked property to that place, and of course the lawyers, by their libels and suits, must and will be benefited, and hence is found the cause of their deep solicitude—their great exertions for the public good.

In some respects I am connected with the firm of P. C. Greene & Company. It is a mercantile house established upon capital, and is in good credit. The island is partly owned by the firm, who, with a view to add to its prosperity have given, rather than sold, lots in town, with a view to its improvement. This firm, to be sure, having an interest may, be benefited by whatever shall conduce to the interest of the island. Theirs, however, is an open, not occult interest. They may be employed as commission merchants, as has already been the case. They may purchase wrecked property, and in doing so will enter into a fair competition with the rest of the world. Beyond these they have no interest, and whatever of imputation or suspicion upon an interest thus declared may be circulated to their prejudice is presumed to be met and overruled by the substantial reasons which are here urged in behalf of the proposed measure. The interest of the commercial part of the community—justice to the wreckers, who venture their lives and property—and, above all, protection on the part of the government to the inhabitants of the island, demand loudly the adoption of the measure that is asked for by the bill enacted by the senate.

JOHN N. SIMONTON.

APPENDIX K

LIST OF JUDGES, DISTRICT ATTORNEYS AND MARSHALS OF THE FEDERAL COURT AT KEY WEST

JUDGES

James Webb of Georgia	1828
William Marvin	March 11, 1839
John A. Bingham of Ohio	June 4, 1863
Thomas Jefferson Boynton	October 19, 1863
John M. McKinney	November 8, 1870
James W. Locke	February 1, 1872

DISTRICT ATTORNEYS

Adam Gordon of Florida	December 29, 1825
William Allison McRea of Florida	January 22, 1827
James G. Ringgold of Georgia	May 26, 1828
John G. Stower of New York	April 20, 1829
John K. Campbell of Florida	April 5, 1830
Edward Chandler of Florida	May 26, 1830
Adam Gordon	October 4, 1834
Wylie P. Clark of Florida	December 30, 1834
William Marvin of Florida	January 13, 1835
Charles Walker	February 17, 1840
L. W. Smith of Florida	July 21, 1840

George W. Macrae.................................August 24, 1842
L. Windsor Smith.................................March 3, 1847
William R. Hackley..............................August 27, 1850
John L. Tatum of Florida.........................March 1, 1858
Thomas Jefferson Boynton of Missouri.............April 5, 1861
Homer G. Plantz of Ohio.........................October 28, 1863
Homer G. Plantz of Ohio.........................May 28, 1868
Frederick A. Dockery............................November 27, 1868
Claiborn R. Mobley..............................June 2, 1869
Oscar A. Myers..................................October 11, 1873
Thomas Savage...................................October 7, 1874
George Bowne Patterson..........................February 6, 1876
Livingston W. Bethel............................March 31, 1886
George Bowne Patterson..........................April 3, 1890
Owen J. H. Summers..............................July 30, 1894
Frank Clark.....................................November 26, 1894
Jos. N. Stripling...............................July 26, 1897
John M. Cheney..................................January 23, 1906

MARSHALS

Alexander Adair of Alabama......................March 3, 1827
Henry Wilson of Florida.........................May 26, 1828
Lackland M. Stone of Florida....................March 4, 1830
Thomas Eastin...................................September 22, 1832
Charles M. Welles...............................June 8, 1836
Joseph B. Browne................................May 25, 1840
Walter C. Maloney...............................September 24, 1850
Fernando J. Moreno..............................March 16, 1853
James C. Clapp..................................April 3, 1861
George D. Allen.................................September 21, 1865
E. B. Rawson....................................September 17, 1872
James G. Jones..................................July 16, 1874
Peter A. Williams...............................March 1, 1879
James T. Tucker.................................March 22, 1887
Fernando J. Moreno..............................February 24, 1888
Peter T. Knight.................................July 18, 1888
Peter A. Williams...............................August 5, 1889
James McKay.....................................July 30, 1894
John F. Horr....................................February 18, 1898

APPENDIX L

LIST OF CLERKS OF CIRCUIT AND SHERIFF COURT FOR MONROE COUNTY AND TERMS OF OFFICE

CLERKS OF COURT

Walter C. Maloney...............................1845 to 1849
James M. Bracewell..............................1849 to 1851
Peter Crusoe....................................1851 to 1861
A. O. Barnes....................................1861 to 1865
Peter Crusoe....................................1865 to 1868
Henry A. Crane..................................1868 to 1873
John T. Baker...................................1873 to 1877
John Sitcher....................................1877 to 1881
Peter T. Knight.................................1881 to 1888
Mason S. Moreno.................................1888 to 1889
George Hudson...................................1889 to 1890
Peter T. Knight.................................1890 to 1893
George W. Reynolds..............................1893 to 1905
Eugene W. Russell...............................1905 to

APPENDIX M

CHESTER, December 29, 1829.

SIR: In consequence of your application to me for my opinion of Thompson's Island or Key West, I have to state, in reply, that since the year 1823 I have, from time to time, been making myself acquainted with the Florida coast and keys—part of the time in command of the United States squadron, and subsequently in command of the Mexican force in that quarter; and perhaps there is no man living better qualified than myself to give an opinion on the subject, as my information is derived from actual observation and practical experience.

The harbor of Key West, in my opinion, is the best harbor within the limits of the United States, or its territories, to the south of the Chesapeake.

1. For its easy access and egress at all times and with all winds.

2. For the excellent anchorage and security it affords both in the inner and outer harbor, for ships of the largest class: Leading to the harbor of Key West are several excellent channels, some affording water for the largest class of ships, the others suited to the vessel drawing ten and eleven feet water.

The advantages which Key West affords in a commercial point of view are:

1. Its vicinity to the island of Cuba and port of Havana, having a ready market for all articles placed there in deposit, or left by the wreckers, of whom this is the rendezvous of those on the coast.

2. It being a convenient touching place for all vessels bound to and from the Gulf of Mexico, Bay of Honduras, and the coasts of Louisiana and Florida.

As a naval station, Key West has decidedly the advantage over all others I have ever known:

1. In its susceptibility of fortification.

2. The ease and number of its approaches with all winds.

3. The difficulty of blockade, as I have proved while in command of the Mexican squadron, it requiring a blockading force equal to three or four times the force to be blockaded, to keep up an efficient blockade.

4. The ease with which supplies may be thrown in, in despite of the presence of an enemy.

5. Abundance of wood and wate

In speaking of Key West as a naval station, I have reference only as to its being employed as a depot for stores, and a rendezvous for our ships of war; but even as a place for the establishment of a navy yard, it has most decidedly the advantage over Pensacola and every other place south of the Chesapeake.

1. On account of the depth of water—Pensacola and all the other places alluded to only admitting sloops of war, and these not with safety—with the exception of the Tortugas, which, although it has depth of water sufficient, is devoid of all other advantages for the purpose of a navy yard.

2. Its more central situation and facility of communication with, and deriving all the advantages by water of supplies from the northern and southern sections of our Union, viz.: provisions from Louisiana, spars and live oak from the Floridas and Georgia, cordage, canvas, iron, gunpowder, shot, etc., from the north. The distance from either being short, the time, risk and expense of furnishing them must necessarily be reduced in proportion.

3. Its salubrity of climate being equal in every respect to that of New Providence or any of the Bahamas.

The malady with which the naval forces under my command for the suppression of piracy was afflicted had its origin in the excessive severity of the duty performed, and the total absence of every description of comfort. The disease was contracted among the haunts of the pirates along the coast of Cuba and not, as is generally supposed, at Key West.

It has since proved that during the worst seasons the inhabitants of Key West have enjoyed as great a share of health as any other in the same parallel, and much more than those of Pensacola, who have been seriously afflicted with pestilence, and compelled to abandon the town, while those of Key West and the Mexican squadron there, have been entirely exempt from sickness. It is found that the salubrity of Key West improves yearly by the filling up of all ponds, clearing the woods, and by adding to the comfort of those who reside there—it will not be surprising if it should hereafter become a place of resort to the inhabitants of our southern section during the prevalence of the sickly seasons.

These facts and opinions are stated after an experience of nearly seven years.

The advantages of its location as a military and naval station has no equal except Gibraltar.

1. It commands the outlet of all the trade from Jamaica, the Caribbean Sea, the Bay of Honduras and the Gulf of Mexico.

2. It protects the outlet and inlet of all the trade of the Gulf of Mexico, the whole western country of Louisiana and Florida.

3. It holds in subjection the trade of Cuba.

4. It is a check to the naval forces of whatever nation may possess Cuba. It is to Cuba what Gibraltar is to Ceuta.

It is to the Gulf of Mexico, etc., what Gibraltar is to the Mediterranean.

Among its advantages as a military position may be enumerated an abundance of free stone for building, which being a concrete of coral and shells, is easily converted into lime. The island is low, not being more than fifteen or twenty feet above the level of the ocean. The channel into the inner harbor runs bold to its western part, which makes wharfs easy of construction. The soil is rich, being formed of a vegetable decomposition mixed with sand and shells. It produces all the plants and fruits of the tropics, with the exception of coffee, and yields abundantly.

On the eastern side of the island is a very extensive natural Salt Pond, which, from every appearance, I should judge, with a moderate capital and enterprise, might be made to vie with any of those in the British Bahamas.

Stock of every description live and thrive well on the island, without requiring any care whatever, as has been abundantly proved by those which I imported on account of the United States from Cuba and the Bahamas.

The thick growth of wood with which the island is covered, and which affords timber suitable for the construction of small vessels, is filled with deer and other game, and the seas abound in the finest fish in the world.

In making this statement respecting Key West, I am actuated by no other feeling than the desire that my country should not by the prejudices, partialities, interested views and errors of others, be induced to lose sight of the great advantages it presents—whether looked at in a military or a commercial point of view. The naval rendezvous has been removed from Key West to Pensacola, enormous amounts have been expended on the navy yard of the latter, and it is found unsuited to the purpose for which it was designed. An effort is now making to form a naval establishment on the insulated cluster of sand keys called Dry Tortugas, which may easily be surrendered by a small enemy's force, exposed to his cannon without entering

213

the harbor, which affords neither wood nor water, nor scarcely any kind of vegetation, and have the insuperable objection of not affording a sufficient area of land on which to form a naval establishment of even a very limited extent.

Nature appears to have formed it for a place of deposit for the eggs of the turtle and the sea birds, and the art of man can make very little more of it.

Key West has been tried and is proved to possess all the advantages which are desirable in a naval depot and rendezvous. It is proved that the only objection, insalubrity of climate, has no foundation in fact. Where, then, is the necessity of making further disbursements on useless experiments, when one has already been made in Key West, and has proved satisfactory?

With great respect,
Your obedient servant,
DAVID PORTER.

(Signed)

APPENDIX N

FORT TAYLOR, KEY WEST, FLA., January 26, 1861.

SIR: I have to report that no demonstration has been made upon this fort to this date. There is no apprehension from the population of Key West, but I have no doubt that a force will soon appear at any moment from the mainland. If my company was filled up to a hundred men, and a sloop of war stationed in this harbor, there would be no danger of any successful attack, or even an attempt at present. The defenses are improving daily.

I am, sir, very respectfully, your obedient servant,
J. M. BRANNAN,
Captain First Artillery, Commanding.

Col. S. Cooper, Adjutant-General U. S. Army, Washington, D. C.

P. S.: I have received no communication from the department in answer to my letter of December 11, 1860.

HEADQUARTERS OF THE ARMY, WASHINGTON, April 1, 1861.
Bvt. Col. Harvey Brown, U. S. Army, Washington, D. C.

You will make Fort Jefferson your main depot and base of operations. You will be careful not to reduce too much the means of the fortresses in the Florida Reef, as they are deemed of greater importance than even Fort Pickens. The naval officers in the gulf will be instructed to co-operate with you in every way, in order to insure the safety of Fort Pickens, Fort Jefferson and Fort Taylor.

April 2, 1861.
WINFIELD SCOTT.
ABRAHAM LINCOLN.
Approved:

HEADQUARTERS DEPARTMENT OF FLORIDA,
KEY WEST, April 13, 1861.
Lieut. Col. E. D. Keyes, Secretary to the General-in-Chief, Washington, D. C.

COLONEL: We arrived at this place this afternoon. Captain Meigs and I have had an interview with Judge Marvin, which has been entirely satisfactory. He, though anxious to leave the place, will remain, having now the assurance of support from the military authority. I have found great industry, intelligence and enterprise in putting forward the works at the fort, and consider it quite secure against any force that can at this time be brought against it. Brevet Major French, the commanding officer, has been untiring in his labors, assisted ably by Captain Hunt, of the engineers, and the officers of the garrison. He and all his officers are, I am happy to say, entirely devoted to the Union and the country, under any and all contingencies.

HARVEY BROWN,
Colonel, Commanding.

U. S. STEAMER CRUSADER,
OFF KEY WEST, April 13, 1861.
Hon. William H. Seward, Secretary of State, Washington, D. C.

DEAR SIR: We arrived here and anchored some three miles below

214

the fort to prevent communication. Going to the fort in a boat, Colonel Brown sent notes to Judge Marvin; to Colonel Patterson, the newly appointed navy agent; to Mr. Howe, the new collector, and to Mr. Filor, the late navy agent. Mr. Clapp, whose commission we brought with us, we found at the fort. To these gentlemen the general policy of the government in regard to the fort and island of Key West was explained, and the assurance of support from their government was received with great satisfaction. I found that Colonel Patterson has lately made himself quite conspicuous by his Union sentiments, and their open avowal. The best feeling prevails between the gentlemen now appointed and the officers of the garrison, and I have no doubt that all will work harmoniously together.

The anxiety to which Judge Marvin has been subjected has preyed upon his spirits and he looks depressed, but he is ready to do his duty and stand to his post, at least until the government is ready to relieve him. His presence for a time, and his influence are, I think, of much importance in eradicating the treasonable spirit which has lately had full and free sway here. He will be able as now supported, I think, to accomplish it without recourse to any harsh measures.

M. C. Meigs,
Captain of Engineers.

Headquarters Department of Florida,
April 13, 1861.

Bvt. Maj. W. H. French, Commanding Fort Taylor, Key West.

Sir: You will use the forces of your command, if need be, for the protection of the officers and the citizens of the United States on this island in the discharge of their public duties, and the pursuit of their legitimate private occupations. You will not permit on the island any person to exercise any office or authority inconsistent with the laws and constitution of the United States, and will, if necessary, prevent any such exercise by force of arms. If unhappy rebellion or insurrection should exist at any time, you will then publish a proclamation, with which you will be furnished, suspending the writ of habeas corpus, and will immediately remove from the island all dangerous or suspected persons. You will before publishing this proclamation take the advice of the United States judge and attorney on its necessity and expediency (its legality has been determined by higher authority) and receive with deference their opinion, giving them that consideration and weight to which their patriotism and legal knowledge entitle them. In exercising the authority here vested in you the greatest conciliation and forbearance must be observed, that while the duty be rigidly performed it may always be done in a spirit of conciliation and kindness.

I am, sir, very respectfully,
Your obedient servant,

Harvey Brown,
Colonel, Commanding.

Headquarters Department of Florida.
Transport Steamship Atlantic,
April 15, 1861.

Lieut. Col. E. D. Keyes, Secretary to the General-in-Chief,Washington, D. C.

Colonel: We left Key West at daybreak yesterday morning (the 14th), and arrived at Fort Jefferson at one p. m. I found this post in the good order to be expected from its vigilant commander. The present armament of the fort is thirteen 8-inch Columbiads and a field battery, and one hundred and four barrels gunpowder, six hundred and eight shells, one hundred and fifty shot, and a vessel now at the wharf is unloading thirty 8-inch Columbiads and twenty-four 24-pounder howitzers, with carriages, implements, etc., complete, with two hundred and fifty barrels of powder, two thousand and four hundred 8-inch shells, six hundred round shot, and a proportioned quantity of fixed ammunition, so that this post may be considered secure from any force that the seceding States can bring against it. The whole lower tier of this work may with little labor be prepared for its armament. Some flagging and the traverse circles are the principal work to be done. On the recommendation of Captain Meigs, chief engineer, I have directed Major Arnold to have four water batteries, mounting three guns each, to be erected on the adjacent keys. This being done, with the support of one or two ships of war, the whole anchorage will be within command of our guns.

I would respectfully recommend that at Fort Jefferson for the 42-pounders ordered 8-inch unchambered Columbiads be substituted, and that the wooden carriages of all three forts be replaced at the earliest possible day by iron ones.

HARVEY BROWN,
Colonel, Commanding.

ENGINEER DEPARTMENT, WASHINGTON.
April 19, 1861.

Hon. Simon Cameron, Secretary of War:

SIR: I enclose the copy of the letter from Captain Hunt, dated Key West, April 11th, which you may think advisable to lay before the secretary of the navy. I may be permitted to add that the danger is a real one that Captain Hunt specifies, namely, the landing of a considerable body of hostile troops on the shore of that island, out of reach of the guns of Fort Taylor. This the fort and its garrison can in no degree prevent. If landed with heavy artillery this force may reduce the fort by siege, because as yet that part of the structure that is to cover its walls from land batteries has not been built, nor can it be erected so as to fulfill its object for a year or more.

In the meantime complete security may be assured by small, quick-armed steamers stationed at Key West, and cruising in its vicinity, provided other demands of the public service will permit the navy department to supply such protection.

I have the honor to be, very respectfully, your obedient servant,
JOS. G. TOTTEN,
Brevet Brigadier-General.

FORT TAYLOR, KEY WEST, FLA.,
April 11, 1861.

General J. G. Totten, Chief Engineer, Washington, D. C.

SIR: Mr. Mallory wrote here, I have been told, by a recent mail, that when the Confederate States army were ready, an attempt to take these works would be made, but I do not believe this would be tried were our assured strength such as to contest the debarkation.

I am glad to say that from what I have heard today the secessionists here have essentially given in and are beginning to see the error of their ways. Judge Marvin has at last been induced, I believe, to hold on to his place, and I trust that all conflict of jurisdiction will now be avoided. It is surmised that Judge McIntosh may conclude not to come here at all.

Very respectfully yours, & c
E. B. HUNT,
Captain of Engineers.

U. S. TROOP-SHIP ATLANTIC,
HAVANA, April, 25, 1861.

Brigadier General J. G. Totten, Chief of Engineers, Washington, D. C.

GENERAL: With all speed possible under the circumstances we made our way to Key West, where, anchoring off the harbor and allowing no other communication with the shore, Colonel Browne, the ordnance officer, Lieutenant Balch, and myself landed by boat at Fort Taylor.

Here, calling the United States judge, Mr. Marvin, the newly appointed collector of customs and marshal, and the commanding officer of the fort, Major French to meet Colonel Brown at the fort, the orders and instructions of the president were communicated to these gentlemen, and the commission of marshal for Mr. H. Clapp intrusted to me for this purpose by the secretary of State, was delivered to Judge Marvin.

216

Several secession flags floated from buildings in view of the fort and upon the court-house of the town.

The president's orders to the authorities at Key West were to tolerate the exercise of no officer in authority inconsistent with the laws and constitution of the United States, to support the civil authority of the United States by force of arms if necessary, to protect the citizens in their lawful occupations, and in case rebellion or insurrection actually broke out to suspend the writ of habeas corpus, and remove from the vicinity of the fortresses of Key West and Tortugas all dangerous or suspected persons.

Orders were also given to the commander at Key West and to the engineer officer, Captain Hunt, to prepare plans for intrenchments to prevent a hostile landing on the island of Key West.

Fort Taylor, with a brick and concrete scarp exposed toward the island, from which it is only three hundred yards distant, cannot resist a landing, and is no better fitted to withstand bombardment than Fort Sumter. The burning woodwork of its barracks would soon drive out its garrison.

M. C. MEIGS,
Captain of Engineers.

FORT TAYLOR, KEY WEST, FLA.,
May 4, 1861.

Mr. J. P. Baldwin, Esq., Mayor, Key West City.

MY DEAR SIR: I proposed on yesterday to print an address to the citizens of the United States on Key West. The address was delayed, and I take the opportunity to say to you, in continuation of the conversation had a few days since, that from circumstances brought to my attention direct, and from reliable sources, it is my opinion that there will be a strong effort made to distress the inhabitants of this key. Isolated and shut up by the water of the gulf, should what I hear prove correct, the distress would be extreme upon the inhabitants of the island. It is in your power to aid in avoiding this contingency, which, whether near or remote, will be terrible when it comes. I have served in Florida during the early wars, and remember the distress of the inhabitants of St. Augustine, to whom the government had to furnish subsistence. It is probable that such may be the case on the key. The government determining to hold it will be responsible for its loyal citizens; and should the necessities referred to arise, it will be necessary to discriminate, and those who do not belong here should be so notified.

It is also essential that it should be generally known that the functions of the commanding officer on Key West, ex-officio, embrace during the present crisis all the military, including citizens desirous to bear arms for the preservation of life and property. It will be necessary for me, in order to combine them with those of the government, that a muster-roll according to the form prescribed should be supplied to these headquarters by any military organization now existing.

I am, sir, very respectfully your most obedient servant,

WM. N. FRENCH,
Brevet Major, U. S. Army, Commanding.

HEADQUARTERS TROOPS AT KEY WEST,
FORT TAYLOR, May 5, 1861.

Col. L. Thomas, Adjutant-General, U. S. Army.

COLONEL: The Illinois, from Fort Pickens, is in coaling, and knowing the anxiety of the government with respect to the insulated forts, Taylor and Jefferson, I communicate direct. This key is in an excellent state for defense. The few suggestions given by me to Captain Meigs are all that will be required until winter. The more men the more disease. I have used my general authority to mount a section of Light Company K, and expected acclimated horses from Havana in a few days, cheap and hardy. With these the island can be patrolled, vedettes kept up, and light guns moved rapidly.

The sentiment on the key is strictly selfish. The Union man of today is the disunionist of the morrow. My effort has been to make it the interest of the citizens to be loyal, to encourage the Union men, and to lift up the faint-hearted. The judiciary (Federal) have had but little to act upon. I call upon them officially, indirectly. Brought up and resident with the citizens it might at this time compromise. I have made myself acquainted with the respectable inhabitants under the same rules and formalities which exist elsewhere. The effect has been to open the trial sooner than might have been anticipated. Everything which should have been for sale, after a refusal, when Captain Meigs passed by on the Atlantic north, is now given—coal, water, wharfage. I am opening propositions through Colonel Patterson, naval officer, to buy out for the government, at reduced rates, water lines, etc. I have asked from the mayor of Key West lists of the inhabitants, extra mouths, etc., which will have to be fed by the United States. Extraneous people will have to leave. Now there are not ten barrels of flour for sale on the island. Military organizations have been directed to make to me (ex-officio) their rolls. No more troops are needed; water is scarce, not doubtful, and the command is equal to every occasion. My position has required me to take responsibility. This I never shrink from. I have the confidence of my officers and the loyalty of the rank and file. Indorse my recommendations, as they are moderate. This place is safe.

I am, colonel, very respectfully, your most obedient servant,

WM. H. FRENCH,
Brevet Major, U. S. Army, Commanding.

HEADQUARTERS DEPARTMENT OF FLORIDA.
FORT PICKENS, May 13, 1861.

Bvt. Maj. W. H. French, Commanding Fort Taylor, Key West.

MAJOR: As the colonel has only your own letters and not the replies nor the special reasons for your action, he cannot judge of the immediate necessity for suspending the writ of habeas corpus, but having the approval of Judge Marvin and of the district attorney, it has his. He desires that you send here all papers in the case.

The island being under martial law, all its citizens must acknowledge allegiance to the government. While the colonel wishes you to be perfectly firm and decided in upholding the laws and suppressing rebellion, he desires that it may be done in a spirit of kindness and conciliation, so that if possible they may be led from error rather than be driven into it by an undue exercise of authority. If, however, any prove incorrigible and refuse allegiance to the government, they must be sent from the island immediately, without respect of persons.

The colonel does not approve of any removal of troops to Tampa or elsewhere from Key West, nor will any be made unless in case of extreme urgency. *Key West is of paramount importance, and must not be weakened for any contingent service*; neither does he think it at all expedient for the Crusader to leave Key West for any such purpose. He intends to address Captain Adams on the subject.

GEO. L. HARTSUFF,
Assistant Adjutant-General.

HEADQUARTERS TROOPS AT KEY WEST.
May 16, 1861.

Capt. G. L. Hartsuff, Assistant Adjutant-General, Headquarters Department, Fla.

CAPTAIN: Since my communication of the 12th instant, the regular time for opening the session of the district court arrived, viz.: the second Monday in May (13th). No court has, however, been held. My order refusing to permit judicial or magisterial functions to be exercised, except by persons who will swear allegiance to the United States, has been carried out, and for the last three days there has been no court for the usual civil routine of a town. I prepared certain rules and instructions to meet this want, intending to have all cases referred to Captain Brannan, to be appointed civil lieutenant-governor of the town, but I ascertained that a citizen (Mr. P. Jister) had been elected a magistrate by the people a year ago, and had declined to serve when Florida passed the ordinance of secession. I sent for him, but he was averse to serving until I showed him that it would be obligatory to use the martial code unless some loyal citizen would act. He has concluded to do so, and I sent for the district attorney, who has proffered his aid and advice.

On Sunday Judge McQueen McIntosh arrived, preparatory to the opening his court under his Confederate States commission. He was waited upon by men of his own party, who represented the precise state of affairs on the island; that everything was going on peaceably and quietly; that his authority would not be recognized by myself, and that if he attempted to exercise his office it would unnecessarily produce difficulties and excitement.

On yesterday Judge McIntosh called upon Judge Marvin at his office. Judge Marvin has informed me that the result of the interview was perfectly satisfactory. Judge McIntosh was strongly impressed with the uselessness of attempting to assert the Confederate States sovereignty here. He was informed how secure the persons and property were on this island, and that the inhabitants preferred to be allowed to remain as they were. Allusion was made to the military officers, and the manner of their obeying the instructions of the government, which had given general satisfaction. Judge McIntosh decided to return, and at the request of Judge Marvin I requested Captain Craven to allow him and his friends to leave the island without applying to me for a permit to do so, there being an order prohibiting non-residents going or coming without my authority, published since the judge came.

Wm. H. French,
Brevet Major, U. S. Army.

Headquarters Troops at Key West.
May 20, 1861.
Capt. Geo. L. Hartsuff, Assistant Adjutant-General, Headquarters Department of Florida.

Captain: I have the honor to acknowledge the receipt of your communication of May 13th. Inclosed is a report made to me by the acting ordnance officer, upon which was based my sending away from the island Ordnance Sergeant Flynn. Lieutenant Closson also made the report indorsed by him. Lieutenant Webber, at the time alluded to, stated that the ammunition in the magazines had been tampered with, and about two hundred 42-pounder cartridges made unserviceable. This, in connection, with his intimacy with a man named Crusoe, a notoriously designing and dangerous man (he leaves the island today), determined me to get rid of him, as I did, or otherwise he would have been hung on the spot, should his treason (suspected) have developed itself by an attack, His example might have spread, and there was no way to keep him aloof from the men.

I inclose two numbers of the *Key of the Gulf*, the last published. When the paper of the 27th of April appeared I spoke to several respectable citizens to have the paper suppressed, and I had an assurance that it would not appear again. To my surprise, that of May 4th came out, more violent and incendiary than its previous numbers. There was great excitement among the Union men, and the rabid secessionists were much elated. After a perfect understanding with the district attorney, and having received by Judge Marvin's views, sent to me verbally by Captain Craven, of the navy, the act of habeas corpus was suspended, in order to arrest without molestation the parties suspected of uttering the treasonable sentiments, etc. The editor has left the island. The Salvor today takes away Mr. Crusoe, the late magistrate of the county, and county clerk; Judge Douglas and family; Mr. Asa Tift and his negroes. Others are preparing to leave, and winding up their affairs.

No martial law has been put in force here. That code has not had to be enforced. The civil magistracy (Union men) has been installed and supported. The habeas corpus act was simply suspended for prospective purposes. Fortunately, in no instance has it been necessary to make an arrest, and as soon as the Union men elect their own mayor and councilmen, and the municipal affairs are arranged on the basis of the paramount sovereignty of the United States laws, the proclamation may be withdrawn. Every voter will be required to swear allegiance to the United States at the polls, and every officer elected must qualify himself in the same manner. Wm. H. French,
Brevet Major, U. S. Army, Commanding.

219

APPENDIX O

"The most important as well as the most gratifying piece of intelligence I have to communicate is that yesterday, by order of General Hunter, commanding the Department of the South, Winer Bethel and William Pinckney, two prominent citizens of this place, and signers of the secession ordinance of the State of Florida, were arrested and ordered to close confinement in Fort Taylor until further orders from the president of the United States. Before saying anything further on the subject, I may as well give an outline of the persons, that the public may know who and what they are.

"William Pinckney is the junior member and the present manager of the firm of Wm. H. Wall & Company, merchants of this place, which firm have amassed a large fortune in mercantile business and wrecking. The senior partner, Wm. H. Wall, has retired from active business, and resides now in New York. William Pinckney was an active participant in all appertaining to secession during the early part of our present troubles, and was elected a delegate to the convention at Tallahassee from this place. On his arrival there, when the convention was organized, he assisted the State out of the Union by voting for and signing the secession ordinance, and afterwards on his return he acted as agent for the commissioners to solicit subscriptions to the loan for the defense of the Confederate States, the books for which subscriptions were opened in the store of William H. Wall & Company. Pinckney remained an active secessionist until compelled to take the oath of allegiance or leave the island, by order of the military commander of this post. Since that time he has remained quiet, knowing that rebeldom had not a ghost of a chance, and if he dared show any outward sign of friendship for Jeff Davis, both his person and property would be endangered.

"Winer Bethel is what we term here a Conch—that is, a native of the Bahamas. Nassau is, I believe, the place that gave him birth, and she has a reason to be proud of her son. Winer Bethel is also a naturalized citizen of the United States, and has been for a long time a resident of Key West, is by profession an attorney-at-law, and was at the time of the secession of Florida judge of probate. Consequently he is better known as Judge Bethel.

"Judge Bethel, as I shall now term him, was also elected a delegate to the convention at Tallahassee from this place, and, with Pinckney, voted for the ordinance of secession, but did not sign it for some days after, for fear, as he said, 'of being tried and hung for high treason.' He signed it, however, and returned here to give secession all the aid in his power. He on one occasion refused to acknowledge the power of the United States on this island, saying that he knew of no authority here except that of the Confederate States. After taking a second time the oath of allegiance, he attempted to practice again as an attorney of the United States court, when our district attorney, Thomas J. Boynton, Esq., moved that his name be stricken from the roll of attorneys of the court. Mr. Boynton argued the case most ably, but his motion was overruled, Judge Marvin restoring Bethel to his former position, on the ground that, having taken the prescribed oath, he was entitled to be considered again as in all respects a loyal citizen. After this decision secesh held up their heads, and considered they had gained a victory, and kept their noses high in the air until the arrest of yesterday compelled them to acknowledge a higher authority than that of Judge Marvin.

"The arrest of these two men will have an important and most beneficial influence. They have been under the impression that they were safe and would escape all punishment for their past misdeeds; but they have, I am glad to say, been mistaken. They discover now that, although more than a year has passed since their great crime was committed, it has not been forgotten, and they will be punished therefor. The people of the North, while wishing to be lenient with the majority, will not permit all to go unpunished, and these men are two of those who were the instigators of this outrageous rebellion, and who are in a measure responsible for all the blood that has been spilled and treasure that has been expended, and must be punished.

"The excitement attending their arrest was very great. It was like a thunderbolt in the midst of our secession community, and afforded much satisfaction to our loyal people; for they felt that we have a president and

220

government determined to punish the guilty; and certainly none more richly deserve it than the scoundrels who have tried heretofore to control this place. Their time has gone by; they have got to the end of their tether, and hereafter they will know, by the lesson of yesterday, that although misconduct may be for a time forgotten, it will be most certainly punished in the end. I only hope there will be no delay in their case, that they will receive their punishment quickly, and that it will be of a character to strike terror among those who desire to do as they have done.

"I cannot close this letter without protesting against the sympathy shown these persons by government officials when arrested yesterday. They appeared to vie with each other to make them (the prisoners) comfortable, and take away from the arrest as much of its character as possible. This is all wrong and would not be countenanced by the government were it known. The officers of the government are employed and paid by the people to crush not sympathize with rebels; and when we see them, for personal considerations, compromise their official positions we may justly consider there is 'something rotten in Denmark,' and form our own opinions. There has been too much of this sympathy during this war, and it is high time where a well established case comes to the knowledge of the government, that the official thus offending should be placed at once on a footing similar to the rebels he chooses to sympathize with. The cap I have just made will fit several in Key West, and they are all at liberty to wear it; and I shall not hesitate in future, should any more cases come to my knowledge, to speak plainer than I have done, and expose the whole affair, that the government and people may know all the circumstances."

APPENDIX P

MEMBERS OF UNION VOLUNTEER CORPS

A. Patterson,
Eldridge L. Ware,
George D. Allen,
James P. Lightbourne,
Henry Albury,
George Demerritt,
Christian Boye,
R. W. Welch
E. O. Gwynn,
S. M. Davis,
William Solomon,
Nathan Niles,
Joseph Almeda,
E. D. Braman,
Frederick Engert,
Hiram B. Dailey,
Joseph B. Kemp,
William Reynolds,
Daniel Davis,
John Gordon,
Calvin Park,
John Gardener,
Joseph Kemp,
Charles Howe, Jr.,
Edward C. Howe,
James Weatherford, Jr.,
Edward F. Papy,
James Egan,
G. W. Ferguson,
Wm. Demeritt,
Henry Williams,
Charles Cox,
Arthur McAllister,

Thomas Lumley,
John Albury,
John O. Braman, Jr.,
Thomas W. Kemp,
Lewis E. Pierce, Jr.,
Lewis E. Pierce, Sr.,
George R. Pearce,
James Pent,
William Sands,
William McDonald,
Wm. H. VonPfister,
John Pent, Sr.,
James Roberts,
Richard Albury, Sr.,
D. Moffatt,
James Simpson,
Joseph Stickney,
Joseph Garcia,
M. Farina,
Shubael Brown,
O. A. Hickey,
Elijah Carey,
Benjamin G. Albury,
David W. Marshall,
William Saunders, Jr.,
Charles Howe, Sr.,
Latham Brightman,
T. J. Boynton,
Cornelius Curtis,
Wm. Marvin,
Robert B. Bingham,
Thomas Albury,
Christopher Dunn,

George Wood,
Robert Sawyer,
Joseph Andrews,
Richardson Albury,
Josephus F. Packer,
William Saunders, Sr.,
William Richardson,
Jeremiah Pent,
Alexander Saunders,
Benj. Bethel,
John Braman, Sr.,
Benj. Albury,
John White,
Henry Williams, Jr.,
Albert A. Johnson,
Henry Williams, Sr.,
Edward Bickford,
Joseph Williams,
G. Wm. Gibbons,
Patrick Casey,

James Pent, Jr.,
Clemente McChow,
Alonzo A. Austin,
Hezekiah Thrift,
Alexander Marshall,
Dennis W. Kelly,
Manuel Gonzales,
Augustus P. Marillac,
William H. Albury,
Peter T. Williams,
John Butler,
Daniel O'Hara,
Henry Demeritt,
William H. Pearce,
John Beck,
Peter L. Jaycocks,
Wm. Marshall,
Francis B. Dailey,
Wm. A. Pitcher,
Benjamin Albury.

APPENDIX Q

U. S. S. CINCINNATI, KEY WEST, FLORIDA,
December 11, 1895.

SIR:

1. I have to report that yesterday about two-thirty p. m., smoke was reported coming from the hatch of Compartment A-20 (V Magazine)— the fire alarm was sounded and an examination made which demonstrated the fact that there was burning wood in that magazine—the urgency of the occasion led me to direct the immediate flooding of the forward magazine (Compartments A-18, A-19, A-20) as well as the leading of all hose to that vicinity.

2. After the flooding of the magazines and there being no further smell of burning wood, they were emptied and all the ammunition passed on deck, then, it was found that many of the shell boxes were badly charred where they had come in contact with the after bulkhead of A-20.

3. This lead to an examination of coal bunker B-8, filled with soft coal and after digging into it a hot fire was found; this was soon extinguished by flooding from the berth deck.

4. There was no gas or smoke to be seen coming from the coal bunker ventilators, as the fire was so near the bottom of the bunker.

5. I have ordered a board to examine and report upon the damage done and all the circumstances incident thereto which will be forwarded by next mail.

6. The alacrity with which all worked is worthy of commendation and I desire to especially mention the efforts of the executive officer, Lieutenant Commander W. N. Everett, Lieutenant C. A. Gove, and Ensign F. R. Payne, as well as the following named men: John Barett, G. M. 2. C.; John M. Ferguson, G. M. 3. C.; W. W. Banks, A. 1. C.; Joseph Steinmetz, G. M. 2. C.; Frank C. Atkinson, A. 1. C.; Charles H. Gray, A. 2. C.; Anthony Merkle, F. 2. C.; George Casseen, G. M. 1. C.; Charles A. Uphoff, G. M. 2. C.; Frank Rorschach, G. M. 1. C.; John A. Riley, M. at A. 2. C.; Joseph Smith, Coxswain, Theodore Morse, Seaman; James O'Toole, Seaman, and Jacob Martin, Seaman.

7. I think very little ammunition has been damaged.

Very respectfully,
M. L. JOHNSON,
Captain Commanding.

The Commander-in-Chief, North Atlantic Station.

APPENDIX R

COLLECTOR OF CUSTOMS

Joel Yancy..............................1822 to December 31, 1823
Samuel Ayres.............. (Acting) January 1, 1824, to January 15, 1824
John Whitehead...........................February, 1824 (Declined)
William Pinckney.......................................1824 to 1829
Algernon S. Thurston....................................1829 to 1831
William A. Whitehead....................................1831 to 1838
Adam Gordon...1838 to 1845
Stephen R. Mallory......................................1845 to 1849
Samuel J. Douglass......................................1849 to 1853
John T. Baldwin...1853 to 1861
Chas. Howe..1861 to 1869
W. G. Vance...1869 to 1873
Chas. M. Hamilton...................April, 1873, to October 31, 1873
Frank N. Wicker..1873 to 1883
Denis Eagan...1883 to 1885
J. V. Harris...1885 to 1889
John F. Horr...1889 to 1893
Jefferson B. Browne.....................................1893 to 1897
Geo. W. Allen..1897 to

APPENDIX S

CUSTOM HOUSE STATISTICS

Total imports of the territory in 1831........................$115,710.00
   Of which the Key West imports were...................... 96,371.00
Total imports of the territory in 1832......................... 107,787.00
   Of which the Key West imports were...................... 67,481.00
Total imports of the territory in 1833......................... 85,386.00
   Of which the Key West imports were...................... 69,070.00
Total imports of the territory in 1834......................... 135,798.00
   Of which the Key West imports were...................... 101,323.00
Total amounts of exports in 1831............................. 30,495.00
   Of which the exports from Key West were................. 27,135.00
Total amount of exports in 1832.............................. 65,716.00
   Of which the exports from Key West were................. 56,724.00
Total amount of exports in 1833.............................. 64,805.00
   Of which the exports from Key West were................. 47,555.00
Total amount of exports in 1834.............................. 228,825.00
   Of which the exports from Key West were................. 80,922.00

Registered, enrolled and licensed tonnage of Florida on the thirty-first of December, 1833, amounted to 378,947 tons, distributed among the four following districts:

Pensacola..177,740 tons
Key West.. 86,375 tons
Apalachicola... 57,764 tons
St. Augustine.. 56,968 tons

On the thirty-first December, 1831, the Florida tonnage was 238,590
On the thirty-first December, 1832, the Florida tonnage was 300,305
In 1875 the tonnage of Key West was 133,862.

There are no detailed statistics at hand prior to 1831, but Mr. Wm. A. Whitehead has furnished a report of the business of the custom house from 1831 to 1835 showing the number of vessels entered and cleared and the amount of imports and exports.

223

	1831	1832	1833	1834	1835
American vessels entered	268	283	201	297	321
Foreign vessels entered	22	20	10	16	10
Of these there were:					
From American ports	118	141	106	135	158
From foreign ports	172	162	105	178	173
American vessels cleared	261	256	205	249	248
Foreign vessels cleared	21	15	11	15	12
Of these there were:					
For American ports	124	94	110	81	89
For foreign ports	158	177	106	183	171

Value of imports from foreign ports were: 1831, $67,863.00; 1832, $108,778.00; 1833, $39,024.00; 1834, $107,856.00.

Value of exports were: 1831, $35,152.00; 1832, $63,943.00; 1833, $35,138.00; 1834, $86,947.00.

The revenue of the custom house of Key West showed an average of about $45,000.00 annually from 1828 to 1832, and in 1835 alone the revenue was $20,000.00. In 1874 the amount of dutiable goods imported into this district was $641,335.00 and free of duty $19,077.00, making a total importation of $660,432.00. In 1874 the total amount of duties paid into the custom house was $222,371.35. Tonnage dues $2,520.83. Hospital dues $2,728.51. Total in 1875, $297,238.96. Total in 1876, $235,514.73.

For the fiscal year of 1900 the custom collections were $337,085.84.

For the fiscal year of 1910 the custom collections were $613,074.28.

APPENDIX T

LIST OF VESSELS EMPLOYED IN WRECKING UPON THE FLORIDA REEF IN 1835

Schooner Hyder Ali of Huntington, Conn.............Captain J. Gould
Sloop Actor of Brook Haven, N. Y..................Captain J. B. Smith
Schooner Whale of Mystic, Conn..................Captain G. Eldridge
Schooner Hester Ann of Key West................Captain J. H. Geiger
Sloop Mystic of Mystic, Conn....................:Captain E. Eldridge
Schooner John Denison of Indian Key...................Captain D. Cold
Schooner Splendid of Key West................Captain G. Alderslade
Schooner Florida of Key West.....................Captain A. Anderson
Sloop Sarah Isabella of Indian Key.................Captain T. Eldridge
Schooner Amelia of Key Vacas.......................Captain J. Bethell
Sloop Brilliant of Groton, Conn.......................Captain J. Egan
Schooner Orion of Key West.......................Captain S. Sanderson
Sloop Thistle of Indian Key..........................Captain H. Brown
Sloop Standard of Huntington, Conn...................Captain J. Place
Schooner Caroline of Key West.......................Captain J. Wood
Schooner Single Sailor of Key Vacas..................Captain R. Roberts
Schooner Edward Thompson of Philadelphia...........Captain S. Young
Schooner Fair American of Indian Key..............Captain J. Shurtleff
Schooner Olive Branch of Key West..................Captain W. Greene
Schooner Blacksmith of Key West....................Captain S. Coombs

Twenty vessels, aggregate tonnage, 103,795.

APPENDIX U

WILLIAM SMITH ALLEN

Mr. Allen, who had been prominent in the business affairs of Key West for many years, died October 10, 1891. He had been in poor health for several months. He was born in Enfield, Conn., February 16, 1823, and was the son of George and Fanny Smith Allen. He was educated in Connecticut and Massachusetts and then moved South, teaching school for some time in Georgia. On February 9, 1853, he married in Ithaca, Tompkins county, New York, Miss Mary Jane Sprague of Lyons, Wayne county, New York, who died September 12, 1869.

Residence of Hon. Joseph Beverly Browne
Key West, Florida

Mr. Allen settled in Jacksonville, Duval county, Florida, soon after his marriage, and was engaged in business in that city until 1862, when he moved to Key West. He then became associated with his brothers, George D., M. A. and B. W. Allen, composing the firm of Allen Brothers, general merchants, whose place of business was on the corner of Duval and Front streets.

At different periods in his life he had held the offices of special deputy collector of customs for the district of Key West, clerk of the United States District Court for the Southern District of Florida, and mayor of the city. He was a leading member of the Methodist church. He is survived by his sons, George W. Allen and John W. Allen of Key West, and Dwight A. Allen of West Palm Beach, Florida.

APPENDIX V

HON. JOSEPH BEVERLY BROWNE

The subject of this sketch, a twin brother of the late Dr. Peter Fielding Browne, son of John Eaton Browne and Elizabeth Ann, his wife, was born at Windsor, James City County, Va., on the 6th day of November, 1814, and died on the afternoon of December 27, 1888, aged seventy-four years, one month, and twenty-one days.

The life and services of Joseph B. Browne intimately and conspicuously blend with the more prominent features of the history of Florida, as territory and State, and of our now progressive city.

He arrived at the then little hamlet of Key West, on Christmas night, night, 1830, when but few small houses, scattered here and there, had been built upon the extreme western point of the island, and as a mere lad, commenced the life, which from the beginning was ever characterized by manly courage and timely devotion to duty, in whatever sphere enlisted.

His more marked and assiduous services to the territory of Florida were as a member of the St. Joseph convention, 1838, which framed the constitution upon which our State was admitted to the Federal Union in 1845. Under the administration of President Van Buren, Mr. Browne was the territorial United States marshal for Florida, and was successively continued in that office under Presidents Polk and Harrison, afterwards being appointed clerk of the United States Court, presided over by Judge Marvin.

He was a member of the legislature of Florida during the sessions of 1866 to 1870, and the subsequent session of 1875.

He was mayor of Key West for several different terms. He was postmaster for four years under the administration of President Hayes, and for many years a warden of St. Paul's Episcopal church, of which he was a communicant.

He was married to Miss Mary Nieves Ximinez, a native of St. Augustine, on the 10th day of December, 1840, and enjoyed an unusual happy married life for forty-eight years, and leaves behind his widow and four children, Mrs. Robert J. Perry, Mrs. L. W. Bethel, Mrs. Geo. W. Allen and Hon. Jefferson B. Browne, to mourn the loss of a faithful husband, and a kind, indulgent father.

Who that knew our island in the charming days of the past will ever forget the retired spot, now and then busy with salvages on wrecks, watering and provisioning vessels, and then relapsing into the serene, ordinary quiet and order, with but one mail, or at most two mails per month, to break the long monotony. The society was most cordial and agreeable. It was in the days of Judges Webb and Marvin, Ministers Adams and Herrick, of Port Collectors Mallory, Baldwin and Howe, and Marshals Stone, Eastin and Moreno. There was then plenty of old fashioned hospitality, with all its true charms; and when everybody knew everybody. It was then that Mr. Browne was best known. With a cordial, kindly nature that never seemed to desert him, he was always popular and appreciated. Coming here, a lad of sixteen, to enter the employ of his uncle, F. A. Browne, one of Key West's honorable and old time merchants, he passed through the various tests of public and private station, to pass away near the close of the third quarter of a century of life respected and mourned by all.

A Jeffersonian Democrat and a Virginian, it was but natural that he should be largely interested in public affairs, and taste and nature fitted him for public life and made him a marked man in the community as well as in the State. He always bore with him the air of the old times of Governor Spottwood, and suggested to one the possibility of some ancient ancestor dropping out from his frame in the ancestral home, and entering upon life in Key West as one who belonged here. He belonged to the times of broad acres and wide hospitality, like a souvenir of the past, a gem of bygone days; yet in companionship with Mr. Browne there was merely the flavor of the antique, which was a delicious morsel, while his sympathies continued quickened to the last act of charity, and his mind aroused to an interest in the last policy of State. Thus through life he held his friends to him as with hooks of steel. He was a born philosopher, and a clear, earnest, vigorous conversationalist. As a friend of Senator C. W. Jones, he, while a member of the Florida legislature, gave him valuable aid and support in his election to the United States senate. As a representative of the people Mr. Browne served with honor to himself and to his constituency. At the first election held here at the close of the war he was an inspector. It was a time of tumult. Questions arose requiring the exercise of a strong mind and conscience. The inspectors were frequently divided. Mr. Browne held to a view that debarred from the ballot some who are today among our first citizens, notwithstanding all his native kindness of heart; and yet the survivor of that board of inspectors believes that Mr. Browne was right, although he then differed with him.

Mr. Browne ventured in mercantile life, but for many years the afflictive loss of sight debarred him from business aims and purposes and from much of his old time social enjoyments. But he warmed to an old friend and was still the cordial companion in his circle; and in his family, where he was ever at home, appreciated and loved.

Mr. Browne was slender in his youth but was stout from manhood. During the stages of complete, then partial, then permanent loss of sight, his bark gradually drifted from the shores of time, and the orbs that saw no light here, saw those upon "the other shore." And the hand that felt its way groped now in darkness because it was the eternal day. And what tribute should be paid at this time to the beautiful, loving devotion of the wife, the companion of forty-eight years, that would not seem sacrilege to name, especially when immured with her husband in darkness in the long struggle to regain his sight? It teaches and preaches the truth that the age of heroism among women has not died, and never will die.

Mr. Browne's death was for some little time expected and when announced was the occasion of very general sorrow. The crowded services at St. Paul's on Friday, at 3:30 p. m., attested the general sentiment, and a large attendance in carriages proceeded to the cemetery to witness the last rites in respect for his memory. The pallbearers were Judge James W. Locke; Commander J. K. Winn, U. S. N.; Mr. W. D. Cash; Hon. Jeptha Vee Harris, collector of customs; Messrs. Whitemore Pinder and James G. Jones.

APPENDIX W

METEOROLOGICAL RECORD FOR KEY WEST, FLA., 1910

Data Given	January	February	March	April	May	June	July	August	September	October	November	December
Mean temperature	68	69	71	74	78	88	83	83	81	77	70	65
Highest temperature	80	81	81	83	87	89	90	92	90	87	79	78
Lowest temperature	55	52	61	64	68	72	71	72	73	59	58	51
Absolute range of temperature	25	29	20	19	19	17	19	20	17	28	21	27
Greatest daily range of temperature	15	15	14	14	14	16	18	16	13	14	17	17
Number of days with temperature 90° or above	0	0	0	0	0	0	0	6	0	0	0	0
Mean relative humidity	80	79	74	71	79	74	74	73	78	79	77	79
Prevailing wind	N.E.	E.	N.E.	S.E.	E.	S.	E.	S.E.	E.	E.	N.E.	N.E.
Total wind movement—miles	7,602	6,725	7,560	7,181	7,424	5,124	6,185	5,586	4,901	10,476	6,045	7,527
Mean hour velocity	10.2	10.0	10.2	10.0	10.0	7.1	8.3	7.5	6.8	14.1	8.4	10.1
Highest velocity	42	25	26	32	24	39	29	19	32	100	31	28
Rainfall—in inches	0.62	0.83	0.35	0.03	0.86	1.06	2.57	3.21	6.42	10.95	1.35	0.18
Greatest daily rainfall	0.32	0.82	0.33	0.03	0.45	0.89	1.09	0.83	1.89	4.12	0.92	0.11
Number of days with rain	5	2	2	1	5	8	12	14	18	14	3	1
Number of clear days	17	21	24	14	14	8	4	6	7	11	24	18
Number of partly cloudy days	12	6	7	15	15	22	21	24	15	11	4	12
Number of cloudy days	2	1	0	1	2	0	6	1	8	9	2	1

H. B. BOYER,
Local Forecaster.

INDEX TO INTRODUCTION

INDEX TO *KEY WEST*

2

Banks, W. W., 222
Barett, John, 222
Barker, John T., 133
Barnes, 22
Barnes, A. O., 211
Barnett, 41
Baron, Charles S., 69, 181
Baron Commandery No. 7, 138
Barranco, Augustin, 117
Barranco, Francisco, 117
Barranco, Manuel, 117
Barry, Father J., 34
Bartlum, George L., 24, 56, 140
Bartlum, John, 183, 184
Bartlum, William J., 31
Bates, William L., 140
Bayard [Thomas?], 20
Beckman, F. A., 46
Beckman, Mrs. F. A., 46
Beehler, Commodore W. H., 23
Beiglet, J. F., 87, 88, 89
Beltzhoover, Lt. Daniel, 22
Beneficencia Cubana, 150
Benevolent and Protective Order of
    Elks, 140
Bennett, Rev. Alva, 21, 28
Berghell, Alfred A., 46
Bernadou, John B., 149
Bernier, Father A. F., 35
Berry, Charles, 97, 98
Betancourt, Benito, 150
Betancourt, Maria Manas de, 150
Bethel, John M., 22
Bethel, Mrs. L. W., 225
Bethel, Livingston W., 32, 69, 126, 132,
    133, 182, 188, 211
Bethel, Mellie, 22
Bethel, William, 126
Bethel, Winer, 13, 22, 56, 69, 90, 91, 94,
    182, 189, 191, 220
Bethel A.M.E. Church, 159
Bethell, Capt. J., 224
Bingham, John A., 210
"Bivouac of the Dead," 115
Blackwell, Jane, 193
Blackwell, W. C., 193
Blount, Mrs. W. A., 189
Bloxham, William D., 132, 135
B'nai Zion, 170
Board, James J., 202
Boarman, Alex, 127
Boesler, August, 108
Bolio, Josephine, 140

Bonachea, Mr., 120
Bonnington, Mr., 22
Bonsal, Stephen M., 146
Bordon, W. C., 149
Borges, Ambrosia, 124
Borroto, Francisco, 117
Borroto, Jacinto, 117
Borroto, Julio, 117
Bostwick, Rev. W. W., 45
Botello, Francisco, 119
Botello, Jose B., 119
Bott, Shirley C., 56
Bottolaccio, Father, 35
Bowers, B. H. F., 154
Bowne, George, 12, 90, 106, 130, 184
Bowne and Curry, 106, 184
Boye, Christian, 221
Boyer, Mrs. H. B., 85
Boyle, John, 180
Boynton, Thomas J., 65, 94, 96, 210,
    211, 220, 221
Bracewell, James M., 211
Braden, Mr., 66
Braman, John, 12
Braman, O. T., 43, 44
Brannan, Capt. James M., 91, 92, 93,
    214, 218
Brannan, John M., 78
Braxton, Mrs. Jacquelin Marshall, 192
Breaker, Miss, 12
Breaker, J. H., 43, 44
Breaker, Lewis, 12
"Brethren of the Coast," 73
Brinas, Miguel, Sr., 121
Bronson, Isaac H., 65
Brooks, George G., 137
Brooks, Hannah, 171
Brossier, F. C., 140, 155
Brotherhood of St. Andrew, 31
Brougham, Henry, 201
Brown, Rev. B. F., 30
Brown, Capt. H., 224
Brown, Harry, 146
Brown, Harvey, 214, 215, 216
Brown, Shubael, 125, 221
Browne, Ann Elizabeth, 22, 188, 191
Browne, Elizabeth Ann, 225
Browne, Fielding A., 12, 13, 27, 51, 52,
    56, 59, 105, 113, 151, 164, 175, 187,
    197, 201, 225
Browne, Jefferson B., 17, 18, 23, 24, 56,
    60, 83, 110, 111, 123, 126, 127, 133,
    134, 137, 140, 188, 195, 223, 225

4

Crain, St. Clair, 31
Crane, Henry, 211
Craven, Capt., 93, 219
Crill, E. C., 195
Crittenden, W. S., 116
Crusoe, Peter, 90, 91, 93, 211, 219
Cuba Lodge No. 15, I.O.O.F., 138
Cunningham, F. J., 22
Cupperberg, Joe, 170
Curry, Alfred Bates, 24
Curry, Allen E., 136, 137, 139
Curry, Charles R., 140
Curry, Mrs. Charles, 98
Curry, George, 41
Curry, J. L. M., 169
Curry, James R., 63
Curry, Joshua, 56, 98
Curry, Mary, 41
Curry, Richard, 212
Curry, Sarah, 41
Curry, Thomas, 149
Curry, William, 12, 30, 32, 56, 90, 101,
    106, 139, 142, 158, 184
Curtis, James, 13
Cussans, R. W., 202

Dade, Major [Francis L.], 58, 84, 197
Dade Lodge No. 14, Free and Accepted
    Masons, 138
Dallas, Commander [Alexander J.], 84
Darley, Thomas, 171
Darnall, Marcy B., 138, 143, 161
Daughters of the King, 188
Davidson, Robert H. M., 134
Davis, Daniel, 96
Davis, George, 96, 97
Davis, Jefferson, 17, 18, 19, 220
Davis, Richard Harding, 144, 145
Davis, Varina Howell, 17
Dawley, Mr., 99
Day, A. H., 27
Day, Rev. Samuel Duncan, 30
Dean, James, 69
Decatur, John P., 165
de Cespedes, Carlos M., 31, 56, 117, 118
de Lamar, Jose, 118
Delancey, John, 172
Delaney, Annie L., 46
Delaney, John J., 101
Delaney, W. J., 181
Delaney, W. L., 100
Delgado, Martin Morua, 124
Delgado, Morua P., 118, 119

De Lipsey, Dr. A. E., 149
De Lono, Angel, 69, 82, 110, 118, 121,
    138
De Mendoza, Alejandro Gonzalez, 118
Demeritt, George A., 212
Demeritt, John, 41
Demerritt, George W., 132, 181, 221
Denham, John, 143
Dennis, William C., 90, 91, 113
De Pass, Rev. J. P., 24, 41
Diaz, Manuel, 97
Dillon, Charles, 181
Dillon, George, 181
Dixon, Mr., 176
Dobbs, Rev. C. E. W., 45
Dockery Frederick A., 211
Doherty, C. J., 161
Domestic Board of Missions, 28
Doolittle, Rev., 44
Dorsett, A. H., 154
Douglas, Stephen J., 13
Douglas School, 22
Douglass, Bettie, 192
Douglass [Douglas], Mrs. S. J., 30, 197
Douglass [Douglas], Judge Samuel J.,
    64, 90, 91, 93, 192, 219, 223
Duffy and Williams, 107
Duke, Druscilla, 44, 85
Duke, Reason, 44
Dupont, Charles, 212
Duval House, 140
Dyce, Rev. Robert, 21, 27

Eagan, Rev., 165
Eagan, Denis, 223
Eastin, Thomas, 27, 141, 211, 225
Easton, Thomas, 11
Eaton, John A., 52
Eaton Street Baptist Church, 45
Eddy, Mrs., 46
Edmonston, L. A., 27
Egan, James, 221, 224
E. H. Gato Company, 125, 128, 132
Eldridge, E., 224
Eldridge, Elim, 43, 44
Eldridge, G., 224
Eldridge, T., 224
Elizarde, Leopoldina, 150
Ellinger, Julius, 128
Elmer, Horace, 123
El Principe de Gales, 117, 125
El Republicano, 118, 119
El Yara, 118

5

Giddens, Rev. John A., 42
Gilbert, Rev. Charles A., 29
Girardo (Giraldo), Antonio, 13, 202
Glass, J., 87
Glassell (Glasel, Glassel), Maj. James
   M., 14, 77, 197, 201, 202
Glassier, George H., 193
Glassier, Urania Neal Geiger, 193
Gomez, Gen. Maximo, 121, 122
Good, Col. T. H., 95, 96, 97
Gordon, Adam, 12, 27, 50, 64, 69, 113,
   210, 223
Gordon, Mrs. Adam, 13, 188
Gordon, Eliza, 188
Gordon, Gen. John B., 194
Gordon, Roger, 176, 177
Gould, Capt. J., 224
Gove, Lt. C. A., 222
Graham, Rev. Andrew, 38
Graham, John A., 22
Granday, A., 110
Grant, Gen. U. S., 19
Graves, Rt. Rev. Anson R., 32
Gray, Bishop, 32
Gray, Charles H., 222
Gray, Frank, 159
Greene, Col., 62
Greene, Pardon C., 7, 12, 14, 27, 51, 52,
   56, 201
Greene, Capt. W., 224
Greene, William C., 201
Greene & Co., P. C., 199, 209, 210
Gregory, John H., 135
Grillon, John Baptiste, 180
Gunn, Francis, 212
Gunn, Judge Hugh, 63, 69
Gustens, Mrs. Maria, 150
Gwynn, E. O., 56, 125, 221
Gwynn, Martin and Strauss, 125, 128

Hackley, William R., 12, 53, 64, 211
Haley, Ellen, 189, 190
Haley, Salisbury, 189
Hall, Dr. W. R., 149
Hamilton, Charles M., 223
Hammersley, Capt., 7
Hanson, Judge G. A., 69
Hanson, Rev. J. H., 28
Hargrove, Ruth, Hall and Seminary,
   25
Hargrove Institute, 25
Harmon, Archer, 82
Harris, J. Vining, 23

Harris, Jeptha (Jephtha) Vee, 132, 134,
   142, 223, 226
Harris, John A., 46
Harris, W. Hunt, 23, 31, 47, 133, 134,
   140
Harris High School, 23
Harrison, Rev. E. A., 41, 136
Hart, Barry, 172
Hart, Hannah, 172
Hart, Rev. R. F., 45
Hart, William, 172
Hartman, John, 193
Hartsuff, George L., 218, 219
Haskins, Henry, 140
Hassan, Father James, 35
Havana-American Company, 125, 128
Hellings, Elenor, 46
Hellings, Martin L., 24, 153
Henderson, Col. John A., 135
Henderson, Sen. John W., 192
Henderson, Sadie, 192
Hendry, George M., 133
Hernandez, Palmenia, 150
Herrera, Martin, 117, 124
Herrick, Rev. Osgood E., 13, 29, 30, 225
Herttell, Clara, 30
Hice, Henry, 41
Hickey, O. A., 221
Hicks, Mr., postmaster, 82
Hicks, James, 13
Hicks, James D., 182
Hicks, Richard T., 212
Higgs, Rev. Gilbert, 30, 31, 82
Higgs, Rev. J. S. J., 29
Hill, Harry W., 155
Hillyer, Rev. J. L. D., 45
Hirsch, Ferdinand, 108
Holy Innocents Church, 31, 32
Horr, John F., 126, 134, 211, 223
House, Rev. W. H., 45
Houseman, Capt., 86, 87, 89
Houston Ice and Brewing Co., 170
Hovey, Edmond Otis, 56, 57
Howe, Amelia, 89
Howe, C. & E., 113, 151, 152
Howe, Charles, 13, 87, 88, 89, 113, 215,
   221, 223, 225
Howe, Charles, Jr., 89, 221
Howe, Edward, 89, 192, 221
Howe, Hannah Watlington, 192
Hudson, George, 83, 131, 211
Hugon, Father, 35
Hunincq, Rev. Fr., 34

7

Hunincq, Father Sylvanus, 35
Hunt, Capt. E. B., 91, 92, 214, 216, 217
Hunt, Mrs. W. H., 189
Hunter, Maj. Gen. D., 23, 95, 220
Huse, Lt. Caleb, 191
Huse, Capt. Henry L., 191
Huselkamp, C. J., 105
Hutchinson, W. H., 143

I
Independent Order of Good Templars, 139
Independent Order of Odd Fellows, 138
Indian Key, 86–89
Ingraham, Edward E., 56
Ingraham, Elizabeth, 41
Ingraham, Joseph, 41
"Internal Evidences of the Authenticity of the Four Gospels," 65
International Ocean Telegraph Company, 103, 194
Island City Guards, 155
Island City Lodge No. 9, Independent Order of Good Templars, 139
Island City Lodge No. 14, Knights of Pythias, 139
Island City National Bank, 109
Isle of the Sea Lodge No. 104, Knights of Pythias, 139

Jackson, Alden A. M., 11, 21, 53, 85
Jackson, Andrew, 52, 58, 201
Jackson, Dr. H. P., 149
Jacksonville, St. Augustine & Indian River Railway, 194, 195
Jaycocks, Clement, 63, 212
Jaycox, Mr., 179
Jenness, L. Y., 19
Jerguson, A. P., 140
Jister, P., 218
Johnson, Mrs., 13
Johnson, Catherine, 44
Johnson, Charles, 12, 192
Johnson, Dr. Charles S., 192
Johnson, Lavinia, 44
Johnson, Mary Watlington, 192
Johnson, Menendez, 133
Johnson, Tom, 179
Jones, Sen. Charles W., 226
Jones, James G. (Jim), 56, 153, 164, 178, 179, 211, 212, 226
Jones, James M., 31
Jones, Mary B., 55
Jose Lovera Company, 128

Kellogg, Mortimer, 193
Kells, Mrs., 30
Kemp, Judge Andrew J., 69, 126, 132
Kemp, Dr. Cornelius F., 24, 139
Kemp, Cornelius J., 56
Kemp, Samuel, 12, 37, 41
Kenny, Rt. Rev. W. J., 36
Kerr, Rev. J. L., 33
Kerr, William R., 126, 127
Ketcham, Charles H., 138
Keyes, Lt. Col. E. D., 214, 215
Key West Baptist Church, 44
Key West Chamber of Commerce, 102
Key West Cigar Factory, 128
Key West Convent Hospital, 148
Key West Council No. 1015, 140
Key West Electric Company, 105, 161
Key West Encampment No. 5, 138
Key West Gas Company, 110, 111
Key West Investment Company, 100
Key West Lodge No. 551, Benevolent & Protective Order of Elks, 140
Key West Lodge No. 13, I.O.O.F., 138
Key West Realty Company, 114
Key West Rifles, 155
King, Dr., 193
King, Rev. H. M., 45
King, Maria Watlington, 192
King, Judge Thomas F., 68
Kinsey, H. J., 46
Kinsey, Theodore L., 46
Kirby, Father J. F., 34
Knight, Frank W., 212
Knight, Peter T., 89, 132, 135, 142, 164
Knights Key, 82
Knights of Columbus, 140
Knights of the Golden Eagle, 140
Knights of Jericho, Astral Lodge No. 18, 139
Knights of Pythias, 139
Knowles, Charles L., 22, 23
Knowles, Clement, Sr., 31
Knowles, Elizabeth, 46
Krome, Mr., 196

Ladd, Frank H., 31, 56
Ladies Missionary Society, 30
LaFayette Fire Department, 151
La Fayette Salt Company, 113
La Fe, Mrs. Esperanza, 150
Laflin, A. F., 105
Lamadriz, Mr., 120
Lamar, President, 11

8

Lancaster, Mrs., 197
Lancaster, Judge Joseph B., 68
Larkin, E. E., 105
La Rocque, Father P., 35
La Rosa Espaniola, 125
Lee, Gen. Fitzhugh, 20
Lee, Taylor, 22, 23
Leon, Joaquin, 31
Lester, Capt. Graham J., 184
Lester, Capt. Joseph G. (Joe), 164, 179
Lewis, Charles C., 43, 44
Lewis, George, 106, 107, 108, 192
Lewis, Noah, 94
Ley, Rev. John C., 40, 41, 42
Lightbourne, Euphemia, 22, 30, 189
Lignum Vitae Key, 86
Linn, Rev. John B., 30
Lipscomb, J. E., 68, 69
"List of Grievances," 67
Livermore, Rev. Arthur Browne, 32
Livermore, Lt. W. R., 113
Locke, Eugene O., 22, 60, 131, 134, 138
Locke, Judge James W., 19, 22, 66, 69,
    101, 107, 120, 130, 142, 193, 210, 226
Locke, R. B., 141
Lopez, Narcisso, 115, 116
Lord and Stocker, 80
Louis, A., 104, 170
Louis, Louis, 155
Louise Maloney Hospital, 149
Lowe, Alfred, 97, 98
Lowe, Charles W., 56
Lowe, Mrs. George L., 31
Lowe, John T., 12, 97, 98
Lowe, Virgil S., 23
Luddington, Lt., 190
Lyne, Rev. Charles F. D., 29

Mabritty, Miss, 12
Mabritty, Michael, 13
McClintock, William, 42, 56, 175
McCook, Rev. W. J., 96
Maceo, Antonio, 121
McIntosh, Judge McQueen, 93, 216, 219
Mack, Rev. C. D., 33
McKay, James, 211
McKeown, Pat, 178
McKinney, John, 65, 210
McLaughline, Lt., 87
McMahon, P. J., 140
McMullen, Capt., 13

McNamee, Robert, 137
Macrae, George W., 68, 211
McRea, William A., 64, 210
Magbee, James, 68, 69
Mallory, Mrs. Ellen, 13, 186, 197
Mallory, Stephen R., 11, 12, 13, 27, 51,
    55, 64, 75, 90, 133, 141, 151, 157, 187,
    193, 194, 202, 216, 223, 225
Mallory and Co., 81
Malone, William H., Jr., 22, 23, 133,
    137, 138
Maloney, John B., 56, 102, 140, 149
Maloney, Mary E., 46
Maloney, Rosalie, 46
Maloney, Col. W. C., Sr., 13, 17, 19, 21,
    54, 55, 56, 60, 65, 69, 91, 95, 96, 97,
    130, 157, 158, 179, 182, 186, 211
Maloney, Walter C., Jr., 55, 56, 60, 64,
    90, 96, 97, 103, 131, 136, 142
Mann, Dr. H., 149
Manning, Dr., 192
Manning, Lt., 14
Manning, Evelyn, 192
Manuel Cruz Co., 128
Marero, Francisco, 155
Maria, 13
Marti, Jose, 122
Martin, E. M., 109, 111
Martin, Jacob, 222
Martin, R., 41
Martinelli, Mary, 13, 189, 190, 197
Martinelli, Nona, 13
Martinelli, Petrona, 189
Martinelly, William, 171
Martinez Havana Co., 128, 159
Marvin, Kitty, 190
Marvin, Judge William, 11, 53, 64, 65,
    68, 90, 91, 129, 174, 186, 190, 210,
    214, 215, 216, 218, 219, 220, 221, 225
Masonic Temple, 22, 89
Mathews, E. May, 46
Mathews, Frederick H., 143
Mathews, H. T., 46
Mayer, John, 111
Mayg, Dolores, 149
Meigs, Montgomery C., 214, 215, 216,
    217, 218
Merchants' Protective Association,
    101
Meredith, Mr., 196
Merkle, Anthony, 222
Merrill, Cassius E., 143
Merrill, Charles T., 106, 142

Messionier, Enrique, 124
Methodist Episcopal Church South, 24, 38, 42
Miller and Henderson, 81
Milord, Domingo, 63
Missionary District of Southern Florida, 32
Mitchel (Mitchell), Henry L., 69, 193
Mobley, Claiborn R., 211
Moffat, D., 221
Mohn, Arthur W., 25
Monroe, James, 58
Monroe Council No. 4, 138
Monroe County Board of Public Instruction, 171
Monroe, Kirk, 168
Monsalvatge, R. Alfred, 56, 101, 107, 109
Monsalvatge and Reed, 68, 107
Montgomery, Dr., 7
Moore, Bishop, 35
Moore, Willis M., 156
Moose, 140
Mordecai and Co., 80
Moreno, Mr., 142
Moreno, Fernando, 189
Moreno, Fernando J., 13, 90, 96, 133, 175, 189, 211, 225
Moreno, Louise, 189
Moreno, Manuel, 118
Moreno, Mason, 106, 142, 189, 211
Morgan, Mr., 143
Morgan, Col. Joseph S., 94, 95, 96
Morgan, Samuel, 97, 98
Morgan and Co., 81
Morgan Line, 81
Morse, Theodore, 222
Mott, Capt. John, 88
Mountain, John, 7
Mouton, Louis, 105, 110
Mulrennan, Henry, 56, 90, 97, 151, 177
Murias Compana Company, 128
Murphy, Father Ed., 34
Myers, Julian, 189
Myers, Oscar A., 211

Navarro, J. M. J., 117
Navarro, Jose M., 117
Nedson, Calvin ("Chief"), 179
Neeld, R. C., 142
Newcomb, Lt. Francis B., 141
Newcomb, Francis D., 27
Newcomb, Henry K., 27

Newcombe, Mr., 197
Newspapers, Key West, 13, 21, 64, 90, 93, 129, 141–43, 146, 151, 156, 167, 194, 219
Nichols, B. C., 22
Nichols, George W., Co., 125, 128, 159
Niles, Nathan, 221
North American Salt Co., 112
North Battery, 79
North Stonington, Conn., Assoc., 43
Northwest Passage reef light, 167
Norwood, Rev. W. A., 45
Noyes, A. B., 130
Noyes, O. S., 138

Oakley, Mrs. Clifford, 192
Ogden, Capt., 37
Ogden, Joseph V., 212
O'Halloran, Teodoro Perez & Co., 128
O'Hara, Father Joseph, 35
O'Hara, Col. Oliver, 12, 27, 50, 56, 174, 201, 202
O'Hara, Col. Theodore, 115
O'Hara & Wells, 151
Oliveri, Marcus, 97, 181
O'Mailley, Father, 35
Onderdonk, Rt. Rev. Benjamin T., 26, 27, 202
O'Neil, Father J. T., 34
Orosco, Mateo, 119
Otis, Samuel, 62, 63
O'Toole, James, 222
Otto, Dr. Joseph, 182
Otto, Julius, 123, 138
Otto, Thomas O., 63
Owens, Theodore, 27
Owls, Order of, 140

Pacetti, G., 97
Pacheco, Col. J. L., 121
Packer, Josephus F., 152, 222
Palmer, J. D., Jr., 86
Palmer, Sarah R. W., 86
Palmer, T. W., 86
Palmer, Thomas, 108
Park, John, 44
Parker, Gen. D., 201
Parodi, Enrique, 117
Parodi, Esteban, 117
Parrott, Joseph R., 196
Partido Revolucionario Cubano, 122
Passlague, Mrs., 21
Patterson, Col., 215, 218

13

Williams, Capt. Courtland, 85
Williams, James ("Crazy Jim"), 89
Williams, Jesse, 171
Williams, Joseph, 222
Williams, Joseph P., 118
Williams, Peter A., 211
Williams, Peter T., 222
Williams, William, 171
Williams, William H., 126
Williams and Warren, 68
Wilson, Mr., 196
Wilson, Henry, 211
Wilson, John, 66
Winn, Commander J. K., 226
Wolf [Wolfe], Col. Samuel J., 135, 155
Wolfe, J. A., 43, 44
Wolfson, Mr., 170
Wolkowsky, Abram, 170
Woman's Board of Home Missions, 24
Wood, Hez. R., 202
Wood, Capt. J., 224
Wood, Rev. William F., 44
Woodmen of the World, 139

Wray, Rev. John A., 137
Wright, W. A., 189
Wyman, Mr., 22

Ximenez, Frederica, 188
Ximenez [Ximinez], Joseph, 12, 188
Ximenez, Mrs. Joseph, 13, 187, 188
Ximenez [Ximinez], Mary Nieves, 12, 188, 197, 225
Ximinez, Josephine, 22, 190

Yancy, Mr., 22
Yancy, Joel, 99, 223
Ybor, Vincente [Vicente] Martinez, 117, 125
Young, Rt. Rev. John Freeman, 31, 32
Young, Adm. Lucian, 75
Young, Capt. S., 224
Young Men's Hebrew Association, 170

Zimmdebaum, A., 170
Ziriax, John G., 75
Ziriax Building, 75

This book may be kept

FOURTEEN DAYS

A fine will be charged for each day the book is kept overtime.

~~1952~~			